WITHDRAWN

A Golden Era

About the Author

Michael Gygax, practitioner at the Clinic of Natural Medicine, is an acupuncturist and physical therapist (see page 282 for more information). Volume 2 of this project will be published in 2017 and will feature Masters athletes born after 1956. Anyone interested in making a contribution to that volume can contact Michael at gygax570@gmail.com.

A GOLDEN ERA

Profiles of Irish Masters Athletes

*(Volume 1 – Athletes born
between 1924 and 1955)*

Michael Gygax

The Liffey Press

Published by
The Liffey Press
Raheny Shopping Centre, Second Floor
Raheny, Dublin 5, Ireland
www.theliffeypress.com

© 2016 Michael Gygax

A catalogue record of this book is
available from the British Library.

ISBN 978-1-908308-94-8

Printed in Spain by GraphyCems.

CONTENTS

Foreword

Eamonn Coghlan

Way back in 1987 I had just won a record seventh Wanamaker Mile in front of an over-excited attendance of 19,000 fans in Madison Square, New York. There to witness the event was my dear friend, mentor and fellow Villanova University alumnus, the great Noel Carroll.

Noel epitomised what Masters running was all about. To me he was the pathfinder in Masters running in Ireland, if not the world. He loved his sport and he inspired many a man and woman to keep it going, or for that matter, not to be afraid to take up the sport at forty years of age or beyond. Noel trained hard almost every day in Trinity College still in pursuit of chasing the clock, but more importantly, he believed that having goals and challenges was the secret to keeping the human spirit alive.

Immediately after that race down on the wooden track in the Garden, Noel suggested that in a few years' time I'd be forty, eligible for Masters competitions and that I should consider keeping it going to chase down what he considered "soft records". I distinctly recall responding, "No thanks Noel, I'd never run in the Masters category, it's not for me". Why? Well I didn't take Masters running serious. I believed that it was something runners did in the hope of just holding on or hoping to improve their times. Athletes who were high achievers wanted to get out of the sport when they considered "their time was up"!

I also recall a certain occasion years earlier, again in the Garden, a certain Jim Ryun and Lasse Viren running in a Masters invitational mile race. I was not impressed. Both ran something in the region of five minutes and I swore I'd never make an exhibition of myself! I wanted my abiding memories of these great champions whom I idolised as a kid preserved, not two old dudes making a show of themselves in front of so many people who appeared to feel sorry for what was witnessed. Masters running was something I did not want to ever consider when I retired from the sport!

All that changed. After two years in hiatus, retired from racing, drinking a few beers and the odd cigar, I felt empty inside. I felt unfulfilled. I knew something was missing from my life. Yeah, I won many a race and reached the highest levels in athletics, but there was a serious void. Playing golf, cycling, walking, and swimming wasn't doing it for me as I approached my thirty-ninth birthday. That void was RUNNING.

I wanted to run again. I wanted to win again. I wanted to dream again. I wanted to get the fulfilment and personal satisfaction of achieving goals. I got the bug. Thankfully, through personal and domestic sacrifices, I returned to training, quietly behind the scenes. I planned, prepared and was willing to give it one more giant lash. I returned to the tracks in America.... The rest is now history.

Master's running completed my story.... Noel Carroll was right! And, I'm now part of a golden era!

This book, *A Golden Era,* is a story long overdue. It gives an insight into life within the athletics family in Ireland over many a decade and is a wonderful tribute to the many men and women who have given their lives to the sport and beyond, not just for the glory, but for the pride and contribution to society.

Michael Gygax and his fellow contributors have captured the history of these great sportspeople, both on and off the track, and brought their lives out in a most meaningful way.

What we learn is not necessarily a history of their successes, but what they have all put into the sport and making their lives and those they've touched most fulfilling. It's a celebration of the great characters and the colourful people we got to know over the years.

It's not just a book outlining the athletic achievements of Ireland's outstanding performers; it's also a story of some of our unsung heros who fill the pages of history like it's never been told before.

As a young child growing up in Dublin I was fortunate to have my father Bill take me along to cross country and track and field meetings. When I entered the sport formally as a twelve year old, I got to hear and learn many of the names of great characters in the sport. I was even luckier when I got to train with and race against quite a number of those referenced in this book. People like Maeve Kyle, Nick Corish, Willie Dunne, Jimmy O'Neill, Hugo Duggan stand to mind, and this book shows the enormous contribution they've made, which was unknown even though people around them for years thought they knew them.

Others featured like the late Jim McNamara, Mick Connolly and Tony Murphy who I had the privilege to train with in Donore Harriers. It was men like these who inspired me and made me believe that one day I could do it! Yet, little did I know the real them until I read *A Golden Era.* Also, the late Padraig Keane ... what a tough man he was. Little natural talent, but he had a huge capacity for hard work. Jerry Kiernan was a close training mate and is a friend to this day. I nearly got him disqualified after he won the Dublin Marathon in 1982 "for pacing him for 30 yards".

The story behind Frank Murphy is enthralling. Described in this book as the George Best of Irish athletics is probably right on! Frank is the one who got me my scholarship to Villanova University. Without Frank I'd never have made it in athletics. I always considered Frank as one on the greatest athletes to come out of Ireland. He was stylish, fast and boy, did he charm the girls!

Then there's "galloping Jesus" a.k.a. Fr Liam Kelleher. What a great man, full of enthusiasm for life and for people. He played a major role in our sport. I recall him saying Mass in Ger Hartmann's home in Florida just before I broke the sub-four minute Master's mile. He did it in 7:58 seconds. The quickest ever!

There are so many others I could reference in this foreword, but instead I'll leave it to the authors to bring their lives to you in this book.

Recently I completed a TV series, *SuperFit Seniors*. My favourite quote that emerged was from a gentleman named Brian Cullen, a 74-year-old F2 car racer. It was:

"Growing old is mandatory, growing up is optional."

This is the spirit captured in *A Golden Era*. It's never too old to start. Running gives you back your youth!

Preface

Michael Gygax

*A*Golden Era* is a book which gives masters athletes and authors a voice. Embarking on this project has given me the opportunity to catch up with the greats of Irish sport. Some are household names, while others exist in relative obscurity. Engaging individuals to chronicle their stories, opinions, philosophies, history and geography has been a great joy. Athletes are a family comprising a diverse range of people, and this work will allow their stories and achievements to be heard.

Excellence in sport can commence in childhood through to adolescence and beyond. This project explores the longevity, span, depth and range of participation in sport. Some individuals come into sport late, excelling beyond their wildest expectations. Others compete at the highest level all throughout their lives. Some individuals win a major championship then hang their socks up at the top.

The criteria for initial entry to the book is to have won a medal at European or World level in an individual event. I also include masters who have won multiple years in their age category and those who hold very impressive Irish all comers' records. A number of domestic masters are also included– those who compete at the highest level locally but not internationally, often beating top seniors and European/World Masters champions in their age category. Participation in this project has inspired them to broaden their horizons beyond local competition. This will potentially strengthen Irish participation at major international championships in the future.

Participants largely live ordinary lives but have something special that allows them to excel. Some have achieved greatness in the midst of illness, injury, economic meltdown or other adversity. Their sport has allowed them to transcend their difficulties through lessons learned in training and competing.

The narratives in this work examine the qualities that make a champion. It gives us insights into training methods, and explores a diverse range of characters in our sport. Athletics is a soup composed of philosophers, eccentrics, academics, fundamentalists, the funny and the bizarre. It comprises the serious and the silly, all of whom are the highest of achievers. Personalities here are a curiosity mix of discipline, diligence, life force and resilience learned through winning and losing.

The subjects of this work whistle with intensity, humour, self-deprecation, love of life, modesty, narcissism, heroism and anti-heroism. Many are key members of clubs, local communities and national bodies. Their role as an athlete is often interchangeable with that of coach, manager, official or guru. This is the story of the athletic family.

A Golden Era is also special because of the calibre of its authors. This work aims to relay an essence of the person profiled, the author and the subject matter. Individual stories are carved out with skill, insight, enthusiasm and love of craft.

The subjects were given the opportunity to nominate a person to write their piece. Some have decided to record their own journey through narrative. A loyal and knowledgeable band of authors has helped make this work inspirational and eclectic.

This book is a valuable memento of athletic greats, their achievements, their authors, communities, families and clubs. It is a cornucopia of wisdom giving an insight into sociological changes in Irish lifestyles and training methods, and it chronicles the great personalities of Irish sport and writing. We are in a golden age of masters athletics in Ireland, where the standard is so high in some events it may be harder to win a national title than an international competition. The stories of Irish masters deserve to be heard, and their achievements need to be recorded.

Excuse Me ...What Age Are You?...

Owen McLoughlin

In November 2003 I linked in with Rathfarnham WSAF AC, unfit, with more than a bit of fat on the bones. I was 39 and was aware of the 40 mark fast approaching. Then I would qualify and run as a master athlete. I had less than a year to attempt to get fit and compete on a level playing pitch with my peers. How exciting! One could claim to be the 8th fastest man in Ireland over 40 to run 400m (that's if 8 such men turned up for the race)!

I had run before in my teens and remember huge fields of hundreds in cross country races in the 1970s in the Phoenix Park where the primary aim was to escape the mass start unspiked. David Ivers (he of Athboy Sports Therapy) was my classmate and he graduated quickly to much faster competition. What happened to me between the ages of 18 and 38 years is for another book. Suffice to say that my 20 year athletic career break left low mileage in my pins!

How naïve I was vis a vis the potential 'lower' standards of men over 40 in Ireland. Not only that but, having diligently built up a strength and endurance over a year, the masters' bar was reduced to 35 years of age in keeping with IAAF regulations. The task was becoming even more difficult. We now had young masters, old masters and ancient masters! For a 49-year-old to compete against a 35-year-old is verging on the ridiculous (except when you mention names like Mick Traynor and Pauric McKinney!). However, you go with the flow and soon you get to know the standards for medalling in road, cross country and track. I didn't have to look much further than our own club to see how high the bar was: Adam Jones ran 2 hours 31 minutes for the marathon over 50 years of age. This is world class and put him justly there at that time of his life 20 years ago. Terry McConnon ran two laps of 60 seconds each for a 2min 800m over 40, so close to almost figure among the immortals. John Farrelly came within seconds of breaking 16 mins for a road 5k over 40 years of age which ain't at all bad. You can see how important your particular age is within the masters section of athletics for the wannabees to achieve bragging rights.

That brings me to the point of all this. Every August, the good the bad and the ugly (present writer excluded) gather in Tullamore for the National Masters Track and Field Championships: Grown men (oul lads!) warming up with the sole preoccupation of medalling in their event. As they limber and chat to each other there is an underlying tension and a query as to which event and category you entered. The inevitable question comes after a few minutes of warm up: "What age are ya now?" How many adult men ask each other their age in society? I had neither stated my age nor proffered an answer to such a question in many a long year. Perhaps in a local disco, as you puff out your chest and pull in your stomach, you might shave a decade off your requested age but in broad daylight? "When did you turn 45? Shit, I haven't a prayer in the 800!"

At registration and number collection a scan of confirmed entrants is carried out by all arriving entrants. "Will it be one race in the 5K?" "The gold is already assured in the 800m M2" (for those not well versed: M1 refers to over 35 years of age and not a motorway, M2 over 40, etc… more later about the intensity of competition in the M10!) "How many have collected their numbers for the M3 1500m?"; "Great news: Johnny X isn't entered. Looks like a potential medal for me." Then the inevitable happens. Johnny X appears out of a car and wangles a late entry in the 1500m which just "shouldn't be allowed". There is a nervous tension ahead of "soon to be called to assemble" on the start line. Men being men we never call it nervous tension and nonchalantly portray either modesty or bravado, both belying the fact that you are sh***ing yourself. I have always questioned myself after as to why there is such tension before the race and during the warm up, in contrast to the absolute relaxed attitude during the cool down, regardless of medal achievement. Fellow competitors start to gather close to the start for fear of missing the gun which would be heart-wrenching!

The biggest catastrophe is to be beaten by a club mate in the same age category! With strangers, the bitter memory is soon erased or just never discussed with family and friends. With club mates, their version of that victory is what is avidly listened to on the following Tuesday and if necessary on every Tuesday for the rest of the year. Funnily, with every re-telling you are gradually appearing in a poorer light. Worse still, if you are 3rd in the M3 800m behind two of your "stablemates"! What kind of an All-Ireland standard is it if 3 out of 3 medals go to your club! No matter what position you come, the colour of your medal or whether there were even more than 3 in the race, your version of the story is embellished on retelling that you came 3rd in the All-Ireland 800m track champs and had a pretty good run. Your savvy teammates will ask how many ran and whether you broke 2-20, which is what you should be doing. The fact that 3 ran and it took you 3 minutes is suddenly irrelevant.

Masters or veterans as they were once known, is not only about the old and the ancient running races against each other, but there is an array of throws, jumps, walks and medals to be won. Patsy O'Connell a Kerry farmer has been competing in these championships for what seems like generations. Ask Pat how he got into the sport and he will tell you the following yarn. "When I was only a garsun, all the schoolchildren played football in the school yard which overlooked old widow Dunne's garden, an old lady we reckoned was the wicked witch of the West. Every time our football trespassed into her plot, she would dart out to the garden, grab the ball and scurry back into her cottage. On occasion when we were playing she would peer over the garden wall and hiss, 'Do you see the smoke coming from my chimney – that is your football gone up in smoke.' One summer's day the ball was loafed into her garden and Patsy hurdled the fence, grabbed the ball, and returned it to the school yard before pole vaulting over the fence, to safety, before the old widow Dunne had time to grab him. During all this commotion the schoolchildren cheered, clapped and whistled. This is the first inkling Patsy had that he had athletic ability and he has been competing ever since." When Patsy and his friends are competing the drama is a mixture of the finest competition and theatre.

At the championships you find the likes of Seamus Fitzpatrick 56lbs weight thrower of distance and over the bar from Portlaoise AC. His interest in throwing started in July 1973 when his family moved from Portlaoise to Emo village. He watched his father Michael throw 56lb weight and practice when he was growing up. Seamus does not train in the conventional way. He trains each day as a labourer on the farm. In addition, he does press ups and sit ups as part of his daily routine. To really test myself he used to put his younger brother William on my back and do pull ups or sit ups with him on it. He does however throw weights regularly, a couple of times a week. He stops throwing two days before an event. Getting ready to compete at a championship and working on the farm was always a difficult balancing act between saving hay and been rested to compete. On many an occasion he would leave the fields to compete in Dublin or Tullamore and to return that evening to continue his work once more after sometimes winning or losing. He can recall flying up the M50 in his car one day for a competition. It had been a bad summer and he was trying to catch up on farm work, as the sun was shining and this resulted in him being late. When BANG! The wheel burst – he had a puncture. So he pulled in and assessed the damaged. He grabbed the spare wheel to find he had no jack. So he lifted up the car as his uncle took off the wheel and put on the new one. With the sweat rolling down his brow, he made it to the Clon-liffe Harriers stadium and pulled up with ten minutes to spare to the start of the competition to find it had been delayed. Luck was definitely on his side! He togged out and competed in the 56lbs weight over the bar event and got placed for a medal. Seamus seems to stand five foot tall and four foot wide.

At road races and cross country there is the post-race analysis, the cuppa tea and brack (thank you Dessie Shorten) and the prize-giving. The latter is most interesting. Masters athletes want their prize and are willing to wait. No problem for the M1 category. Sooner, rather than later, the great announcement is made that you came second over 40. However, the analysis over whether you came 3rd over 65 can take longer and the hall is emptying faster than a drunkard's pocket! The younger you are the bigger the crowd in the hall to witness your tremendous achievement. The older you get the less people will see you hobble up to collect your winnings, sometimes less than you paid to enter and sometimes involving carrying bulky electrical goods you could do without doubling up with in your home! "Where were you all day?" "But darling, look at the oil-filled radiator that I just won!". "Just put it upstairs with last year's one!" Jack and the Beanstalk how are ya!

I have come home with toasters, irons and the above mentioned oil-filled radiator (anoraks guess the race!). In team prizes I have opened a 3 pack of sports socks with my compadres to take a pair each. Did I care about worth? Never have those astute organisers known that the receiving of the prize in front of your peers far outweighs its monetary value…

So what have we learned? There are times that being asked your age as a 50 year old is extremely important to the questioner. It's good manners to wait until the last prize is given out (you too will be 80 some day). Having paid 15 euro entrance fee and received a brown envelope prize containing 10 euro is a fantastic thing…

The last word must go to Brendan Earley and Nicky Corish. I don't know these gents particularly well but I talk about them a lot. The camaraderie and rivalry intensified as they both entered into the 80+ category (M10). They togged out in the dressing rooms (shorts and singlet with their bib numbers pinned on) on cold winter cross country courses, chatting amiably with all and competing avidly. Wow, an inspiration to all in society! Nicky is known to count aloud the runners passing him in a cross country race to selflessly give them their current position because they are all lapping him (he is over 80!) Brendan is still a yearly entrant in the Rathfarnham 5 road race. They never lost it!

It is a mathematical imperative that if one lives long enough, maintain an upright position and is able to waddle – one can become a world champion by outliving fellow competitors. Everything has a beginning, middle and an end, and so it is with masters athletics that the number dwindles as the age categories increase. Numbers participating peak at forty, forty-five, fifty years of age. The natural fall is incremental in the older age categories. Athletes get sick, injured and die. As a master athlete trips towards a century he or she can become a champion of the world in their age category. These sorts of musings often entertain the light hearted amongst the older member of our athletic tribe. It is not unusual for athletes to measure up to their rival's condition or ailment that might knock them off the podium. The race to stay healthy is as important as reaching the end line in first, second or third place.

So, when you walk down the road and a strange man of your vintage asks you your age, be afraid, be very afraid… He may be on the start line with you next August in Tullamore. People never really lose their inner child and that is a good thing. Masters athletes are competitive to the end, a great thing to witness. Surely that is what makes the world go round!

JIMMY BENNETT
Date of Birth: 25/5/1940

Gentle Jim

By Cillian Lonergan

"Sport allows us to transcend our personal limitations"

Big Jim or Gentle Jim? Both names have often been used to describe Clon-liffe's Jim Bennett. Standing 6ft 2inches tall, and with that, there could have been a measurement mistake, Jim Bennett is one of the great examples of a Masters athlete that didn't come up through the ranks of traditional Junior and Senior athletics. For that reason Jim and those like him are a tremendous advertisement of the fact that it's never too late to start training, join a club and see where it brings you.

Football was Jim's first love, playing inside left midfield at various levels with Dublin's Home Farm FC for over 20 years. From the age of 12, crossing paths occasionally with John Giles' Stella Marist team, Jim was a very capable player. At under 15 he had a trial for the Irish schoolboy team, and it was two years later at 17 that he made the Home Farm first eleven for the first time.

Born in the same year as Pele (1940), he was fascinated to watch and read about the Brazilian youngsters conquering of the world in 1958. Jimmy was extremely excited about plans to hit the Continent himself with Home Farm the following year. Regrettably, due to injury, he missed this trip and struggled

Jimmy Bennett

somewhat in the following years to get his place back on the senior team.

In the days of heavy boots and even heavier pitches, the "fitness" training orchestrated by most football clubs consisted of a few laps around the pitch. Jimmy says he was "always well able to hold the pace of anyone at the club" and indeed won an open sports mile race around this same time. This race was his first foray in the athletics world.

However, this toe dipping exercise didn't win Jimmy over to athletics just yet. Volleyball took on the mantle of his back-up sport. Playing for the "Olympians" for years, his skill, fitness and persistence was rewarded in the winning of the 1979 National championship title. Jimmy continued to play and indeed coach up to 2012, when he was 72! The coaching highlight being his Elm Mount Under 16 girls' team victory in the National championship.

The inaugural Dublin marathon of 1980 took many active sportsmen down a new path and Jim was one such adventurer to throw his hat in to the ring. Working in Dublin city centre, he was able to avail of both the Phoenix Park and Trinity College for lunch time runs. Joining the start line of whatever races were on around the city and combing these with one long weekly run, Jimmy was firmly hooked in to the running boom. A great team spirit surrounded his group training spins out to Ringsend Park in the winter and it was this more than anything that kept Jimmy committed to his training. This regime saw him complete nine marathons, seven of which were in Dublin, one in Limerick and one "out the Naas Road somewhere"! Notably he stopped the clock under 3 hours twice for the classic distance.

After a decade long lover affair with the 26 mile event, it wasn't long before Jimmy shifted his attention to the shorter distances, but not without joining a club first. One of his colleagues in Dublin Castle was Clonliffe's Mick Kearney, a lover of the 800m distance. Their friendship had seen them jump in to the Liffey together on the way back from the Phoenix Park on more than one occasion. So, when Mick suggested to Jim that he should join in a few easy runs on the track, how could he say no? Thus the routine for the next 15 years was now set. Under Mick's advice, Jimmy joined in on a few group track sessions in Santry stadium in the early 1990s.

Faith soon intervened and after a few notable appearances at these training sessions, the infamous Laro Byrne cajoled Jimmy into the joining Clonliffe Harriers. Immediately taking to the shorter distances, or in truth, being "strong armed by Mick", Jimmy latched on to the 800m as his event of choice. Racing Indoor and Outdoor competitions whenever possible, he also mixed in some cross country appearances for good measure, but it was the two lap event that he favoured most.

With decades of stamina and endurance to call on, Jimmy focused the majority of his training sessions on speed. Based around 200s, 300s and 400s, he successfully embedded himself within groups consisting of younger and faster athletes. His least favourite training sessions were a series of hard 400ms where the goal was to run each one faster than race pace. On the other end of the fondness spectrum, his favourite sessions were a series of 6x300m and 4x200m. On off days, these group sessions were often supplemented by a lunch run in Santry stadium as well.

In 2001 Jim won his first National title with a 2.34.76 800m win in Tullamore. This was the start of numerous titles over the next 7 years.

As he approached his 65th birthday in 2005, Jimmy set his sights on representing Ireland at the World Masters Championships in San Sebastian. With this new goal looming ever brighter in the near future Jimmy's training intensity in the preceding months provided a solid indication that his form was better than ever.

Doubling up at that year's National Championships brought two Gold medals. With performances of 2.38.79 for the 800m and 5.29.43 for the 1500m, it was time to take on a bigger challenge. By the time the team arrived at the Championship had completed some specific training in qualification tactics, aimed at getting in to the final first and foremost.

So, it wasn't down to good luck that Jimmy qualified for the final with a season's best time of 2.31.10. Unbeknownst to Jim at the time, this was also an Irish age group record! Jim wasn't too concerned with records but on hearing from Willie Dunne that he had set it, he drew confidence for what lay ahead in the final.

With less than two seconds separately the top athletes in Jim's heat, he was delighted to have qualified as a faster loser. All was to play for in the final. Jim's plan had always been to get close the leaders on the first lap, run with them for the third quarter and then see what was left for the last furlong's sprint. This time the pace was extreme from the gun and when Germany's Willi Klaus pulled away down the back straight the second time around, there was nothing Jim could do. Still, he finished a creditable 7th in his first international event in a time of 2.31.30, just outside his newly minted record.

With a taste for the big time Jim continued to plot his training diligently over the following months. That November, he wore the green of Ireland once more that the British and Irish Master International Cross Country held in on home course of Santry. The 2006 indoor campaign saw Jim pick up two more gold medals, though this time in the 800m (2.54.30) and the 3000m (12.47.00). Repeating the medal haul at the outdoor equivalent, this time in the 800m (2.40.20) and 1500m (5.37.40), Jim travelled to Poznan, Poland for the European Masters, in confident mood.

The camaraderie amongst the team, built up with team dinners and post dinner activities made this trip Jim's favourite. With such a positive frame of mind, it's no wonder Jim was able to pull out his best performance of the year when it counted. Trusting his tried and tested tactics of sticking to the leaders for as long as he can, Jim powered down the final straightaway to capture a bronze medal in a time of 2.37.44. With the German winner and Spanish runner up less than 1 second in front, it was one of the races of the Championships.

Not sitting on his laurels Jim toed the line for the 1500m as well. This time Jim was stretched to the limit, managing to qualify for the final as a fastest loser, with a season's best time of 5.15.17. Jim's ability to raise his game when it counted saw another season's best with a time of 5.12.11, to finish 8th.

With his European medal in his back pocket, even the notoriously modest Jim appreciated it had been a memorable Championship.

Returning to the domestic scene Jim continued to pick up National medals over the coming hears. In 2007, there was another double with 2.39.77 and 5.42.2 winning efforts.

The 2008 outdoor championships stands out for Jim as one where that 6'2 inch frame helped him more than ever! Having pocketed the 800/1500m double during the indoor championship, it was fair to believe Jim would have things his own way in the outdoor equivalent. Planning to execute his standard tactics, Jim found himself in the battle of the Championships down the home straight. Crossing the line neither athlete could have known the winner, but it was Jim edging it by 1/100th of a second, in a time of 2.45.72 to 2.45.73. Returning for the 1500m later that evening Jim collected the 1500m win in a time of 5.51.07.

It's important to remember the athletic exploits outlined above as a Master were achieved by Jimmy despite a relatively late introduction to structured racing. How many more potential National and European medallists are out there, needing only the encouragement, motivation and dedication to try?

Major Master Achievements

National 800m and 1500m Master champion 3 years in a row
Master European Championships

PAT BONASS

Date of Birth: 12/5/1944

Fitness – The Thread that Keeps the Fabric of the Mood Buoyant

*"For many a flower is born to blush unseen and waste its
sweetness on the desert air"* – Thomas Gray

"Where genius arise a cacophony of fools will rise up against it"
– To paraphrase Jonathan Swift

Fitness, the thread that keeps the fabric of the mood buoyant In the poem "September 1913", W.B. Yeats takes a swipe at the traders of Dublin who "fumble in the greasy till/And add the halfpence to the pence/And prayer shivering prayer" stereotyping business people and entrepreneurs as a hypocritical class of people without pride of community or nationalism: "For men were born to pray and save:/Romantic Ireland's dead and gone/It's with O'Leary in the grave."

Ireland in early twentieth century was a much divided place, where tensions between the have and have nots, the businesspeople and workers were greatly amplified by the lockout of 1913. Yeats' sentiments reflect the deep bitterness of a period when the employers won the battle hands down and workers were dismissed when they joined unions, many blacklisted by big employers, never working again.

These words of Yeats could be quoted by artists to convey their sense of moral superiority over those working in economics and business. That attitude, some believe, hindered enterprise and innovation, making it difficult to start up and succeed in business, at least until Sean Lemass came along in the 1960s, and realised – unlike Eamonn de Valera – that Ireland must start promoting local enterprise and creating business links with the outside world if the drain of talent from the country that had begun in the 1930s was to be halted. In the Ireland of that time, generations felt doomed to recreate the lives of their

11

Pat Bonass

parents, whether as part of a thriving family enterprise, or as a doomed underclass, whose only option was to leave the country. Wealth and position was acquired through inheritance, while poverty and unemployment created a cycle that was difficult to break; for ninety per cent of people, third level education was not a realistic option; indeed few stayed in school after the age of fourteen.

Pat Bonass is one of the Lemass generation – a self-made man and a leading entrepreneur in the 1960s; a hard worker, a natural born leader and organiser who, with his sharp wit, enjoys the conversation and company of like-minded people. He is a man of many talents: a musician, a man of romantic ideals, and a fiercely proud nationalist. His patriotism is not expressed through marching and shouting slogans but in following and taking part in sport, music and cultural events. He delights in Ireland beating the British in international competition, while acknowledging that the British are great supporters of Irish athletes, a compliment which is not always returned.

Pat's father was a gardener and, as an eleven year old boy, he started working himself thinning turnips in the fields of Clonee, providing much needed cash to pay for school books and clothes.

After he left O'Connells Secondary School with his Leaving Cert, Pat went to work with Philips, an electrical supply company that provided him with the opportunity to study business and management at night in Rathmines College. After five years, he moved to Glenabbey Clothes and started to study engineering, design and fashion. Never a man to let the grass grow under his feet, he bought the "reject shirts" at knock-down prices from the company, redesigned the sleeves and sold them on at a handsome profit. With the capital he acquired, he set up his own manufacturing business and, from 1966, was soon employing nearly 400 people making children's clothes.

He sold the business in 1978, becoming an importer and travelling all over the globe. While this was enjoyable, it greatly hindered his involvement in sport and so, after ten years, he stopped his travels and began building up a chain of retail stores selling children's clothes and equipment. In 2004, at the age of sixty, he decided to retire.

As a twelve-year-old boy, Pat had watched enthralled as Ronnie Delany won Olympic gold in the 1500m at Melbourne 1956. Like many of his generation, he was inspired to take up athletics, although not a natural talent; he still recalls the occasion he dropped the baton in a relay race where he was representing his school St Bridget's in Castleknock. Never a man to give up, he persisted with his training; running regularly in the Phoenix Park and devouring anything and everything he could get his hands on about athletics. Peter Purcell, a business acquaintance and coach and later husband of the great Mary Purcell convinced him to join a club and learn how to run properly. He joined was Clonliffe Harriers, the club to which he has now devoted close to fifty years of his life.

While Pat Bonass would never feature on Clonliffe teams at Dublin or national level as a senior, his great gift was his ability to squeeze from himself the very last ounce of potential, training consistently and hard and dreaming of the day when he would wear the green jersey and represent his country as a master. On his 40th birthday, Pat celebrated his arrival in the masters' ranks by running a time of 2 hours 52 minutes in the London Marathon After he began to feature in local masters' races, he saw the potential of organising Irish teams for the major masters championships at European and world level.

One of his inspirations was his good friend Tadhg Lynch, a founding member of the Irish Masters Athletics Association, and soon, Pat found himself elected to the committee of the IMAA, founded in the 1980s and affiliated to Athletics Ireland. In 1989, some of Ireland's great master athletes travelled to Oregon, USA for the World Masters Athletics Championships and, to help fund the trip, Pat secured £5,000 in sponsorship from Dublin businesses as well as a grant from the Department of Defense. It was the first of many trips away.

When the British and Irish Masters' Cross-Country International was held in Malahide Park in Dublin 1995, all members of winning teams (not just the scorers) were presented with medals thanks to a deal Pat struck with Adam Jones who was generously sponsoring the medals. This innovation gave all team members an incentive to travel.

Running can be a metaphor for life, and in Pat's world there is no such thing as failure, just feedback. In November 2010, Pat's wife Sylvia passed away after a life-long struggle with ill-health. His son Pat Bonass junior, who had battled alcoholism, died soon after his mother. Through rough times and smooth, Pat has kept up his sport and his music. In 2013, he was diagnosed with prostate cancer and set about treatment and recovery in a stoic and organised way. He kept up his training and in August 2014, won the Irish M70 5000m title. He continues to train and to improve and in 2015, finally realised his dream of winning a major international Masters medal when he won the bronze individual medal in the European Masters' cross-country in Torun Poland.

Pat is a fine example of a dedicated senior athlete who came to excel in the masters' ranks through good planning and dedication.

Major Master Achievements

Senior: Best Time – Marathon: 2.52; Half Marathon: 1 hour 17
Master Road Times: Half Marathon Age 65 1.32
5 age group Irish records
First Clonliffe member to win an international masters medal,
winning gold all Ireland medals in all 5 running disciplines
(Track, x country, indoors, mountain and road running)
4th in the European cross country in Holland
4th in 2000 meters steeplechase in Hungary in a new Irish record
3000 meters steeplechase 045 – 11.26.00 Irish record
2000 meters steeplechase 060 – 8.53.98 Irish record
2000 meters steeplechase 065 – 9.00.2 Irish record
3000 meters indoors 065 – 11.39.12 Irish record
2nd in British indoors championships breaking the Irish record by 40 secs
4th European championship 2000m 065 in Hungary setting a new Irish record

JOHN BUCKLEY

Date of Birth: 17/8/1945

From Teenage Star to Masters Champion

By John Walshe

"There are no short cuts"

Just across the bridge that bears the name of arguably Cork's greatest sporting legend, Christy Ring, the sign outside the building proudly proclaims 'John Buckley Sports – Ireland's No 1 Running Specialists'.

Much like the iconic hurler whose inter-county career with Cork spanned an incredible 25 years, John Buckley too has excelled on the cross-country courses, roads and track of his native patch and further afield for a similar time span.

A native of Cloghroe near Blarney, Buckley first got involved in athletics at the age of 16. Three years later he became the youngest-ever winner of the Cork Senior cross-country title, something no other 19-year-old has achieved since.

"That race took place in Millstreet – the home of my ancestors, as my mother and father came from there," he recalls. "It was over a distance of seven-and-a-half miles and I beat Pat Coleman from Youghal, who I think was favourite."

It was through a Millstreet connection – Fr Paddy Byrne – that Buckley was offered a scholarship to Nebraska State University. "I was all for it at first, but very few had gone to the States at that stage and you could say I got cold feet and didn't go. There were 10 of us at home and none of us had strayed too far away and I had left school fairly early, only going as far as the Inter Cert."

In 1967, the year that BLE (Bord Luthchleas na hEireann) came into being, Buckley won the All-Ireland cross-country, the first Corkman to do so. The following year he represented Ireland at the International C-C championships in Tunisia. As Buckley finished in the middle of the pack, local hero Mohammed Gammoudi was winning the race. He would go on the following October to take Olympic 5000m gold in the rarefied air of Mexico City, but for both of them their paths would cross again sooner than expected.

On St Patrick's Day, 1969, around 7,000 spectators braved the wet conditions and headed to Ballincollig where the International Military Cross-Country Championships were taking place. Known as the CISM Meeting, eight national teams took part including squads from Tunisia and Morocco, the latter having finished in the top three for the previous six years.

The Irish challenge was made up in the main from members of the FCA. "I suppose you could say we were headhunted because of our running talent, I can't say we did much military training," recalls Buckley with a smile. "There was a fair bit of pressure coming up to the race and great hype when we heard that Gammoudi was coming. I felt good before the race, the confidence was high and of course we had huge support on the day which gave us all a boost."

Buckley got away with the leaders and as the race progressed he knew from the crowd that the Irish were in with a chance of making the medals. He was the leading Irishman and ahead of Gammoudi which really spurred him on. Up front, the Moroccans were well in control with the 22-year-old unknown, Ou Moha Bassou, defeating his countryman Haddou Jabor to win by a foot in a thrilling sprint.

Buckley crossed the line just 23 seconds later for a brilliant ninth position, two places ahead of his teammate Sean O'Sullivan with Gammoudi following in 12th place. When the points were tallied Ireland had a total of 105, giving them the silver medals ahead of Tunisia, France, West Germany, Italy, Belgium and the fancied USA.

In 1972, after finishing third behind John Hartnett and Donie Walsh in the Cork cross-country championships, Buckley went on to win the Munster, the Inter-Counties and the Inter-Clubs titles. After such a great season, he was then selected on an Irish team for a tour of Germany which would have a profound affect on his running career.

"A big team of about 40 went out and we had three track races in three different venues. I had never seen a tartan track up to that and the facilities were out of this world. I think I ran around 14:11 for one of the 5,000m races out there but when I came home I became disillusioned with the sport. I was working as a commercial traveller for Batchelors Beans at the time and would spend two or three nights a week away from home and I couldn't face going out into the dark strange roads to train anymore."

For the remainder of the 1970s, John Buckley did very little running, missing out on what should probably have been his best years. Then in 1979 he, along with his wife Mary, decided on the big gamble of opening their own business, a small supermarket at the top of Strawberry Hill. A couple years later, out on a social run someone enquired of the best place in Cork to buy running shoes and for John Buckley it was a Eureka moment.

"When I came home that night I decided as we had some space over the shop to diversify and go into the sports gear. We were very lucky when we started as we were the first shop in Cork to get leather basketball boots – they were called Nike Legend and as the sport was huge in Cork at the time they sold like hot cakes."

Now, with a set routine and working for himself, Buckley decided on a comeback. It was the start of the running boom and the second Dublin Marathon saw him finishing in a respectable 2:52. Back to his regular 100 miles a week training, the times continued to tumble and by 1985 – having reached the masters category – he was down to 2:26:50 which won him the M40 title at Dublin.

"Training at the time would be twice a day and based loosely on the Arthur Lydiard system with say a 10-mile at lunchtime with a group and maybe five miles at night. Once a week I would do a track session, such as interval 400s or 1000s with a hill session on another night. On Sunday, it would be a long run of 15 miles and all would be at an easy pace, except for the two speed sessions. Most of my best races were run off my hardest training and I am also a great believer in racing frequently."

At the 1987 European Masters in Spain, Buckley tool silver in the road 10km and bronze in the 25km and two years later another bronze – this time over 5000m – and a fourth place in the marathon were achieved in Sweden.

By 1991, he had graduated to the M45 grade where he recorded probably the best performances of his career, winning National, European and World titles. At the European road championships in Italy, he took gold in the 10km with his time of 31:20 also placing him ahead of all the M40s. The following day, another gold followed in the 25km.

Sonia O'Sullivan and John Buckley

This led on to the World Veteran Games in Turku, Finland, the scene of his greatest triumph. Over five days he ran four races, winning the 10,000m in 31:30.42, the 5000m in 15:04.07 and the cross-country on the final day.

"Going out there, if I had got a medal I'd have been over the moon. I had never run a 10000m on the track before but as the race progressed I was getting stronger and I pulled away with about a mile to go to win. Then I had the heats of the 5,000m, followed by the final which I won, and then the cross-country which was probably my best race as I finished second overall with only one M40 ahead of me."

A big homecoming celebration followed, including a civic reception in Cork City Hall. After that, John Buckley continued to race locally up to 50 years and he still loves to run, although racing is now a thing of the past. "I do something every day; either go for a run of 30 minutes, go for a walk or go for a cycle," he says.

His thoughts on injuries and diet are also worth noting. "I never had a major injury, apart from shin splits on one occasion. Like everybody, I got aches and pains but I'd say the easy running pace had a lot to do with. Before I went to Finland, I was at my lightest weight ever. I was always convinced my racing weight was nine-and-a-half stone but in Finland I was down to eight stone, 12 pounds. I wasn't trying to lose weight, but something I put it down to was a brisk walk of an hour or so I would do maybe five nights a week."

Nowadays, the sports shop emporium he runs with his business partner Conor Kavanagh is booming, thanks to the huge upsurge in running and races in recent years. As well as dispensing advice on gear and footwear, it's also a meeting place and source of advice and gossip on the local scene.

John Buckley Sports is also to the forefront in contributing to the sport, as seen from their 5km flagship promotion which is the biggest event on the Cork BHAA calendar, the St Finbarr's Half-Marathon in September and their sponsorship of the Graded T&F Leagues, along with associated sponsorship of numerous other events including the prestigious "Top 100" T-shirts for the Ballycotton "10".

"It's nice to be in a position to put something back in as running has been good to me," says Buckley. With almost a half-century of involvement in the sport he has graced with distinction, the enthusiasm is still evident and as great as ever.

And for anyone running the Cork City Marathon on the June Bank Holiday Monday, the man at the bottom of Mulgrave Road giving encouragement over those final agonizing metres knows what it's all about – because he's been there and won the medals, although now, instead of the T-shirt, he wears the yellow marshals' jacket.

Major Achievements

3 World Masters Gold

2 European Masters Gold

1 European Masters Silver

2 European Masters Bronze

3 All Ireland Senior Cross Country Gold (Inter Club/County/NACAI)

2 All Ireland Senior Track Gold

3 All Army Cross Country Gold

3 Munster Senior Cross Country Gold

3 County Senior Cross Country Gold

Ran 2 World Cross Country Championships

Ran for Ireland on Road, Track and Cross Country

NOEL CARROLL
7/ 12 /1941 – 23/10/1998

From Eccentric to Expert

P.J. Browne

"Ni bheidh a leitheid aris ann"

"To me a great track performance is a work of art. It is the culmi-
nation of training, talent, astuteness, mental and physical resil-
ience – a whole series of things coming together in one statement
or performance. It is short but tremendously intense. The 800m is
the fastest race not run in lanes; there is physical contact and ma-
neuverability as well as blazing speed. It is the putting together of
a whole orchestra of inputs and getting them together for less than
one minute and fifty seconds. It is, at its finest, art, and a real
runner knows that and gently reflects on it." – Noel Carroll on
his favourite subject, track performance.

"He's my horse." – Jumbo Elliott after Carroll had anchored
Villanova to a World Record in the 4 x 800 2 mile relay.

It was evident from an early age that Noel Carroll was going to make his mark in athletics. "I was foolish enough to think that I'd be the next Irish runner to get to Villanova after Ron Delany," he said. Looking back it is tempting to second guess but his observation reflects a time when such thinking would have been laughed at.

On the other hand, it illustrates how pervasive was the influence of Delany in Ireland in the sixties. "Everybody has a hero when they are young. Mine was Ronnie Delany. I remember my father telling me the unbelievable news on a dark morning in December 1956. "Delany of Eire" had won the Olympic

1500 metres in Melbourne. He had heard it on the BBC. It was about 7.00 o' clock in the morning, but I can remember it as if it were yesterday."

Noel Carroll came from a poor background. Poverty was pervasive in post war times and the sense of staying within one's class had not changed much since the days of John Joe Barry. Having extravagant ideas contrary to one's station were frowned upon.

"My childhood memories are clouded with nostalgia because by and large I had a happy childhood. My mother died when I was young and my father was left with a young family to raise. My parents would have been encouraging people. My father had no interest in running but worse than that running around would have been regarded as a slight on the family. Each family is allowed an eccentric but my father would have felt why was my son so eccentric. There I was at a fairly young age with no interest or hobby other than running. He quietly ignored me. My granny (on my father's side) lived next door so we were close to all of my father's extended family. I had a brother Patsy born in the same year as me and two sisters Kathleen and Helen. I came to the attention of some athletes who had heard of this youngster mad keen on running. Eddie Jones was my first coach at St. Peter's AC (Drimiskin) and I started training with them at fourteen. It was all farmers in the club so training and races had to be fitted around the work on the farms. I was tall for my age and rangy. The highlight of those years was winning the Louth Senior Championships in 1957."

The youngster left school at 13. "Between the ages of 13 and 17," he recalled, "I left school and got work as a labourer in the buildings and bits of farming in the locality to get a few shillings. I was running all the time; I'd race my brother home from school every day. I had no interest in any other sport so there was very little going for me. Secondary school was out unless you could afford it or had a scholarship."

Carroll's early education ended prematurely but he was an intelligent young man. His sisters remembered him as being very bright at school. "Everything he did, he did well, he was always motivated and helped us with our homework." Even so he was determined to find a way to better himself. "I had this urge to get out of the place I was in and do something. Joining the army was the next logical step for me, a means to an end."

He joined the Army in February 1959 and was assigned to the Motor Squadron in Gormanstown Army barracks. For the first time in his life he was able to run and train in a structured and supportive way. He was guided by John Kelly who looked out for the young man. He was a big young man and growing, so extra milk, eggs and brown bread – very difficult to come by

Noel Carroll

in those austere days – were found to build him up. He responded well to his improved circumstances.

His transition from cross country runner to track athlete began in the Army. He was reluctant to wear spikes for any kind of running and preferred to run barefoot. It took some persuasion before he was comfortable in spikes. His running ability was quickly noted and he won a World Military 800m title. Broadcaster Jimmy Magee remembers hearing about "this young fella who was the talk of the army with great potential." He sent postcards back home from the various places he was stationed all over Europe.

He came to the attention of Jumbo Elliott at the 1962 Millrose Games. Elliott was impressed with the big man's ability to race on the boards and he was offered an athletic scholarship to Villanova. It was an opportunity too good to pass up and Carroll once again saw it as a means to an end. "I was very conscious of the tradition there and of course Ron Delany. The opportunity to follow in his footsteps was the fulfilment of my wildest dream," he noted.

It was an opportunity that came about when Ron Delany, Basil Clifford, Noel Carroll and Derek McClean undertook a 7 meet tour of the US with Billy Morton. The previous summer the four athletes set a European 2 mile relay record of 7.21.4.

"We would like to run individual events as well as the relay," Delany told the *New York Times*, "but the truth is that at this point we're shy of training. There are no board tracks indoor or out in Ireland. And except for Carroll, who just got out of the army, we all have jobs.

Because of this we have been limited to running on roads or grass, when weather conditions permitted, during our lunch hours and on the hard packed sand on the beaches on weekends." Delany was particularly enthusiastic about the 20-year-old Carroll, "a strapping, black haired youth from County Louth, who packs 196 pounds on his 6 foot 3 inch frame".

"This fellow makes me feel like a novice by his cool, level-headed approach to competition. He has run the quarter mile in 47.3 secs and the half-mile in 1.48.5, and he really doesn't know his own strengths yet. I'm sure he'll be great before he's through." (NYT, 30 January 1962) Needless to say, Jumbo Elliott was quietly apprised of this.

Villanova

Going to Villanova University was a considerable challenge for Carroll. Lacking the formal educational background he was required to make up for the non-existent secondary preparation. "I was fully aware of how difficult it was to get into Villanova and I had to create a situation where Villanova wanted me. The army enabled me to become a better runner and that got me a foot in the door at the university. All I had to offer, my only advantage if you like, was my athletic ability. Jumbo accepted me on that basis with the understanding that I would fulfil the academic obligations." It was not an orthodox admission to university life as Carroll explained. "I was doing college courses and high school courses simultaneously. I didn't feel inferior to any student. I viewed it as a challenge, a disadvantage that I had to overcome. It never became a source of discontent because I had too much work to do. It was very hard alright but I enjoyed it and that was a big help."

His initial courses involved maths, economics, "subjects that didn't involve long winded reading and study. As I progressed in college I was able to pursue subjects that interested me. I focussed a lot more on English and Philosophy." The eccentric of the family was gradually becoming a person to be reckoned with. His reading in Literature and Philosophy – which remained a lifelong passion – broadened his mind, raised more questions than answers and heightened an already innate compassion and humility. Jimmy Magee would rightfully describe him as being "handsome, mannerly, with a lot of very nice traits."

His running career at Villanova was a pronounced success as his performances indicate. Elliott got an athlete who contributed hugely to Villanova's relay success and Carroll graduated with a very broad degree. He adjusted to college life quite quickly. There was no strong hint of homesickness largely because Carroll had scarcely any free time with his training and studies. "I enjoyed my time at Villanova and I did adjust well. I wanted to be there, I really went all out to make the best of the educational opportunity. What more could one ask for – all I had to do was study, train and race."

A clash with Elliott was inevitable given Carroll's intelligence and his insightful attitude to athletics. His love of actually going out and running probably averted many an argument.

"Of course I didn't agree with everything Jumbo said or did. More important were the things he didn't do. He'd show up and all eyes were on him, and he knew it. He thrived on the control that he had. On the other hand he could build you up if you were the type of individual who was receptive to that." Carroll had his own ideas, was self-assured and confident, but for the most part kept his silence. He was, however, beginning to show the traits (honesty of thought and opinion) that became his trademark in later years.

As the 1968 Olympics approached, Carroll was widely perceived to be a legitimate medal prospect. He wasn't under any illusions, however. "I'm determined to do well but it won't break me if I don't. I don't compete for good results. I compete for enjoyment." At 26, he was Ireland's most exciting prospect since Delany, and the reigning indoor half mile champion and AAA title holder. "I have never trained harder and I have never felt as fit in my life." He didn't hesitate to criticize the lack of government support for athletics in Ireland, a theme he would return to repeatedly in later years.

"This little country of ours must surely rank among the most conceited nations in the world – she expects success on a shoestring budget. If an Irishman wins a medal at Mexico, the credit will belong more to the US than Ireland. Most of our leading athletes must go to the US on scholarships because there are virtually no training facilities in Ireland." *Farmington* (New Mexico) *Daily Times*, 8 October 1968.

Perhaps his biggest difficulty with the coach had nothing to do with athletics. Two years into his scholarship at Villanova he was introduced to his future wife. Brendan O'Reilly was interviewing him at the RTÉ studios and introduced him to Deirdre O' Callaghan, the receptionist at the station. Carroll was drawn to her immediately and they began to date. Her musical career took her to many countries.

One of those tours brought her to the USA where they met and the relationship became stronger. They got married before Carroll graduated. When the athlete showed up with his wife Elliott was not pleased. There was growing tension between the coach and Carroll.

After graduation, Carroll and his wife returned to Ireland. Deirdre wanted to live in Ireland and raise a family in Ireland. Carroll liked America and he was returning to an Ireland with limited prospects. He left behind untold opportunities in America but was happy to do so. He returned with a degree in accountancy but it was also backed by a broader well rounded course of studies.

His international career may not have reached the heights he had scaled in college. He went to two Olympics at a time when Ireland won nothing in athletics. He was possibly too young and inexperienced in 1964, and the altitude worked against him in 1968. "He had the talent," Jimmy Magee pointed out. "It was a very barren era for Irish sport in the Olympics. He more than made up for it in other ways if you look at the range of his achievements."

Carroll's memories of competing against Delaney are remembered with fondness. "I only raced against him a few times but how often does an athlete get a chance to race against and run with his boyhood hero. My first serious race against him was in 1961 in the final of the AAA 880 yards in the White City. That race was won by George Kerr of Jamaica in a slow time (1:51.9) with Ronnie second (1:51.9). I was fourth (1:52.1)

"A few days later I raced Ronnie again in Santry. He finished third and I was fifth. However, the times for that same 880 yards were stunning. Peter Snell won in 1:47.2 (the fastest 880 yards in the world for 1961), Ronnie's time was 1:48.0 (an Irish record – his 1:47.8 in California was never recognized). I finished 5th in 1:48.5 (a personal best and the world's fastest ever for a 19-year-old).

I never did race Ronnie after that, although we did team up with Derek McClean and the late Basil Clifford to set a European record for the 4x880 yards later in 1961. We clocked 7 minutes, 21.8 seconds – just 2.4 seconds off the world record held by a US team. The result of this race was an invitation to run in the US indoor circuit in early 1962.

This tour was to begin my international career in earnest as I accepted a scholarship to Villanova while in the US. Sadly it was to be the last of the great Ronnie Delany. He ran some marvellous relay legs in the US to the absolute delight of capacity US audiences but an unfortunate Achilles tendon injury recurred on the tour and put an end to one of the greatest careers in world athletics. It was a privilege to race and be associated with him.

The roles were reversed you might say twelve years later in the summer of 1974. That was when Eamonn Coghlan won his first All-Ireland Senior Championship in the 800 metres beating me in 1:50.2. My career was winding down at that stage (I was 33) and Eamonn regarded me as a hero so there was a nice congruity at play in all of those events."

Carroll's place is the history of the Irish at Villanova cannot be overstated. He solidified the reputation established by Ron Delany; he added to the tradition and provided an important continuity in the link or "Irish pipeline". He inspired others to follow the same path and was generous with his support and advice especially to a homesick freshman named Frank Murphy.

Carroll continued to train and race and had an outstanding career in International Veteran's competition. He is synonymous with the Dublin City

Marathon and was the driving force behind its emergence. Ironically, he was better known as a voice of wisdom in the new mass participation marathons than he was as a serious 800 metre international star. It was a role he was happy to fulfil but he had no aspirations to be a serious marathon runner. Noel Carroll continued to run and race in the 800metres his specialty. "You don't tell the punters about it," he wrote. "They would wonder what the hell you were talking about."

The introductory paragraph to his "Runner's Book" is an apt summation of Noel Carroll the runner. It is deceptively simple yet intimates the underlying complexity of the man.

"I used to be an eccentric: now I'm an expert. I was once tolerated now I'm consulted. I have graduated from being somebody who should know better to somebody who knows better. The oddity I practiced was running. The only wisdom I can now claim is that I continued to run."

Frank Hearns Remembers

Noel Carroll was born in Annagassan, County Louth on 7 December 1941 and received his initial education at the local National School. His mother died when he was 14 years old and soon after that sad event he left school and went to work with the St. John of God Brothers at St. Mary's, Drumcar. The following year he joined the local St. Peter's Athletic Club and for the next three years he participated mostly in cross-country competitions.

By the age of seventeen Noel was becoming aware of his talent for running and decided that a career in the Army might be a step in the right direction in developing this talent. He enlisted at Cathal Brugha Barracks, Dublin and on finishing his recruit training he was posted to the 2nd Cavalry Regiment. At the same time he joined the Civil Service A.C. and met legendary coach Frank Duffy. Noel always spoke of this "stroke of good luck" and loved relating how Frank introduced him to the rigour and suffering of "real" training. He never forgot the discipline and commitment demanded by his first coach.

Under Duffy's tutelage and encouragement Noel began to blossom as an athlete. Following his victories in the All-Army 440 yds and 880 yds in 1959, the then Director of Training, Col. Jimmy Quinn, recognised his burgeoning talent and arranged to have him posted to the Ordinance Survey in the Phoenix Park. Here he took up the post of pay clerk, commenced studying and caught up on the education he had missed since leaving school. He revelled in training in the outstanding facilities right outside his door.

I first met and competed against Noel Carroll at the All-Army Championships in 1960. Even then he was an imposing figure. Standing 6'2" with massive shoulders, barrel-chested and with legs like sapling oak trees he cut a commanding figure. I would have fancied my chances against him the previous year. However the rigors of cadet training in the Military College and the physical and mental demands of three weeks field training in the Glen of Imaal prior to the Championship left me with no realistic chance of defeating Trooper Carroll. I was happy with two silver medals and a gold medal when leading the Curragh Camp Medley Relay Team to victory over Noel's Eastern Command Team. At the post meeting meal we met and chatted. We did not meet again for twenty two years.

All the while his comrades in the Recruit Platoon were posted to various units within The Eastern Command and commenced careers as peace time soldiers at home in Ireland. Then in mid-1960, out of the blue came a request from the United Nations for Ireland to contribute a battalion of soldiers to the peace keeping force in the newly independent Congo. In due course the 32nd Irish Battalion set out for Africa amid great excitement. While Noel continued to focus on his future as a student and athlete many of his young friends from the Recruit Platoon volunteered for the mission in Congo. Sadly, a number of these fine comrades were to lose their lives in the cause of peace in the ambush by Baluba warriors at Niemba. Noel often spoke of this tragedy and how in different circumstances he may have suffered a similar fate.

In 1961 Noel repaid the Army by winning the 800m at the World Military Games in Brussels –the first Irish soldier to win a medal at these games. Soon after this notable victory Noel came to the attention of legendary Villa Nova coach, "Jumbo" Elliott, who offered him a scholarship. He readily accepted and thus fulfilled one of his life's great ambitions. Noel, under the watchful eye of Elliott, dramatically improved his athletic performance and went on to forge an outstanding career in athletics. In addition to being an Olympian at Tokyo (1964) and Mexico (1968) he had the distinction of winning three successive European Indoor Championships (1965,'66,'67), three British AAA titles and fourteen Irish Championships. It is worth recording that his first Irish 880 yds title in 1961 was won in 1.52.5 and his last 800m title in 1977 in 1.52.35! In 1964, *Sports Illustrated* described Noel Carroll "as one of the best middle distance runners in the world".

All this time Noel Carroll, the supreme athlete, was assiduously developing his academic and business talents. On his graduation from Villanova he engaged in business with the same enthusiasm as he displayed in his sporting endeavours. As PRO for Dublin Corporation, between 1972 and 1996, he earned a reputation as an outspoken and tenacious defender of his employers. He was controversial on occasions when dealing with aggrieved citizens and critics of the Corporation but his loyalty to his organisation and his sense of humour were admired by friend and adversary alike. Noel spent the last two years of his all too short life as CEO of Dublin Chamber of Commerce.

When they both were in their early twenties Noel met and fell in love with the beautiful and talented singer and harpist, Deirdre O'Callaghan. They married in 1964 and they with their four children were a very happy and united family.

Noel Carroll contributed to the welfare of many sections of Irish society. He will be remembered for his role as Chairman of GOAL and in particular for his part in organising the now world famous Christmas Day Goal Mile. He is equally remembered for his leadership of the group which helped launch the Dublin City Marathon. Without his exceptional passion, belief and drive, it is doubtful this annual event would ever have been inaugurated and become such a huge success story. It is truly fitting that the Noel Carroll Memorial Trophy is presented to the winner each year.

When we met again after twenty-two years Noel and myself were to become training partners for eight years and good friends for a further eight years. Once again I finished behind him at the Irish Masters Championships at Tullamore in 1982. Now it was my turn to learn about "real" training. A typical weekly schedule would have been:

- Monday: 8 x 200 – one minute interval
- Tuesday: 7 mile cross-country run
- Wednesday: 4 x 400 – one minute interval
- Thursday: 7 mile road run
- Friday: 2 x 200 full effort
- Saturday: 3 x 600 – two minute interval
- Sunday: rest

Noel was a firm believer in speed training and short intervals. This belief stood to him well. As a master athlete he was unbeaten in domestic championships. At European level he was a gold medallist in the M40 800m at Strasbourg in 1982 and silver medallist in the M45 800m in Verona in 1988.

I treasure the memories of our sessions in Ringsend Park, Belfield and College Park with our good friends and outstanding 800m runners Aisling Molloy and Mary Reilly. Noel always referred to our winter cross-country slogs in the Phoenix Park as the "agony in the park". On our travels around Ireland, the UK, Europe and further afield he loved to engage in discussions on philosophy, history (particularly Roman and military history) and literature.

What I achieved as a master athlete I attribute in no small part to the advice and encouragement of Noel Carroll.

My utter shock and devastation on hearing of his death on 23 October 1998 were immense. I had spoken with him the previous day at Belfield where I was training and he was coaching his young aspiring 800m athletes. Encouraging as ever he had shouted "looking good Frank".

So how do I remember Noel Carroll? I remember and admire him as a self-made man, as an outstanding athlete, and a wise and shrewd business person. Noel was a man of integrity who never shirked the difficult call or to speak his mind no matter how unpopular his views might have been. Most of all I recollect his enthusiasm for life, his loyalty to his friends, his love of running, his commitment to his profession and projects and his love for Deirdre and their children.

Major Achievements

Sub 4 minute mile
Winner of world military Games
2 Olympic Games
14 national track titles
4 x 880 world record holder
Three times European champion
3 times AAA title
European Master champion Strasbourge 1982 V 40
European Silver medallist 1988 Verona 1988 V 45
Noel Was part of a 4 x 880 yds World record team with Villanova

SHEILA CHAMPION

Date of Birth: 11/9/1935

Sheila, Champion of the World

By Michael Gygax

"The only thing stopping us achieving excellence is ourselves"

Seeing a mature woman driving a car with a pole vault strapped to the side of it is a bizarre enough sight. Seeing two mature women, identical twins, with two poles is surreal. This is the scene I witnessed in Berlin in 2002 when

Sheila Champion and her twin and Dorothy McLennan picked me up at Berlin airport to bring me to Potsdam to compete in the European master championships.

Oscar Wilde declared that imitation is the best form of flattery. My children Fionnuala and Fiachra both expressed an aspiration to be like Sheila Champion when they get older. They had met Sheila when she volunteered to coach a group of young Raheny athletes when they were in their early teens. This petite, white haired woman, with her exuberance and fun way of teaching and training made a big impression on them.

In her own working life, Sheila ran a pre-school at the back of her house in Kimmage. She kept rabbits, hens and dogs – her own little zoo – for the children, a place of botanical beauty and diversity, a wonderful playground.

Sport was always central to her life. She was a national gymnastics coach for twenty three years and introduced a new style of gymnastics into Ireland. Like many coaches, she became involved through her three sons. Her lads were all high achievers, propelled no doubt by example of Sheila and her husband Barney who shone in their respective sports; Barney was a top class table tennis coach and player.

Each year Sheila goes to Wimbledon for the tennis, a passion she shares with her twin sister Dorothy who lives in London. She loves to watch the great and the strong; each decade bringing a new batch of champions, personalities and role models. She never grows weary of the queues, the conversation, banter and gossip.

There are very few sports Sheila does not like and she has excelled in tennis, table tennis swimming, pitch and putt, race walking and running. She has run twenty marathons, nationally and internationally. How many people would you know who have won European and world championship medals at events as diverse as race walking, pole vaulting, steeplechase, javelin and shot putt? Sheila has. Sheila has travelled the world in pursuit of competition, usually traveling with her twin sister Dorothy, who also competes for Ireland. During their heyday, Serge Bubka, Michael Johnson, Usain Bolt were hot favourites when they competed. When it comes to masters pole vault, the "Irish twins" fit into the same category, often finishing first and second. Sheila has a drawer full of silver medals for the pole vault. Rarely has she gone to a championships and not come home with a medal.

Sheila's married name is a good description of her character. Sheila does not give up. She has fallen but always gets up, never losing heart. A Kilkenny native, she was one of three children and attended Holy Faith secondary school before getting her first job.

Sheila Champion

Until 2011 Sheila trained with the top vaults in Santry Stadium. Witnessing a 75-year-old woman vaulting with a huge pole provokes a variety of responses – from awe to genuine concern for her health and safety. The young guns, girls and lads training with her, love her. They admire her dedication, spirit and ability. "She is the most inspirational person I have ever met," says David Donegan, the national pole vault champion. Sheila loves breathing the same air and walking the same ground as national champions. They are her friends. She shares their dreams, feels their exhilaration and disappointments. She loves watching them compete.

In her fifties Sheila became a champion pole vaulter at world and European level. Since there were no facilities in Dublin at the time, she would travel to Nenagh three times a week; the word "cannot" does not exist in her vocabulary. If you want it enough, you can make it happen she believes. One of the most extra ordinary things about Sheila Champion is not alone her lifestyle, her athletic achievements, her good humour, love of life but all of these things combined. That's despite having suffered three strokes over a ten year period. Sheila eats well, rests adequately, is positive and, of course, exercises; all the ingredients for perfect health.

The strokes she suffered may be genetic in origin. Her first stroke in 2002 left her badly paralysed down one side, with her face distorted and her speech slurred. It forced her to give up the degree course in psychology she was studying for at the time. She could not walk correctly for six months. Her usual training programme was replaced by a rehabilitation routine, including intense acupuncture treatment which she feels transformed her recovery.

Her second stroke she saw as a blip; If she could rehabilitate before, she could rehabilitate again. If you fall down, there is not much choice but to stay down or get up. When she fell in during a training session for the pole vault, breaking her shoulder, it transpired that she had suffered a third stroke. Her vaulting days were over and instead she joined the group training for the javelin and shot putt. Keeping her feet firmly on the ground seems to be better for her health. Recently she has entered European and world championship medals as well as winning national titles in these events.

At the age of 78, Sheila retired after winning the world championships in the javelin. She wanted to retire at the top and wants to be remembered as somebody who reached the top by training, perseverance and was still able to compete with people half her age using her hard-won skills.

Sheila Champion

31

Sheila Champion

Sheila Champion white haired petite gregarious gentle lady
Heaven bestowed multiple gifts talents skills determination
Energy extraordinary enthusiasm will of Hercules
Implodes with wild sense of laugher fun mischievous
Lifestyle of professional sportswoman, ageless, engages young and old
Astounding peers with audacity of youth, a septuagenarian female
Champion of life, overcoming three strokes paralyses emotional mayhem
Hurdling life's obstacles with determination and grace
Aura of invincibility accentuating positivism
Mythical magnanimous masterly cherub
Peddling dreams imaginings usually cherished by a younger generation
Iconoclast overcoming humanities most profound human fragilities
Overwhelming mortals of mediocrity
Nature nurtures extraordinary feats heights in athletics and the pole vault.

(Michael Gygax, 19 July 2009 – Acknowledging Sheila's warm personality,
inspiration and kindness)

EAMONN COGHLAN (1)
Date of Birth 21/11/1952

Eamonn Coghlan

By P.J. Browne

"Number one is just to gain a passion for running. To love the
morning, to love the trail, to love the pace on the track. And if
some kid gets really good at it, that's cool too."– Pat Tyson

"It was a great time for running. Domestic competition was strong. All around the country you had great meetings and relays. There were night when you could come out to a graded meeting and find yourself running against the likes of Noel Carroll and Fanahan McSweeney. And this was on a Wednesday after a day's work…Tommy (Gregan) was like Herb Elliott in that he would try to burn you off if he could get away with it. He was tough to run against, a great runner, and I earned every victory. I nearly had to run a personal best every time to get in ahead of him. And then Eamonn came along and began to make his mark. When he started to make an impact, I began to see the writing on the wall for the domestic athletes. The gap between the American-based athletes and ourselves began to increase, and then Eamonn made a quantum leap from four minutes to 3:53, and we could not cope with that." – Kevin Humphries

Eamonn Coghlan wrote the definitive story of his life, *Chairman of the Boards: Master of the Mile*. It is comprehensive, soul searching, and no aspect of his athletic and personal life is unexamined. His Villanova years are very well documented but even so the contribution and legacy to his beloved alma mater are hugely significant.

His early years are remembered with affection and the close bond with his father is rendered with tenderness and appreciation. The tension between the father and the son are both ancient and familiar. It can boil over at various points. Arguments surfaced from time to time. The passion for athletics that bound them also became a chasm that divided them. The relationship between Bill Coghlan and his son Eamonn could be almost any father son relationship.

His youth as remembered is part of a vanished world. Long before he ever had any interest in athletics he met the legendary Ron Delany at an All Ireland final in Croke Park. His father, an electrician, had the contract for the sound check on big match days and invariably Eamonn was given a seat where he met priests, politicians and celebrities.

"One day (1967) I met Ron Delany at one of the All-Ireland's when the match was over. Ron was the superstar the big name. I clearly remember my father bringing me over to meet him. I really didn't know much about Ron or his Olympic achievement. I followed the Dubs football team with a passion and also that great Chelsea side of the late 60s. I learned more about Ron later when I started to progress in athletics. My Da was so proud. 'Ronnie one of these days he's going to be like you.' I was looking for an autograph but he got distracted by other friends or admirers. It wasn't a snub or anything like that. It's happened to myself; your attention is caught at the wrong time.

It was ironic that over the years we became good friends. There was never any jealousy on my part towards him or vice versa, ever. I still have one hundred percent respect for what he achieved and he has loads of respects for my accomplishments. He would have probably felt really bad for me that I never won an Olympic Gold medal. Life is funny in how it brings people together. We became close and worked on projects together."

Coghlan started running as an 11 year old in the Phoenix Park with Celtic Athletic Club. He knew well that his father Bill, passionate about track and field would be pleased. Success came early and winning seemed easy against his 13, 14 and 15 year old rivals. He was however, ambivalent about athletics and played soccer. Like many youngsters he might have drifted away from the sport. That he did not is due to the influence of Gerry Farnan who invited him to join Metropolitan Harriers.

"Gerry took me under his wing and looked after me like I was one of his own. He had a kind disposition and connected easily with youngsters. He was a psychiatric nurse at one point and that gave him a unique insight and awareness. But he was passionate about athletics. He didn't just talk about the sport either, he ran himself, twice a day sometimes, and still managed his fruit and vegetable wholesale business. Without Gerry Farnan I would not have had the wonderful career that I had."

Before Farnan entered his life, Coghlan had his sporting heroes in various sports and he recalls one inspiring moment. "There was one veteran athlete who made a profound impression on me and I remember him vividly from the Stephen's Day 10 mile cross country race put on by Donore Harriers. It was a handicap race and he was there for what seemed like hours in the cold. That was Tommy Hopkins, Emily Dowling's father. I'll never forget looking at him year after year, with jock rash and blood pouring down the side of his legs. As a kid the man impressed me, because instead of dropping out of the races, he kept on going to the end. I was impressed where other kids might be turned off. I gained a lot of knowledge about track and field through going to all those races with my father."

When he was changing secondary schools, and reluctant to go at one point, Farnan was aware but didn't want to get involved. The youngster was mitching increasingly from school. "Gerry understood the difficulties I was having and what he did do was bring a bit of needed perspective to the situation as it pertained to me. My father knew Gerry was able to get through to me. Similarly Gerry knew how to deal with my father, if he was getting on my case. He was the go between and not just for me and my father but several kids at the club.

When I was getting ready to go to Villanova this was when Gerry Farnan was at his best. He knew of Jumbo Elliott and his achievements, the great tradition of Irish athletes there. Gerry's attitude was unambiguous. Jumbo Elliott would coach me during the four years at Villanova and Gerry would stay in the background. During that period we'd write, talk about the training I was doing, but he never once interfered. During the summers he'd be with me with the watch. In truth I didn't run a lot; some summers I'd stay in America and Yvonne would come over."

Eamonn Coghlan

Coghlan was very unsettled when he first went to Villanova. He was homesick, missing his girlfriend. Tom Gregan was still in Ireland after his father's sudden death. The 19 year old Coghlan was struggling academically, and becoming disillusioned. After six months he returned to Ireland. Effectively that should have ended his career at Villanova.

Coghlan didn't anticipate the intensity of the reaction back home. His parents were upset, Jumbo Elliott was unhappy, Yvonne was livid, and even Gerry Farnan could not hide his displeasure. Then Jumbo Elliott gave him an unexpected and indeed unprecedented break. He called Bill Coghlan and told him he felt he could do something with Eamonn and he wanted him back.

Coghlan was still reluctant to return until he sat down for a chat with Gerry Farnan. This was a defining moment in his life and he has often quoted Gerry's advice that 'a quitter never wins and a winner never quits.' Nobody, he reminded him, gets a second chance from Jumbo Elliott. Besides, Yvonne threatened to end the relationship if he refused to go back. She didn't want to spend the rest of her life being blamed for his quitting college. As Coghlan often said, that was the killer blow! He made a fresh start and returned to Villanova.

This time it was different but he found the training regime hard to adapt to even though Elliott eased him into it. "When I got settled in Villanova I progressed to training twice a day and logging 90 to 100 miles a week whereas

I might have only been doing 25 to 30 miles a week as a kid. When I ran 20 x 400 intervals for the first time in my life I was crippled. I never felt such pain, that's how tough the training was." Coghlan's mindset was totally different though; now he was more mature and prepared to do everything possible to realize his potential. Also, the arrival of swimmer Chalkie White from Drimnagh provided Coghlan with the presence of a neighbourhood friend. Ironically, they met for the first time in Villanova and become very close friends. Another piece of the puzzle was in place as Coghlan acknowledged.

There was no place to hide when Elliott had the hard work scheduled as Marty Liquori explains: "Jumbo advocated hard work but that lasted for about six weeks out of the whole year. But when he gave you hard work it was really hard work. At the start of cross country season we still kept up the distance work but we'd come on track one day a week and do pace work, 20 quarters something like that. We'd usually start at 70 seconds and come down a second a week until we got to about 60 second pace per quarter. The other track sessions were a variation of this workout.

We trained for our indoor season on the board track outdoors. On the board track, out in the cold, in the wind snow and everything where it's 30 degrees, we'd be doing 15 three-lappers, which is about 60 yards farther than a quarter, in about 65 seconds each, with a quarter in between. During the big meets there was no hard work. Jumbo knew what he wanted to do with his runners and he could do it with them over the whole year. He could bring guys along at a high plateau from indoor season right on through the outdoor season. I don't blame the Irish guys for not wanting to race when they went home in the summer. Many times they had to after a long collegiate year."

Elliott had plans for the returned athlete and he began by providing special tuition when needed. This allowed him to focus better on athletics. He was eligible to run cross country and trained with John Hartnett who was then the Number One runner at the college. His confidence grew as he stayed with the senior runners over varying distances. The squad was deep and talented and Coghlan absorbed the lesson while becoming a regular on the team.

After the cross country season Coghlan began his track career in a pressure-free progression. He was hidden in relay teams for the next two years. Elliott wanted him to improve his 800m times without fanfare and picked him for the 4 x 800 relay team. This was a wise strategic decision; Villanova had the best relay team in the country and Coghlan was exposed to the big time arenas that he would eventually dominate. Significantly, he was a "natural" on the boards, cold winds, snow and ice notwithstanding.

For his first outdoor track season Elliott introduced Coghlan to quarter mile interval training. The coach was relentless in instilling a sense of pace in his athletes. Invariably, the intervals were run within a tenth of a second of each other. Elliott might vary the number of intervals, the speed or the recovery until it became second nature to the athletes. Rhythm and relaxation became the mantra.

As this progression was taking place the athletes were learning something more important. "Jumbo taught us to think bigger and believe bigger. He taught us how to be individuals from the point of view of looking after ourselves and not having to be spoon-fed. He taught us how to coach ourselves if he was not around. He taught us how to act and behave. He insisted on a short back and sides haircut and a collar and tie when we travelled with the team. He taught us a lot about self-respect and respect for others."

The coach raced Coghlan a lot, week after week on relay teams. His first big win for Elliott came in the Penn relays in his freshman year, when he lead off the 4 x 1 mile team (running 4:09).John Hartnett and Ken Schappert were on that formidable team and they went on to win. It was Coghlan's first Championship of America and he went on to win 9 titles at Villanova and was voted Outstanding Athlete of the Championships on two occasions. At the end of his first year, Coghlan was regarded as one of Jumbo's elite.

When he returned for his sophomore year Coghlan continued to improve. Elliott entered him in an open mile In Cleveland where he took Dave Wottle, the defending 800m Olympic champion, right down to the wire in a disputed photo-finish. They were both timed at 4:03.9 – Wottle got the win but newspaper pictures showed Coghlan crossing the line ahead. It mattered little; this race proclaimed Coghlan's arrival in the big time. In his sophomore outdoor season he ran his fastest mile in 4:00.9. That he would break the 4 minute barrier was now a foregone conclusion.

After Hartnett's graduation Coghlan was regarded as the college's best miler. His first official sub 4 mile was achieved 10 May 1974, but two weekends earlier he ran two sub 4 miles at the Penn Relays, with his father in attendance. He ran 3:56.2 in a relay team that set a world record but because it was a relay it didn't count. That same month in Jamaica, he chased Filbert Bayi home lowering his mile time to 3:53.3, breaking the European record. It was the culmination of a brilliant three weeks of sustained excellence by the Irishman. He was now a world class miler and the interviews and profiles came with this new status. He made the cover of *Sports Illustrated* for the first time.

His final year at Villanova was marked by continued success. The 1976 Olympics was uppermost in his mind, but Coghlan finished his collegiate career winning the NCAA 1500 in 3:37.1 in Franklin Field, appropriately.

His Olympic and World Championship exploits and his success at the Millrose Games would follow on after his graduation from Villanova. Jumbo

Elliott's faith in the youngster's potential was amply rewarded. It did not come easy for him; he was hugely talented but Elliott turned him into a winner through sheer drive and persistence. It was a characteristic that highlighted his life after college.

The question who was the greatest of the Villanova Irish is not easily answered, and perhaps an answer is unnecessary. There are four athletes who stand out above all the rest. Coghlan is one of the four as is Ron Delany, Marcus O'Sullivan and Sonia O'Sullivan.

EAMONN COGHLAN (2)
Date of Birth: 21/11/1952

One Eamonn Coghlan

By Kevin Humphreys

When Eamonn Coghlan stepped off the track at the US Indoor Championships in 1990 unable to complete his event, a magnificent career as one of the world's best middle distance runners had come to an end in an apparently, most unfulfilled manner.

Coghlan's story is well known of two Olympic fourth places in the 1500 metres in Montreal in 1976 and the 5000 metres in Moscow were redeemed in Helsinki in his famous 5000 metres World Championship title. However, it is as an unbeatable indoor miler on the US Circuit that Coghlan truly carved his name as a running legend. For a glorious period from his European outdoor mile record in 1975 when he broke the record of France's Michel Jazy, who had taken the silver medal behind Herb Elliot in the Rome Olympics of 1960, to his three world indoor mile records of 3.52.6 in 1979, 3.50.6 in 1981 and his staggering 3.49.78 in Meadowlands in 1983, Coghlan brightened up the dreary trouble filled period of Irish history with a production line of drama, heartache and glory in a variety of scenarios.

Though still the darling of the track fans as the "Chairman of the Boards", Coghlan could command a decent living from race promoters, shoe companies and TV stations, but his body was crying "enough". Years of high mileage foundations in the winter and intense interval sessions for the indoor and outdoor track, had taken its toll on his body. Groin strains, hip strains, Achilles tendon injuries, all contributed to the decision to retire from competition at the 1990

Championships. Though there was plenty of goodwill towards Coghlan from race promoters and the business end of the sport and a good living could still be made, it had always been his intention to return home to Ireland. Following the death of his coach Gerry Farnan, Coghlan, his wife Yvonne and their four children returned to live in the beautiful house in Porterstown that he had built with the help of his friend and fellow Olympian, the late, lamented Fanahan McSweeney.

Coghlan was then invited at the instigation of another former great Villanova athlete, Noel Carroll, to apply for the position of Chief Executive of the governing body of the Irish Athletics Board, Bórd Lúthchleas na hÉireann, (BLE). What followed for Coghlan was, in his own words, "144 days of misery for both himself and his family".

That particular saga is not the subject of this article but, Coghlan and BLE parted ways in the business sense, after a very short duration. In November 1991, Coghlan took a position with the Children's Medical Research Foundation in Crumlin just down the road from his parents' home. He had begun to train with his old club Metropolitan Harriers, and the aches and pains of the previous years had eased enough to achieve a very high level of fitness. This he demonstrated by running 30.04 for ten kilometres in a Metro Club race in the Phoenix Park. He was then invited to run in the "Legends" while in

Eamonn Coghlan, three times Olympian –
"Ronnie, can we swap medals?"

Edinburgh against Sydney Maree and Nick Rose. He ran 4.04 for the mile on the road.

He was so happy again doing "what I do best". At this time, Masters Athletics was as he describes it himself, somewhat "gimmicky", with Lasse Viren and Jim Ryun running on the US Indoor Circuit in mediocre times. He took part in the Bill Rodgers International Meet in Manchester, Connecticut and an unhappy history at that meeting recurred when he was injured there repeating the events of 1979 and 1983. The possibility or running a sub four minute mile aged over 40 now became a realistic target. A coterie of great milers was now eyeing this possibility – Rod Dixon, Dave Moorcroft, John Walker and Thomas Wessinghage.

Not unlike the race to be the first sub four minute miler in the early fifties with Roger Bannister, John Landy and Wes Santee, the most likely to achieve it was, the fact that John Walker, Dave Moorcroft and others were contemplating a sub four over forty which provided Coghlan with the motivation to achieve the fulfilment he sought at last. Basing himself in Florida with his, and many other top athletes' physiotherapist Ger Hartman, Coghlan embarked on a regime which would cause many a senior international miler to flinch even today. Leafing through his training diary sessions like: am 30 minutes easy then sitting on an ice block to try to ease the pain from an injury to his hamstring followed by seven miles pm; am 30 minutes – ice, pm 3 x 1200 metres in 3.17, 3.19, 3.24, short jog then 4 x 200 metres in 28, 28.28.27, building to one of his last sessions before his race series to 8 x 400 in 61-62 followed by 4 x 200 in 27.28.

Coghlan, although running through pain, was on an ascending performance curve in the main indoor meets with Coghlan destroying the over 40 marks for several events. The world record for the mile over 40 stood at four minutes 13 seconds. In Gainesville he ran 4.08, at Madison Square Garden 4.05 and in Fairfax Virginia 4.02. In February 1993 in Madison Square Garden, he ran 4.01.3. He also set world records for 800 meters and 1500 metres indoor.

A unique opportunity then presented itself. When Bill Clarke lay on a veteran's mile in the Massachusetts High School Indoor Championships at Harvard, a strange coincidence occurred in that, in July 1953 at the Surrey Schools Championship an Invitation Mile was laid on for Roger Bannister, unlike the Coghlan story he ran 4.02.03. In conjunction with his sponsors Foot Locker, and veteran members of the New York Athletic Club (NYAC) the race was planned. Stanley Redwine an 800 metre runner was to lead until 1200 and then Coghlan would try to take it home. On the Friday before the race Coghlan ran five miles in the morning followed by a 15 minute jog and then 2 x 300 metres in 43 and 1 x 200 metres in 27. The stage was now set and on the Saturday morning Coghlan ran a few laps in his spikes to test the track. In its own way, this was reminiscent of New Zealand's Jack Lovelock in Berlin in 1936 not letting his spikes touch the track until race time wanting "the track to fall fresh and inviting under his spikes".

On the Sunday morning with snow falling in Boston, Coghlan invited Redwine to Mass, but being a Baptist he said he would rest in bed and give it a miss. However, Coghlan's lifelong New York friend Johnny Mauritz who ran a garage business where Coghlan would carry out car servicing, where he could unwind out of the glare of publicity at the height of his "Chairman of the Boards" period attended. During his homily, the priest referred to people struggling to achieve milestones in life and used climbing Mount Everest or running a sub-four minute mile. Astounded, Mauritz, an Episcopalian, turned to Coghlan and said, "coach, if you do this today I'll convert". Delayed in a snow storm on the way to the track, Coghlan relaxed, Mauritz reminding him that they could not start without him.

In front of the 3,000 high school students crowd the Masters Mile was called. Coghlan had felt no twinges of pain in his warm up. Redwine took it out as planned passing the quarter in 59 and the half in 1.59 and then, to Coghlan's horror, Redwine stepped off the track. Alone Coghlan raced on passing the three quarter mile mark in world record pace. However, this had happened five times previously, Coghlan drove the second last lap as fast as he could and hoped the last lap would take care of itself. At the last bend he

Greta Weitz, Michael Gygax, Eamonn Coghlan, New York Marathon 1994
Michael administered massage and acupuncture to Eamonn before Seoul Olympics
and in the summer of 2003 Prior to his departure for U.S.A where he cracked the 4 min. mile

relaxed and crossed the line in three minutes 58.15 seconds. Surrounded by his friends from the NYAC, including Pat and Margaret from the Old Stand in New York familiar to all those who have run the New York Marathon for Crumlin, a smiling Coghlan left Harvard thinking of the setting from the film *Love Story*. When asked if he would be taking part in an attempt in Iffley Road Oxford on 4 May, the anniversary of Bannister's race, Coghlan reminded the *New York Times* that it would be too late, as the sub-four by a veteran had already been achieved. Invited to compete at the Sunkist Invitational Meet, Coghlan declined all further offers to run. He left the indoor miling and the track and field world on his terms, a first, fulfilled.

There are no further entries in Eamonn Coghlan's training diary. There is only one Edmund Hillary, one Yuri Gagarin, one Neil Armstrong, one Roger Bannister and one Eamonn Coghlan.

P.S. Johnny Mauritz did convert.

Major Achievements as a Senior

4 NCAA titles with Villanova College
European record mile 3.53.3 [1975]
World record indoor mile 3.52.6 [San Diego, 1979]
World record indoor mile 3.50.6 [1981]
World record indoor mile 3.49.78 [Meadowlands, 1983]
World record 2,000 M 4.54.07
7 Wannamaker miles wins 1977 to 1987 aged 34
European Silver medal 1500 behind Steve Ovett [1978]
European Indoor Champion 1979 Vienna
83 sub-4 minute miles
World Champion 5000m 1983 Helsinki

Major Achievements as a Master

World record: Mile indoors 3.58.15
World Record 1500 m indoors
World record 1,000m
World record 1500 outdoors
World record miles outdoors
World record 800m outdoors

PAT CONBY

Date of Birth: 19/12/1941

An Authentic Voice

By Jim Kelly

"Challenges are what make life interesting and overcoming them is what makes life meaningful." – Joshua J. Marine

From a very early age, I was interested in sport. I played some Gaelic football but gave up in my early twenties to concentrate on athletics. The decisive factor was my good friend and advisor Matt Maloney, a teacher and runner at Drimnagh Castle CBS, who got me to join Brothers Pearse A.C. in the 1960s. I am still an active member.

In those years, hammer throwing was a lot more popular and was a regular event at meets. I took up the hammer with a workmate of mine called Mick Brennan and we got on very well. We trained after work. We worked for Roadstone and this meant that we could easily find suitable places for training. I got hooked on the hammer – it's a very difficult discipline; some would say one of the most demanding of all. It's worth noting that when I lived in Raheny, I trained in St Anne's Park at a quiet spot where there was a concrete area ideal for the throws. That would not be possible nowadays.

In the early days, sports days were very popular around the country, with lots of opportunities for hammer throwing. Every Sunday, you had a choice of venues, with meets held on grass tracks in big towns in the days before tartan tracks and all the related nets, circles, pits and safety conditions. Sad was the day this ended.

Rules and regulations have meant that promoting the hammer and other field events costs too much for small clubs; for instance, the hammer and discus must take place in specially constructed circles surrounded by elaborate and expensive safety nets. That means that, in present times, you have very few opportunities to compete as a thrower, unlike runners, who have road races and cross country, as well as the track. Ireland is a small country, with Gaelic

Pat Conby

games dominating. Yet despite the relatively small number involved in athletics, Ireland does well internationally.

Being a thrower requires strength as well as technique so weight lifting played a big part in my training. I can credit a lot of my success to the Hercules Weightlifting Club in Dublin's Lurgan Street, which is organised and run by the members themselves. It's the oldest weightlifting club in Ireland and has produced many world and European champions.

In my early days, I trained for two days at weights and two days at throwing and then competed on Sundays. As you get older, the weights you throw grow lighter every ten years, which means you can remain competitive and I have won a number of Irish and Leinster titles over the years.

As a master, there is far more in the way of competition for throwers and I have travelled to events in Germany, Italy, Spain, Denmark, Austria, Greece, Switzerland, Portugal, Malta and Luxembourg. At the British Championships, which I have attended most years since I became a master, I have picked up gold, silver and bronze medals. My best British win was with the 28lb hammer where I broke the record with 16.50m throw.

My best European performance was in Lugano, Italy in 2011, where I won a bronze in the hammer and silver in the weight pentathlon. In Europe, there are a number of weight throwing disciplines as well as the hammer, shot, discus and javelin. Among them are the weight for distance and the weight for height, which are still relatively common in Ireland, as well as the 28lb hammer, the stone throw, the grenade and the Goulding hammer.   I

As long as the body permits, I have no thoughts of retirement, especially since I enjoy the social aspect of competing. So I will soldier on, although sometimes injuries restrict me from training. I am now like a vintage car, with parts wearing out that need a good mechanic to keep the show on the road.

Top Achievements Senior
National Championship Hammer NACA
Master European Championships, 2011, Italy, Hammer M70, Bronze
Weight Pentathlon M70 Silver

MICHAEL CONNOLLY

Date of Birth: 30/09/1938

Nights of Dark Cold Rain and Snow Transmute to Gold

"Worthwhile goals will only be achieved through hard work, single mindedness, sacrifice and even selfishness."

Like most boys who attended Christian Brothers schools my main sporting interests throughout my early school days were Gaelic football and hurling. I was moderately good in that I was able to make the school teams. My greatest football claim to fame was playing in Croke Park for Synge Street CBS in either 1955 or 1956 in the final of the senior Leinster colleges against St Josephs Marino (Joeys). We were ignominiously defeated by a cricket score. Joey's team included Lar and Des Foley, Blackie Coen, Buster Leaney and several others, who played for the Dubs minor team which subsequently won the All Ireland minor title.

I mention this as background to the fact that there was no serious interest in athletics at CBS schools. When the football season ended there was a scramble by the games master to assemble an athletics team for the Leinster CBS championships. Somehow I found myself selected for the mile. Without any formal training or being a member of an athletic club I won the race. A couple of weeks later I ran the mile in the Leinster colleges and won in 4.32.6 which knocked 12.1 seconds off the existing record. I did not know how to race. My first lap was 62.00 seconds!

I was selected for the European Catholic student games team which was to compete in Lisbon (first time out of Ireland) where I won the 3000 metres. Again this was without training. In hindsight I recall when I was about 10 or 12 years of age playing on the streets and laneways in Crumlin, For some reason we were not playing football as we normally did (possibly the Gardai were in the vicinity), I remember about 10 of us running around the laneway at Bangor Road, a square of approx 4 x 400 yards. We ran continuously for a long time, maybe 2 hours, going home for dinner and immediately coming back,

Michael Connolly

reassembling and continuing for another hour or two. On reflection we must have covered between 12 or 15 miles. No ill effects.

In the autumn of 1956 (aged 17) I decided to study evening courses in Trinity and joined the Dublin University Harriers, I ran some races with DUHAC and won the AAU and NIAAA version of the Irish University championships. However the Christmas holidays arrived and everybody else on the college team went to their homes, all of which were either in Northern Ireland or England. This left me without a team for the cross country season. If I wanted to compete I had to join another club. By chance I joined Donore Harriers. This was in January 1957. I came under the tutelage of Eddie Hogan. Then I learned what training was. Within a few weeks of joining Donore I was on the Donore team which won the All Ireland Cross Country title.

I was starting to train with real athletes and I loved it. There was a competitive edge to the training and it was hard. A whole new vista opened up to me. The camaraderie and team spirit was new to me and I revelled in the training. An example of the type of training indulged in was 14x1 mile. This was run on the footpath between the Islandebridge and Chapelizod gates to the Phoenix Park. There was a timed interval between each mile of 5 minutes and the target was to run each mile in under 5 minutes. This was generally achieved.

At this stage I was working full time, studying for insurance exams, approx 9 hours per week and training 6 days per week. We normally had Friday off. I was lucky in that my (then) girlfriend (now my wife) Jean with whom I had been courting, since my school days was very interested in athletics. She acquired a stop watch and travelled many times to Santry Stadium and other venues to record my lap times in major races. Some of these documented times are available today (55 years later).

I completed my exams in 1960 and for a couple more years devoted more time to training. This was the period (1960 to 1962) when I got 3 international cross country singlets and 5 All Ireland track titles. Jean and I got married in February 1964 and moved to the South Dublin suburbs. In setting up house so far from the Donore head quarters, I found that I did not have the time to travel to Islandbridge. When you bought a new house in those days you generally moved in to a shell, and over a period of years acquired floor covering and household utensils over a period of years. Gardening, painting decorating curtain hanging etc became more important that athletics training. I did not take partake in athletics for about 6 years.

I came back to Donore about 1969 but for 3 years I was plagued by a constant barrage of injuries, hamstring, achilles, calf and back problems. Whilst I was running reasonable well during this period I was constantly getting injured. So I decided to stop running and started into what I then thought were enjoyable pastimes like badminton and squash. I played both sports to a reasonable standard. My general fitness helped. I then realised that I would only improve my standard if I got fitter than everyone else. I started back training in 1978. Back to the schedules of the 1950s and early 1960s. I started back with Donore and realised (a) that I was not far off the standard I had been at in the 50s and 60s and (b) I was not getting injured. The fact that I did not run much between 1964 and 1975 may have helped for what came later.

In 1979 when I had just turned 40 I ran the world Veterans Road Running Championships in England and I finished 4th. In 1983 when I was 45 I ran 15.04 to finish 4th in the World Championships.

Many were the days or nights of running for a couple of hours on my own when I was relaxed enough to think of and often solve work problems in my mind. This happened more and more during the last 20 years of my running career when business pressures were increasing.

The heavy schedule was taking its toll on the body and little injuries began to manifest themselves again. It was time to reel back but continue to train hard enough so as to not get injured. This I was able to do for another 15 years. Then when I was about 60 both knees became sore (wear and tear) and I was forced to stop running. Now 15 years later I can look back at what were glorious days, but they were not achieved without the bitter sweet days and nights of dark, cold ,rain and snow. This was more so in the earlier days of the 50s and 60s when you met and trained with your clubmates and the commitment by all to the training irrespective of weather conditions. This was in contrast with my later years, from about aged 40, when a large part of my training was on my own.

I had a schedule which by and large I adhered to, but I was freer to tailor the training to times which were more amenable to me. In the 50s and 60s it was not unusual to train twice per day, perhaps one day per week but when training on my own I regularly trained three times per day. The 10 mile run was nearly always with a group of good class athletes who all lived locally. This group consisted of about 10 athletes who could all run 10 miles in 60 minutes comfortably in training.

When running on my own I found that my mind drifted. Sometimes I imagined I was involved in racing world renowned athletes and tried different tactics (in my mind) to get the upper hand. But generally I found myself thinking about work problems (factual stuff) and throughout the run tried and often succeeded in solving problems, or working out tactics to solve situations where I would have had more difficulty when my mind would have been more cluttered.

To sum up, I would say that to be a successful athlete, you must be dedicated, almost to the point of being selfish in that dedication. This obviously affects your lifestyle and the lifestyle of all others around you. I know of several good athletes whose relationships with their partners broke up because of this "dedication" (selfishness!). We must pay tribute and say a grateful "Thank You" to those who stuck with us and saw us through the tough times.

Finally – was it worth it ? Yes, a resounding yes!

Major Accomplishments
1981 New Zealand 5km world Champion

NICHOLAS (NICK) CORISH
Date of Birth: 3/9/1924

A National Treasure

By Ciaran O Coigligh

"Keep going as long as the body allows"

Nick Corish was born on 3 September 1924 in New Ross, County Wexford. He was educated by the Christian Brothers at primary and secondary level where he was involved in hurling and Gaelic football. Have completed his Leaving Certificate in 1943 he gained summer employment in a local engineering works owned by Andy Minihane. This became more permanent as he unsuccessfully sought alternative employment more suited to his qualifications. After a period of years which approximated to an apprenticeship and at the suggestion of Andy Minihane, Nick applied for and was offered a place on a teacher-training programme in metalwork in Ringsend Technical Institute, Cambridge Road, Ringsend, Dublin 4.

After two years Nick qualified as a metal-work teacher in 1948 and commenced teaching in Capel Street Technical School from where he moved after a year to Marino Technical School. In 1955 Nick was appointed Vice-Principal of Clogher Road Technical School. A year later he moved to Killester Technical School (now College of Further Education) as Vice-Principal.

On commencing his teaching career he took up running and also refereeing at second-level Gaelic football and hurling matches as a strategy in order to maintain a level of fitness. This often involved refereeing two matches in succession in Terenure or Whitehall, both locations in Dublin.

In 1954 Nick married Pheny Power, a Home-Economics Teacher from County Laois, whose acquaintance he had made while on an Irish-language course in the Carrowroe, County Galway Gaeltacht (Irish-speaking area).

On being appointed Principal in 1956 he could no longer guarantee his availability to act as referee. He therefore increased his commitment to running in order to compensate for the loss of exercise he enjoyed as a Gaelic games referee.

Nick came to know Pat and Dick Hooper through his wife Pheny's family connections. This led him to become a long-time supporter of Raheny Shamrock Athletic Club. However, Nick did not begin to run competitively in a serious way until he achieved the masters' category which then was over-40. Nick acknowledges the Business Houses Athletic Association (BHAA) and the Irish Masters Athletic Association as having been important influences on his running career.

Nick's preferred distances were 5000m, 10000m and marathon. He also won quite a number of 5k and 10k races at National level. He ran seven marathons in all with a personal best of 4.10 or "3.70" as he says himself! He ran his last marathon at sixty-four years of age.

Nick and his close friends Sheila Champion and her twin sister Dorothy McLennan discussed specialising in one or other area in order to achieve success at national and international level. Sheila and Dorothy opted for pole-vaulting while Nick chose the steeplechase. Nick donned the Irish jersey for the first time in 1987 for the track and cross-country events in Melbourne. Nick's choice was providential and he achieved great success for club and country, winning Bronze in Puerto Rico, Central America, in 2003. This was followed by a Gold medal in Poznan, Poland in 2006 in the European Masters. In 2007 Nick won Silver in Italy and again in 2008 he won Silver in Slovenia. He also won Bronze in the 800m and in the 1500m in Hungary in 2008.

Nick Corish

Nick's involvement in sport was not confined to Gaelic games and athletics. Early in his teaching career he qualified as a swimming instructor with Irish Water Safety which subsequently became Swim Ireland. He taught swimming and water safety to the pupils of those schools in which he happened to be teaching. His achievement in this area is extraordinary when one thinks that he taught swimming and basic lifesaving to every pupil in Killester VC throughout his teaching career.

Nick had always danced – initially in Ballyedmund, Wexford. Within a year of moving from Wexford to Dublin he met his future wife Pheny and then began a lifetime of involvement, as a couple, in ballroom dancing in the National Ballroom in Parnell Square, Dublin 1. Their repertoire of dances included the Quickstep, the Foxtrot, the Slow Waltz, the Old-Time Waltz and a variety of Latin American dances. Nick who will be ninety (90) in September 2014 continues to dance.

Nick has always been of the view that the application, discipline, and dedication required for sport and physical exercise, including dancing and swimming, on the one hand and for education and academic attainment on the other hand, reinforce each other.

Nick commenced canoeing and boat sailing in 1977, under the auspices of the City of Dublin Vocational Education Committee, in Cloher Road Vocational College. Subsequent to his retirement, at sixty years of age, Nick took on a part-time position in Outdoor Education. He added a number of adventure activities, including hill walking, rock-climbing, orienteering, and dinghy sailing and board sailing or windsurfing to his suite of outdoor activities. He borrowed a Topper sailing boat and a wind surfer and built up a stock in Cahore, County Wexford, where he had already taught swimming in summer time all his adult life.

In acknowledgement of his contribution over such a long time and on a completely voluntary basis the people of Cahore erected a commemorative place in his honour with the legend:

To Mr Corish to thank you for teaching us to swim for fifty years.

What a wonderful achievement and what a fitting, simple and sincere acknowledgement.

Nick continued to run competitively at national and international level until 2012 when he was eighty-eight!

A publication entitled Symposium of Road Safety, Dublin 1964 Department of Local Government, 1965), includes an address (pages 248-251), by Nick Corish, representing Cumann na nGairm-mhúinteoirí (Vocational Teachers Association). The piece is extremely polished and displays a passion for safety and a depth of knowledge, including impressive references to statistics and strategies particularly from Sweden and Norway, other countries relevant to the theme of the symposium. The address highlights the crucial role of health safety in complementing road safety.

Commenting on the Road Safety precept, "Man mind thyself", Nick suggested that this is very laudable in itself, but in a Christian society such as ours should we not do something more, for having survived all the dangers inherent in our modern environment is it not incumbent on us all to be in a position to help others less fortunate than ourselves? To teach our pupils to show care and courtesy on the roads is good, but to teach them in addition the elements of First Aid necessary to save a life in an emergency is to add charity to common sense.

During the course of the article Nick explains how in the two previous school sessions all pupils in his school had been taught oral resuscitation using a Resuscianne Manikin, a full-sized inflatable model, with movable head and jaw sections which had been donated to the school by the Red Cross Society to which the school was associated as a Junior Link.

Nick finished his piece as follows: "Whatever little experience we may have gained in this field is freely at the service of anyone who wants it, and while we may never see the fruits of our labours in this life, perhaps we all may console ourselves, as we teachers always do, by hoping for it in the next."

The generosity of the author is evident in these faith-filled words. Fifty years after they were spoken, the theme is as relevant as ever to education and life in general in Ireland. Thankfully, Nick has in fact seen the fruits of his labours and that they have been acknowledged by people in a range of locations and walks of life. Recent awards presented to Nick include the Seán Bannon award from Trinity College and a certificate as a competent Toastmaster. This must surely be a great cause of satisfaction to Nick Corish.

Nick's sons have followed professions which reflect their father's enthusiasms: one, Denis, is a metal worker, another, Liam, is a landscape designer, and a third, Cormac, is a fish advisory officer. His only daughter, Assumpta (Sammy), is a bank official.

My first contact with Nick Corish was when I lapped him in the RTÉ 5 mile race and he helpfully and encouragingly informed me of my place in the race! In acknowledgement of that typical courtesy I finish with an acrostic poem I composed in 2008 as part of a series of poems to celebrate the 50th anniversary of the founding of Raheny Shamrock Athletic Club: Pat Bonass describes Nick Corish as a National treasure.

Nick Corish

Natural ability and indomitable ardour
Integrating running with ballroom dance,
Countering the pessimism of the old at heart,
Kick-starting a post-elder revolution!

Constant, courageous and courteous,
Offending only those too dour to dream,
Record holder, record breaker,
In you we image our future selves,
Senior citizen, servant to dedication,
Hero to all who come within your generous reach.

*On Saturday first of June 2014
Pheny Corish passed away [R.I.P]*

EMILY DOWLING

Date of Birth: 27/9/1950

A Sporting World

By Michael Gygax

"Champions keep playing until they get it right."
– Billie Jean King

With Emily Dowling's father and her two brothers deeply involved with Donore Harriers athletic club, it's not all that surprising that Emily (then Hopkins) took up running – though with Avondale not Donore – at the age of seventeen.

Remarkably, after only a few months training, she made the Irish senior cross-country team for the international race which would evolve into the world cross-country. Emily's father, Tom Hopkins, an Irish international athlete, was hugely supportive of his daughter as he was of his sons, Jimmy and Tommy who both went on American athletic scholarships to Louisiana and still live in the USA.

In 1973, at the age of twenty-three, Emily married the Olympic boxer Mick Dowling. Their four children would grow up in a sports-mad household, with health and fitness a central theme in their lives.

From the 1970s to the 1990s, Emily competing with Dublin City Harriers, then the top club in the country, was part of an elite squad which won thirteen straight national cross-country titles and the European Clubs Cross-Country Championships twice. At international level, she represented Ireland five times at the World Cross-Country Championships, but perhaps her finest moment came at the 1982 Dublin City Marathon when, at a time when women distance runners were only coming into the athletics mainstream, she won the women's race in a time of 2 hrs 48 mins. Later, as a master, she took W50 silver at the World Masters' Cross-Country.

In 1983, just before the first Dublin Women's Mini-Marathon, Emily and Mick founded Sportsworld Running Club, based in Bushy Park – a peace-

Emily Dowling

ful oasis in Dublin's south city suburbs; the name came from the sports shop run by the Dowlings in Terenure. Adopting the "Meet and Train" ethos of the mini-marathon, the club was open to runners of all standard at a time when athletics was considered an elitist sport.

In 1992, Sportsworld registered with BLE (now AAI) and started competing in championship races and, these days, has a membership of two hundred plus, men and women, unlike the early days when it was mostly women who signed up.

Sportsworld is well able to hold its own in the south Dublin area where Rathfarnham WSAF, DSD, Crusaders, Blackrock, Brothers Pearse and Tallaght are among the other active clubs, each with its own distinct personality and catchment area. With no junior members, the club concentrates on developing senior runners of all standards, with its "Meet and Train" section still thriving.

In recent years Emily has put most of her energy into coaching. She's a natural and instinctive coach leading and inspiring runners of all shapes, sizes and levels. Witness a rainy winter's night and see how many turn up to be coached by Emily. Now witness the same night if it is known she won't be there (a rare event!). Yet she remains unassuming and even diffident, shunning applause, gratitude and the limelight.

The Women's Mini-Marathon, now going for over thirty years, is especially indebted to Emily. Every spring, women in their dozens turn up at Bushy Park to prepare for the big day in June. They are all welcome and Emily patiently guides them from their first few faltering laps to the full 10km distance. Some have gone on to achieve national and international honours, notably Sandra Gowran, Bernie White, Eimear Martin (who married Seamus Power) and Lucy Darcy.

There have also been many team honours on the roads and in cross-country at all levels, with many members of Sportsworld taking gold, silver and bronze medals at Dublin and national level as well as in the annual Meet and Train summer and winter leagues.

In 2015 came a clubhouse in Bushy Park, the pride and joy of all Sportsworld members, partly funded by the Sportsworld 5-mile road race first held in 1985 and these days called the Terenure 5.

Attracting up to 2,000 starters each May, the race is firmly established as one of the most prestigious high quality races on the athletic calendar, with generous prize money attracting high quality competition up front, and the cup of tea, biscuits and cake for everyone afterwards.

Emily is supported all the way by her husband Mick, a Kilkenny man brought up as one of sixteen children with a father who drank more than was good for him, who found consolation in athletics and later boxing.

Wiry and sharp, Mick, a bantamweight, was the dominant Irish boxer of his time and a double Olympian, only losing out on a coveted medal by a split decision in 1972. His record of nine times national titles, with eight of those titles consecutive, was only bettered by Kenny Egan. At a time when Irish boxing was in the doldrums, he was twice a European bronze medal winner helping to inspire a golden era for the sport, which has seen it firmly established as Ireland's most successful sport at international level. He has continued in the sport he loves as a coach, manager and become well known through his television appearances.

There have been hard times. In 2005, a shock diagnosis revealed that Emily had cancer, which effectively brought a great runner career to an end and involved months of chemotherapy and treatment. For the 2006 National Senior

Kenny Egan, Jimmy Magee and Mick Dowling

Cross-Country, Emily was poorly and confined to bed and so when the race started, Mick called her mobile and relayed every step, move and battle. Emily listened intently and advised on tactics. Her athletes did not disappoint and brought home medals. Even in sickness the coach could not stop coaching!

Today Emily is still doing what she does best, shouting, yelling and encouraging. After a long lay-off, she runs regularly with her clubmates in the Phoenix Park. She can run nonstop for three miles. It is clearly tough going but the qualities that mark her out kick in. You can see her smile. That says everything there is to say about Emily Dowling.

Major Achievements
Irish senior international
World cross country participant
Winner Dublin City Marathon
Prolific cross country runner with DCH
World Master champion 5km Budapest 1990
Sivler medal cross country Brisbane Australia 2001
Prolific road racer
Best Marathon 2.47

HUGO DUGGAN

Date of Birth: 14/10/1946

A Jumping Success

By Hugo Duggan and Michael Gygax

"Remember, it's only sport"

When I joined Cranford Athletics Club, which was affiliated to the NACAI, with my close school friend Paddy Marley in 1964, it had only been in existence for three years and was the only athletics club in the county. I was lucky to live in Milford just three miles away.

In 1965, we entered the NACA Junior Championships which would take at Clogher Road in Dublin. To get there, we hitched a lift as far as Balbriggan with the local garda superintendent and then got a bus to Dublin, staying in a B&B and competing the next day. I won the long jump and loved the thrill of competition. The following year, I won both the 200m and the long jump; I remember Phil Conway, who was to qualify for the 1972 Olympics, also had a double in the shot and discus.

Those early years saw the Cranford lads travelling all over Ulster and I won many Ulster junior and senior 100m, 200m and long jump titles in those years. One Sunday, I travelled to Belfast to compete in the Ulster decathlon, with all ten events taking place that day. I won with 5,330 points and travelled back to Donegal afterwards.

Joining the FCA gave my athletics career a major boost. Sean Hurley had recruited Danny McDaid, Paddy Marley, Patsy McGonagle and me into the Western Command reserves. We lads joined for a bit of adventure, some free grub, a uniform and free transport, so it came as a great bonus when we found we had the opportunity to train and later compete in athletics against other regiments. Each year, the all-army championships were held in the Curragh and, in 1966, I won the General Mulcahy Trophy awarded to the best athlete of the meet. This was calculated on points and I scored in every event I entered.

The Beginning of BLE

The amalgamation of the NACAI and the AAU saw the birth of BLE and a bright new beginning in the history of Irish athletics. In Ulster, matters were not so simple, with the Northern Irish AAA remaining affiliated to Great Britain. So the Ulster Sports Council was formed to allow those who wished to compete for Ireland the opportunity to do so.

At the first trials to select an Irish team for the 1967 Europa Cup in Santry, I won the long jump, but was not selected although I was first reserve. With no Donegal representative on any national committee, one had to be extremely good to make an Irish team. I realised that having a proper structure in place is as important as talent and training, if one is to progress as an international athlete.

When the first choice long jumper Cyril O'Regan from Waterford was injured, I made the team and was the first Ulster athlete to do so. I justified my selection by winning the long jump at the first BLE Championships that year as well as winning the famous Guinness 100 yards. This was the first of a record seven Irish titles in the long jump as well as four silver medals. I also went on to compete fifteen times for my country. In 1967, I set a Donegal and Ulster Sports Council record of 7.39m for the long jump in Emyvale that still stands today and I won national senior titles with Cranford, Clonliffe, Lifford and Finn Valley, which makes me, I'm told, the only athlete to win with four different clubs.

When Paddy Marley, Danny and Frankie McDaid and I came to Dublin in late 1967 seeking work and adventure, we had joined Clonliffe Harriers. I had a few enjoyable years with the club, although I was surprised to find that there was no specialised coaching for jumpers and I was left to my own devices. By contrast, the runners were well catered for with training groups and coaching. So although I competed with Clonliffe, I did most of my training with my friends in Raheny Shamrocks – Paddy Noonan, Paddy Fay, Anto O'Connell and many more. I also had a love for soccer and played for Telephones United.

I remember competing in the two-day George V. Ryan Trophy the first year Clonliffe won it. On the Saturday, I accumulated points in the 100m, triple jump, high jump and 4x100m. On Sunday morning, I played a match for Telephones and, that afternoon, was back in Santry picking up points in 200m, long jump, javelin and 4x400m. Championships in those days were social gatherings and, after the last day of competition, athletes from different clubs would go to the "Hole in the Wall" in Sutton for a swim and a few beers.

In Donegal, a county board was formed in 1971 and athletics became more structured with county championships in track and field and cross-country. Athletics took off in the county, and soon the number of clubs had mushroomed from one to fourteen. The sport was promoted largely through the newspapers, but pirate radio and local radio played a very important role in advertising every aspect of athletics. Athletics began to take pride of place in many a Donegal heart. Today, Donegal athletics is strongly represented at national level by Theresa McDaid, Eamonn Harvey, Eamon Giles and Patsy McGonagle, who have long been part of the executive and coaching structures of both BLE and Athletics Ireland.

I remember on one occasion when I saw an international meet advertised for Ballinasloe. I had won the long jump there a few years earlier so travelled down. On my arrival, I discovered that there was no long jump but one of the officials told me that there was a spade at the pit and I could dig it and have a few jumps. Tom O'Riordan reported this in his column in the *Irish Independent* and another story was headlined 'In Ballinasloe they call a spade a spade'. The *Sunday World* picked it up and it ran for about four weeks with comments and replies each week.

In 1970, I returned home to Donegal delivering bread from Milford Bakery to depots all over Ulster and as far south as Dundalk. I normally loaded my truck at 7.00 pm, drove it to Ballybofey where I would train with the lads and eat something with Patsy McGonagle before resuming a twelve-hour round journey. I did those late night journeys for thirty years, six day a week. The roads were poor in the early days but they improved over the years making life more comfortable. Of course for two decades, I had to be careful, since the

Troubles were at their height during the seventies and early eighties. Thankfully I never ran into any real danger.

My training was specific: circuits, speed drills and dynamic sprints, yet I always mixed football and other activities with my athletics. Today I see children specialising from a very young age, confining themselves to one discipline, excelling and winning championships but, more often than not, never competing as seniors never mind masters. I thank God I had a great longevity in sport. Do these youngsters not realise that they are only in the spring of their athletic lives? Sport is fun – it helps us to stay young. Danny McDaid and I only started training hard

Hugo Duggan

and competing when we were seventeen years and older. We were at the top of the sport in our forties. I have been part of the coaching structure which has witnessed these developments, so I am not critical of it in any way. I just wonder sometimes how to keep our youngsters in sport.

Becoming a Veteran Athlete

I turned 40 in 1986 and since I was still competing with Finn Valley, and having won my last national senior title in 1984 as an over 35, it was an easy transition. I won my first masters title in 1986. Early in 1987, I had knee surgery and, in June, won the long jump at the British Masters in Corby setting a British record of 6.80m. When the World Masters in Melbourne was first mentioned, I wasn't going to travel. I had my wife Brid and eight children to support and four weeks away meant no money coming into the house. With support from Patsy McGonagle and the Finn Valley club, a local committee was formed in Milford town and organised a few fund-raising dances to cover my expenses. I was Australia-bound.

Patsy McGonagle remembers Hugo training on an inclement evenings with the wind howling and the long jump pit waterlogged. Hugo emerged from the pit muddied and saturated from head to toe. "If I can jump in these conditions, then Melbourne can hold no fear," Hugo quipped before heading for a shower before setting off on his night's work.

In the long jump in Melbourne, jumpers were divided into three pools with three attempts initially and then another three for the top eight. Conditions were difficult with the run-up into a strong breeze. I fouled my first two attempts and standing at the end of the run-up for the third, I knew that it had to be a valid jump and also get me into the top eight. This was to be my winning jump of 6.60m. Winning the gold was an unbelievable feeling and a great relief knowing how much support I had got at home. "Hugo Duggan, Ireland, gold; Osamu Panaka, Japan,silver; Michael Reigner, France, bronze." How good that felt.

A week after the World Masters in Melbourne, I competed in the first Australian Masters Championships in Hobart, Tasmania. I was the only Irish person entered so I flew out alone and won again. My jump of 6.76m is still a championship best performance. When I returned home, there was a large reception for Brid, my family and me. I was like the horse that won the Derby; everyone had supported me, and so now had a share in my win. It was great for the community."

Word had travelled quickly that Hugo was world champion. From the bridge in Letterkenny, he could see celebratory bonfires of turf on the surrounding hills. It took him some time to compose himself. The Donegal people were welcoming back their hero, a tradition that has gone on in rural Ireland for generations.

"One of my best performances came in 1988 at the first National Senior Indoor Championships in Nenagh. I finished second, twenty-one years after winning the first BLE outdoor championships. In 1988, I won the Irish then the British Indoor titles in Cosford and outdoors in Wales and was runner-up at the European Championships in Verona. I went on to win many more national, British indoor and outdoor medals.

I have had a fantastic life in athletics and sport. In soccer, I represented Donegal in the Oscar Traynor Trophy inter league; I played rugby for Letterkenny and was on the Ulster fly angling interprovincial team. As an administrator, I chaired the Donegal juvenile athletics board and was also Donegal Community Games PRO for over ten years.

After the Milford athletics club was formed in 1987, I served as coach for twenty years until I retired in 2007, although I am still a member of the club. We had some outstanding athletes who were winning national medals from 1990. All my family took part in athletics with national success. I have made lifelong friends through sport and remember with gratitude Eamon Giles of Cranford who introduced me to athletics, John Kilmartin, my first coach and Patsy McGonagle of Finn Valley. My advice to anyone in competition is to know what you can do and then do it. Enjoy every moment and always remember that it's only sport."

Top Achievements: Senior

National Senior Champion Long Jump 7 times
4 times silver medallist Nationals
Best: Distance 7.39 Meters
3rd Triple Jump 1969
Ulster Senior Sports Council Decathlon
200m 22.8 seconds, 100m 11.00 seconds
15 times international vest
World Champion long jump 1987

Top Achievements: Master

Australian Master Champion
British National Champion
National Master Champion
2nd indoor national senior aged41
Master European Championships

WILLIE DUNNE

Date of Birth: 15 September 1933

Beyond Brotherhood

By Neil Farrell

*"Champions aren't made in the gyms. Champions are made
from something they have deep inside them – a desire, a dream,
a vision"* – Muhammad Ali

On a summer's day many, many years ago, young Willie Dunne was taking the long way home from St. Kevin's boxing club on Merchant's Quay in Dublin. Passing by Trinity College, he looked into the grounds and saw a commotion down on the playing fields. It was College Race day. Willie's curiosity got the better of him and he clambered over the railings into College Park. Track and field athletics would have been nowhere on Willie's radar in those days, boxing was his sport.

Willie was coached by brothers Jack and Joe Foley, notable Dublin boxers of the 1930s and 40s, whose names featured prominently on fight posters in Dublin, Belfast and Liverpool. When you think of famous sporting siblings of today like the Klitschko brothers, or the 3 Christle brothers from Crumlin in Dublin who boxed in the 70s, or indeed Jack and Bobby Charlton or Venus and Serena Williams, the question begging to be asked is could we ever have had one without the other? Is it even meaningful to consider their achievements in isolation? Would Jack Charlton have stayed working in the mines, or maybe fulfilled a onetime ambition to become a policeman, if Bobby hadn't set down a marker with his success on the football field? Would it have occurred to World Cross Country Champion and Olympic silver medalist John Treacy to start running the 10 miles home from school if his older brother Ray, a highly successful athletics coach in the US today, wasn't already a runner?

Siblings have much more than the same blood in common. They have the same first associations, the same family habits and enjoyments, especially in those early formative years. As siblings we are part of a system in which everything is connected to everything else. Change one piece of the family mosaic and everything else changes at the same time, often in ways that aren't predictable. No doubt natural talent, athletic physique, coaching and dedication to training are important elements that contribute to individual success in sport, but you'd have to suspect that what's zipping around in the family feedback loop must have a lot to do with it too. Moreover, when the system produces more than one outstanding achiever, it's pretty obvious that the sum of the parts is a woefully inadequate explanation of the whole story. Willie Dunne shared those early years with nine brothers and a sister. His parents, Mary and Thomas Dunne were tenants of the Guinness sponsored Iveagh Trust, and raised their children in a flat in Kevin Street, in Dublin's inner city.

In 1890, the immensely wealthy Edward Guinness, Earl of Iveagh, founded the trust that still bears his aristocratic title. The Trust cleared slums and built hundreds of houses and shops in Edwardian Dublin. At that time middle class comforts were unknown to large swathes of Dublin's population whose lives were circumscribed by low wages and poor quality housing. Well into the 1930s tens of thousands of families lived in one-room in degraded tenement buildings, where infant mortality was as high as twenty percent. For a few pennies, a "pint of plain" gave short-term remission from the daily drudgery of working class life and it made the Guinness's fantastically wealthy. All too often it added its own special dimension of misery to the mix. While Willie himself is a lifelong teetotaler, the irony is that the Dunne's story critically intersects, at more than one point, with that of the famous brewing family. Willie and his brothers were born in the Coombe Hospital, which had been extended and rebuilt by Lord Ardilaun, who was Arthur Guinness, great-grandson of the original brewer and Lord Iveagh's brother. Although politically conservative, the Guinness's have been inclined to philanthropy from the time of the first Arthur Guinness who founded the brand in the eighteenth century. The Iveagh Trust continues to provide over ten percent of the social housing in central Dublin and Willie is a tenant there to this day.

Going back to the summer's day that Willie gate-crashed the College Races, an annual event organised by Dublin University Harriers. It was 1949. In recognition of the many sizeable donations made by the Guinness family to the university, the post of College Chancellor was occupied by Willie's landlord, the 2nd Earl of Iveagh. Couple this with the fact that modern formalised athletic competition in Ireland was inaugurated on the very same spot in 1857, and Willie pitching up in there on the anniversary of this event, begins to look less random and more like something that was meant to be. In those early days and well into the 20th century, athletics, like golf and sailing, was the preserve of the middle classes. Club membership fees were substantial to keep it that way.

Curiously it was the university rugby club that sponsored the first so-called "foot races". Only five events were held: 150 yards sprint, 440 yards, 3 miles, high jump and long jump. Spectator numbers at athletics meets today, pale by comparison with the reported attendances. In 1874 some 37,000 tickets were sold over a two-day meet in Trinity's College Park! One of the first chairmen of these foot races was a certain Mr. A. Stoker, better known today as Bram Stoker, author and creator of Dracula. By the mid 1940s, spectator numbers were still in the region of 10,000 on College Race Day. However, such matters were of little concern to Willie Dunne as he threaded his way through the crowd, enjoying their champagne and strawberries and cream.

Near the running track, Willie's attention was attracted by a man offering half a crown for an all-comers winner at 440 yards, one lap of the track. Willie fancied his chances so he took him on, beat the field and pocketed the loot. At 15 years old it was the most money he'd ever had, about the equivalent of €25 in purchasing power today. Moreover the winnings came with an introduction to Donore Harriers.

For many decades Donore was something of a moveable feast. It had based itself in the premises of several pubs in and around Kilmainham and Dolphin's Barn, until it finally settled in its own premises at Islandbridge in 1948. Change was in the air and the 1950s would be a boom time for Irish athletics, now opening up to a much wider demographic. The record doesn't show that Willie's cash prize was shared when he got home to Kevin Street,

Willie Dunne

but his introduction to Donore Harriers was to have a considerable impact in the Dunne household.

Subsequently every one of the boys joined Donore and running became the Dunne thing. While Patricia, their only sister, was sporty too and played soccer, throughout the 1950s the boys featured at all levels in cross country and distance running. George and Paddy Dunne ran in club races, Val was on Donore youth teams, Bernard won intermediate team medals, Kevin won medals on senior teams and Joe and Brendan were junior cross country champions. However, in the midst of all this success, there is no argument as to who the front runners were. Willie and his brother Tommy Dunne became highly competitive distance runners and went on to represent Ireland many times. While Willie ran cross country races, Tommy was the cross country specialist. He was on the Irish Cross Country Team no fewer than 6 times and he finished 5th in the 1958 World Championship.

1960 was a watershed year. In March, Tommy and Willie both ran in the World Cross Country Championship in Wales, but Willie had a bigger call later in the year. He was selected for the Irish Olympic Team to run in the marathon alongside teammates Bertie Messitt and Gerry McIntyre. From our vantage point in the 21st century, it is astounding to think that athletes in those days, who were fortunate enough to be selected for the Olympics, had to negotiate with their employers for time off from work! Of course this meant a loss of earnings allied to which was a liability for covering at least half of their own expenses in getting to and from the games. Olympians in the pre-television age really were amateurs, for whom sport came without the benefit of sponsorship, fees for product endorsement and certainly no celebrity as we know it today. Different times indeed.

Willie Dunne had trained as a silversmith with Charles Lamb of Temple Lane. Lamb had been in the silver business in Temple Bar since the late 19th century and was getting on in years. Willie remembers working on alms dishes which were "left lying around the place" until he realised that they came from St Patrick's Cathedral. They were antique silver pieces that may very well have been as old as the cathedral itself! By 1960, when he was chosen for the Irish Olympics Team, Willie had moved on to Weir's Jewellers of Grafton Street.

The Eternal City was chosen as the venue for the Olympics in 1960. Rome was adjacent enough to make the practicalities of travel and funding more feasible for Irish athletes, unlike the previous games of '56 held in Melbourne or the succeeding Tokyo Olympics in '64. Willie sought and was granted permission from Weirs to go to the summer games that ushered in the Olympics as we know them today. Although it would still be a couple of years before Ireland had its own TV station, the Games of the XVII Olympiad were the first to be commercially broadcast. Coverage was extensive throughout Europe and in the US.

The site selected for the Games, on the ancient Roman road, Via Flaminia, was an area along the flood plain of the Tiber that had long been used for sporting events. In the wake of World War II, extensive reconstruction was still ongoing and the Olympic Village was a showcase project. Designer Pier Luigi Nervi integrated the new build for the Games with pre-existing facilities in the Via Flaminia area. One of two new stadiums, the Palazzetto dello Sport, quickly became a favourite of Willie Dunne's during the long wait for the marathon at the end of the Olympic programme. The Palazzetto was the venue for the boxing competition and Willie had retained an interest in the sport, since his early days being coached by the Foley brothers.

In Rome Colm McCoy boxed at light heavyweight for Ireland but didn't make it into the second round of the competition. However Willie and just about everyone else were tracking the progress of a young unknown American boxer who was storming through the opposition on his way to Olympic Gold. Willie kept returning to the Palazzo to watch the 18-year-old whose speed and unique style put him years ahead of the competition. Appropriately he rejoiced in the wonderfully ancient Roman name of Cassius Marcellus Clay. He was to become one of the iconic figures in 20th century sport under his Muslim name Muhammad Ali.

In the 1950s, winning times in the Olympic marathon had only just dipped below 2.30, a time that was well within the compass of the Irish athletes. On the evening of Saturday 10th September 1960, wearing consecutive race numbers 58, 59 and 60, Willie Dunne, Bertie Messitt and Gerry McIntyre took their places at the start of what unfolded as one of the stand-out sporting events in the history of the Olympics. The course was a triangular loop that took in many of the wonders of ancient Rome including the Caracalla Baths and the Appian Way, with the finish located under the Arch of Constantine. Unlike all other Olympic Marathons, the race in 1960 neither started nor finished at the Olympic Stadium.

Beginning at 5.30 pm, much of the marathon took place in the dark, illuminated by burning torches. On pedestals at the top of the steps of Piazza del Campidoglio, one of the Seven Hills of ancient Rome, the mythological brothers Castor and Pollux presided over the start. Inseparable and fearless in battle according to legend, the twin brothers always acted together and were worshipped by Greeks and Romans alike as the patrons of athletes and athletic contests. Long distance runners take note: characteristically they intervene at moments of crisis to aid those who honour or trust them. Also there is a curious Dublin literary connection to the aforementioned Guinness brothers, Arthur and Edward. In *Ulysses*, James Joyce satirises them as Castor and Pollux vying to see who could do the most good in their native city. In other circumstances, their brotherly rivalry might have been expressed in the boxing ring or on the running track. From this confluence of the classical and the modern another sporting icon of the 20th century was about to emerge at the Rome Olympics.

The marathon was won by an unknown Ethiopian who, incredibly, running barefoot shaved a full 8 minutes off the previous Olympic record. Abebe Bikila had been added at the last minute, as a replacement for one of Ethiopia's only two track and field competitors, both of them entered in the marathon. Among others with known form in the race, were two previous Olympic Marathon champions, while Bikila was on nobody's radar. The Ethiopians had a Swedish coach, who noted that his athletes ran efficiently and clocked better times when barefoot. He encouraged them to condition their feet by going barefoot, even about the Olympic Village. This, it must be said, caused some sniggering among the other athletes. Neither of the Ethiopians spoke Italian or English, so there was a language barrier too. Shoeless and speechless, Bikila, and his team mate Wakgira, were somewhat isolated. Willie Dunne, then as he is today, a genuine and personally modest man who is dedicated to helping others in the sport, could not leave that situation unchallenged. He made a conscious effort to be open and friendly to the Ethiopians. Conversations of a sort took place involving much sign language but connection was established and the compliment would be returned some years later when Bikila and Willie met again at the Zarautz marathon in Spain.

As race day approached in Rome however, and with national pride in mind, the Ethiopians certainly didn't want to appear among the nations as being too backward to wear running shoes. Although much has been made subsequently of the fact that Bikila ran barefoot, it wasn't unheard of in those days, even for Irish runners, to train and on occasion to race in bare feet. In the turn of events, Adidas the shoe sponsor for the marathon were unable to provide Bikila with suitable footwear so that settled the matter. He raced without shoes and the rest is the stuff of legend. Thus began the African dominance of long distance running in world athletics that has lasted for more than half a century.

With mass communication still in its infancy in 1960, an unknown winner finishing after dark, at a distance from the Olympic Stadium left many of the athletes likewise in the dark about the identity of the winner, until they got back to the Village. Willie was astonished to find that the quiet African he'd struggled to chat with had been sensationally transformed into an international sporting celebrity. It was an inspirational moment. In the pomp and circumstance of ancient Rome that day, Willie had discovered what it was like to run with the best in the world.

Willie Dunne and Michael Gygax

As the 60s progressed, Willie Dunne was the man to beat in Irish marathon running. He had a string of firsts from 1962-67 in Dublin and Belfast. In 1966, Willie competed against Bikila again at the Zarautz marathon in the Basque Country of northern Spain. The Ethiopian was by now one of the most celebrated runners of all time having won gold again in the Tokyo Olympics of '64, the only athlete in history to successfully defend the marathon title. The starting line at Zarautz was narrow and runners jockeyed for position crowding each other out. Willie ended up being jostled into a ditch that flanked the track. Bikila came over to help Willie back on to his feet and they set off together. This time Willie came home in a creditable 4th place behind the seemingly unbeatable Ethiopian. The following year Bikila was injured and didn't run at Zarautz. Mamo Wolde, another Ethiopian and soon-to-be gold medalist in the '68 Olympics, took the laurels on that occasion, but again Willie finished well up the field in 5th position. His career best for the marathon was 2.17, a time that would have seen him in contention for a medal back in 1960. It came in 1972, at the ripe old age of 39!

Still running and in top form in his mid 40s, Willie competed in the 1979 Boston Marathon, M45 category. In the general melee that accompanied the departure of the athletes at Dublin Airport, Willie was swept on to the plane and it wasn't until he was preparing to meet with US Immigration that he realised he had travelled without his passport! An Irish American police chief who became involved in the debacle that ensued at Boston's Logan Airport had a quiet word with Willie and assured him it was a problem that could be sorted. It was also an opportunity to make some mischief. There was consternation when Willie was whisked away for a destination unknown, by the grim looking police chief. Was Willie was on his way to Sing Sing Prison? Actually he was "taken into custody" at the police chief's home while waiting for his passport to be flown out from home. Released from custody, on race day Willie came home first in the M45 category, winning in a time of 2.31. Thrilled to be hosting a winner, Willie was feted and entertained around Boston by his police chief buddy!

In these days when African marathon runners are getting faster and faster with the WR time converging on that Holy Grail, the 2 hour mark, it is curious that elsewhere in the world, including Ireland, the pace of things seem to be slowing down. In the 2014 Dublin City Marathon no Irish runner finished in the top ten and the fastest time on the day, by an Irish competitor was 2.25; in the M45 category Willie Dunne's Boston time from 36 years ago would have made him an easy winner.

Now in his 82nd year, Willie remains active, coaching and mentoring at Donore. He joined the ranks of the unsung heroes in society: the scout leaders, choir masters, community games organisers, mentors, coaches and all those who volunteer their time to engage young people in sport and other pastimes. In fact, by their efforts they do nothing less than build an essential component into the life skills required for meeting life on life's terms. Award ceremonies rightly bestow honours on those who stand-up for the homeless and the addicted but it is our unsung heroes who nip trouble in the bud. If we had more of them, it's fair to say that Fr. Peter McVerry, the Simon Community and others on the front line, would be a lot less busy.

Willie Dunne places little emphasis on personal achievement and past glories. He discovered he could run that day in College Park and he has been running ever since – "these days I run better than I can walk". Through him, running became the currency in the Dunne household. Nowadays it's all about the coaching at Donore, his second family. Everything that went into the making of Willie Dunne, from his early days in the boxing club on Merchant's Quay, through representing Ireland at the 1960 Olympics, and subsequently his many winning performances in the marathon, is conserved in the man that he is today. May it continue to nourish and enrich the coaching experience of young athletes at Donore for many more years to come.

Senior: Best Time

Marathon: 2.14.3 BLE National Marathon
Half Marathon: 65.40

Master Road Times:

Half Marathon Age 0/50 71.30

Top Achievements: Senior

Rome Olympics 1960 Marathon
National Champion Marathon1963/64/65/66/67
Silver National Marathon[d] 1960/61
4 Cross Country internationals 1958/59/60/61
14 team titles with Donore Harriers
National Champion twice 6 miles

Masters Achievements

Boston Marathon 1979 0/45 2hours 31 min Winner age category

JIM FANNING
(Date of Birth: 23/5/1946)

Beat the Bookie

If you can fill the unforgiving minute
With sixty seconds of distance run
Yours is the earth and everything that is in it
And what is more, you'll be a man my son – Kipling

High jumping was always to the fore in the Fanning family. My father Pat and his two brothers enjoyed participating in the country sports that were commonplace in the 1930s. With Pat winning the inaugural A.A.V. High Jump Championship in 1937. My three brothers were all fine athletes, but turned more to rugby in their twenties. My brother Declan captained the Leinster rugby team for four seasons in the 1970s and also captained the Ireland B team. His son Darragh is currently on the Leinster Rugby squad.

After leaving school, I broke my left thigh bone playing rugby. I was put on traction tied to a bed in the Meath hospital for 10 weeks and left hospital having grown an extra 5cm! Over the next few years while at UCD I combined rugby and athletics and won the Irish Universities championship in 1967, jumping 1.85cm.

I then started weight training to build up my legs and showed great improvement over the next few years. I was selected to compete for Ireland against Romania and a German selection in 1972. Having played a rugby match the previous Sunday, I won that High Jump at 2.01m beating Brendan O'Reilly's 18 year old record. I gave up the rugby as the two sports were not compatible, as I was about 8kg heavier than other high jumpers of the same height. In 1973 I increased the record to 2.06m in the British AAA championship.

In 1974 I won the British indoor championship in Cosford and got selected to compete for Britain against USA and Russia. However, Maeve Kyle intervened to inform the selectors that I was from Southern Ireland and not eligible. Over the next few years I was honoured to be selected for Ireland to compete in the high jump, triple jump, 110m hurdles and javelin. Not many can boast of representing their country in the jumping, throwing and running disciplines individually!

In 1974, having won the British Indoor Championship, I qualified for the European Indoors in Gothenburg in March but BLE said they had no money to send anyone. Mitchelstown Creamery sponsored me to the tune of £100, so I took a few days holiday leave from Calor gas where I then worked as an accountant. Being the only Irish representative there, I carried the Irish flag at the opening ceremony and at the post competition banquet sat at the table of Prince Carlos of Sweden (now the King). I finished down the field in the high jump but then assisted Liam Nolan with RTÉ's live coverage of the games over the next few days.

My flight home was diverted to London due to fog and I decided to stay there for two days with my sister. Gold Cup day at Cheltenham was on, so I went there backed the Gold Cup winner and enjoyed the buzz.

Ten years later, I bought a bookmaker's office off Baggot St. and now I am an on-course bookie operating at most Irish racetracks.

My most enjoyable masters trip was the World Games at Eugene, Oregon in 1989. There was a large Irish group of over thirty competitors and family including Jim McNamara, one of the star performers and Emily Dowling with her husband boxer Mick. The Eugene people treated us like royalty with parties, barbeques and river rafting.

The stadium filled with about 10,000 knowledgeable and enthusiastic spectators creating a great atmosphere. I finished joint fourth in the high jump, but the most poignant event was the men's over 90s 200 metres in which the 94 year old Korean held off the partially blind American. But the American, unsure of where the finish was, kept going for about another 100 yards and the Korean unwilling to let the challenger pass ran on as well until the official intervened. The spectators erupted as the old competitors would not give in to each other, just as they had not given in to age or the smothering thought of defeat.

Master athletics is about sportsmanship and about staying young and setting goals, working hard and having fun.

My love of athletics and competition kept me focussed and I embraced Master athletics with enthusiasm. At 41 I was 2nd in the World Veteran's Championship in Melbourne, jumping a record 1.87m. The following year I won the European championship in Verona, clearing 1.85m. I enjoyed the camaraderie and socialising with fellow athletes in travelling to the various games. Among the com-

Jim Fanning

petitors I met over the years was Valeri Brumel, the Russian Olympic High Jump champion of 1964, who raised the world record six times to 2.28m. His last record stood for eight years. In 1965 he had a serious motorcycle accident, shattering his right leg. After 29 operations and four years, his leg recovered and he resumed high jumping but at a lower level.

In 1998, an Irish team was invited to compete in the Russian Indoor Master's Championships. I won the O/50 high jump beating thirteen Russians. I met Brumel there for the last time that competed in the O/55 event, but without success. But his greatest pride came from his recovery from his accident and was grateful to be able to jump again. Sadly he died of an illness in 2003, aged 60.

Arthritis has been my nemesis over the last twenty years, having had eight leg operations over my life. Reluctantly, my legs hint to me they've had enough, and I retire with many good sporting memories.

The thrill and buzz of competing rarely deteriorates with age. Master athletes can live the illusion of being 25 years old as they run or jump or throw with the feel good factor outweighing the ageing factor.

Major Achievements
Irish High Jump Champion 1972-74 record holder from 1972-1980 at 2.06m.
British Indoor champion 1974.
Represented Ireland in the High Jump, Triple Jump, Javelin and 110 metre hurdles.

Major Achievements as a Master

World Masters Silver Medallist (1.90m), Melbourne 1987.
European champion, Verona 1988.
British Masters High Jump champion on 5 occasions
Held British championship record 0/40 at 1.87m.
Russian indoor 0/50 champion 1998.
My final event finishing 3rd in British O/60 H.J. in 2007 at 1.40m
– arthritis was setting in.

HUGH GALLAGHER

Date of Birth: 1/8/1924

Never Mess with a Gallagher

By Neil Farrell

*"Do you know what my favorite part of the game is?
The opportunity to play."* – Mike Singletary, former Chicago
Bears football player

Hugh Gallagher is the grand old man of Irish Master's Athletics. In fact, look across the spectrum of all sporting activity in the nation and probably you won't find a more senior competitor. Almost the same age as Irish independence itself, the man turns 90 this autumn. Hugh's story reaches back even further than those 90 years and intertwines with seminal events in Irish history.

In the 1870s Hugh Gallagher's Grandfather James, and his four brothers, had their Donegal homestead razed by Lord Leitrim on one of his rampages. William Sydney Clements, 3rd Earl of Leitrim, was one of the country's biggest landowners in the 19th century. His enormous 100,000 acre estate, granted to the Clements family by Oliver Cromwell, straddled Galway, Leitrim and Donegal. William Clements was a ruthless landlord and pitiless evictor. Sometimes referred to locally as the "oul debaucher", he behaved like a feudal overlord, intruding and interfering in every aspect of the lives of his hapless tenants. The spirited Gallagher brothers, in the words of grandson Hugh, "refused to bow to him" and suffered the consequences. Dispossessed of their land near the County Donegal village of Carrigart, the family took the boat to America and the story of the force of nature that is Hugh Gallagher today was already running into the sand.

Some years passed. James and his brothers set about building new lives in Pennsylvania. However, the Gallagher Clan has been in Donegal from the time of St. Patrick and Niall of the Nine Hostages, a thousand years before Cromwell installed the Clements family. With the advent of the Land League and men like Michael Davit and Parnell, the page of Irish history was set to turn again. Moreover the parochial dispute between the Gallaghers and their landlord, was about to re-ignite.

In Cratlagh Wood in the spring of 1878, while on his way in to the village of Milford, the despicable Clements and two of his party were killed in an ambush. We can get a sense of how the locals felt about the demise of his lordship from the apocryphal Ballad of Lord Leitrim which tells us that "the devils ate him, rump and stump"! Meanwhile, on the other side of the Atlantic in Philadelphia, the game changing news reached James Gallagher. Gathering his belongings, James headed for the boat back to Ireland and his unfinished business with the estate of his former landlord. By now the Land War was raging, especially in the west and northwest of Ireland where tenant evictions were being fiercely resisted. Those who took over properties from evicted tenants were boycotted and ostracised. Rural Ireland was rapidly becoming ungovernable by the landlord class.

Hugh takes up the narrative telling how his grandfather's arrival back at Creevy, the family home place near Carrigart, was marred by the sight of Leitrim's cattle on the land. Adding insult to injury, James recognised stones from the old homestead had been used to build a new house for Leitrim's land steward. The formative influence of these events, on succeeding generations of Gallaghers, is evident from Hugh's story of the encounter between his grandfather and the land steward.

James identifies himself, enters the steward's house, sits down and refuses to leave. A standoff ensues. Midnight comes and goes and the two men continue to eyeball one another. Who knows what threats and counter threats were made during that long night but in the morning the land steward took his cattle and left. James had made good his return by repossessing the old homestead and it has remained in the Gallagher family ever since. Hugh's father Dannie took over the farm from James and in more peaceful times it became the training camp that launched Ireland's most successful sporting family: Hugh and his 12 children have bagged over 4,000 medals and trophies to date, a tally which continues to be revised upward after every competition season.

Martin, Hugh and Bernadette Gallagher

If strength is forged in adversity, the Gallagher family are the people to know it. Hugh was the youngest child of Dannie's brood of six. The children attended the local one teacher school and Hugh remembers that then, as now, bullying was a problem. On the advice of his bothers, Hugh trained hard to be fit for resisting the school bullies as much as for competition. Sports equipment had to be improvised like the punch bag made from a sack filled with sand. Growing up to be a young man of superior fitness and strength, Hugh had a keen competitive spirit. As he says himself, it didn't take long to find out that bullies have big mouths and not much else.

Times were hard in the 1920s and 30s, when the Irish Free State was in its infancy. DeValera's Government, on taking office in 1932, refused to continue reimbursing Britain for loans made to Irish tenant farmers to enable land purchase. These arrangements dated back to the time of Hugh's grandfather and the Land War that brought him home from America. The ensuing Economic War with Britain caused severe damage to the Irish economy during the 1930s. The repercussions were felt by all: Hugh left school at 14 and worked for a local farmer earning £1 a month. Many long hours were spent saving turf on the bogs to keep the home fires burning. An early riser, Hugh trained from 6am before work every morning. Cycling was the chief mode of transport in those days and Hugh travelled to track and field events all over northwest Ulster. Hardly a surprise then that he also became a highly competitive cyclist, winning many races and, on occasion, beating Ulster champions in the process.

Hard on the heels of the Economic war with Britain came World War II, quaintly known in Ireland as "The Emergency". Hugh joined the Local Defence Force (LDF) in 1940, giving his age as eighteen years although only sixteen at the time. Later, when the Irish army took over the LDF, it became the more disciplined and professionally structured Army Reserve (FCA). Hugh liked the army drill and held his comrades and the army trainers in very high repute. Reflecting this and not least the lack of employment in Ireland at the time, Hugh remained in the FCA after the war into the mid-1950s.

Medieval hiring fairs survived in Letterkenny into the 1940s. Young men sold their labour to English and Scottish farmers as potato pickers or "tattie hokers". Hugh left to go to Yorkshire "pulling beet" and digging potatoes in a team assembled by his brother-in-law. They worked from dawn until dusk covering 2 acres per day. When word got around of Hugh's cycling successes back in Ireland, the organisers of a local 25 mile race offered to provide him with a bike if he would take part. He lined up with some of the top cyclists in the north of England and his tactic was simple: follow the police car that led out the race as closely as possible. The plan worked and he finished an easy first receiving a standing ovation later at the presentation. Hugh also went to Scotland and worked 12 hour shifts in all weathers on the huge hydroelectricity projects which were rolled out in Britain's post war reconstruction. His employer, Wimpey Construction, mentioned in Dominic Behan's famous song McAlpine's Fusiliers, built the Lairg Dam on Loch Shin in the mountainous NW Highlands.

Hugh met his wife-to-be, Rosemary McGee, on a return visit to Donegal. His mother had fallen ill and he tried to find work in Ireland to be near home. Jobs were scarce and the wages were poor. After Hugh and Rosemary married, they went to live in London where prospects were better but all the while, the lure of Donegal remained strong. Three years passed. Rosemary and Hugh decided to return and make their family home in Creevy, the hard won seat of the Gallagher family over generations. Although putting bread on the table forced Hugh back over to the UK to work for a time every year. His fitness and strength meant that finding work was never a problem but construction sites are dangerous. In those days site safety was not a premium concern and fate is a cruel arbiter.

It determined that the man with a wife and young family back in Donegal, the man who didn't smoke or drink, who cultivated fitness and a healthy lifestyle, be the victim of a random work accident that left Hugh with a broken back. The doctors, at St. George's Hospital in London, told him he would never walk again. Hugh speaks of being frightened for the first time in his life. He was in severe pain and, alone with his thoughts, he felt it might be the end. He wondered about his remains going home to Rosemary and the children in Donegal. It was a dark time. His entire body was encased in plaster and now, adding more stress to the mix, the wards were filling up with British Soldiers coming back from Northern Ireland. Against all medical advice, Hugh determined he would have to return to his flat.

A taxi brought him home to his flat where a whole new set of challenges awaited – getting in and out of bed, getting dressed, struggling down to the local café once a day to try and eat something. As Christmas drew nearer, Hugh planned to return home and insisted that the doctors remove his body cast. They told him it needed to remain on for another 3 or 4 months, at least, and that if they cut it off, he would never be able for the journey home. Needless to say the cast came off and Hugh made it home. Unable to carry anything, he paid for help with his bags and presents. At home, when his local doctor saw his medical report, he reiterated the warning about lifting and advised Hugh that life in a wheel chair beckoned if he continued to ignore the warnings. With the support of Rosemary and their family of 12 children, Hugh began a programme of mild exercise and a slow but real recovery was underway.

Employment was out of the question so Hugh turned his attention to training his family in athletics and began a long association with the Community Games. Thus commenced a most remarkable story of family endeavour in which the Gallagher family's haul of medals and trophies runs into thousands. Hugh served as President of Donegal Community Games for many years while his children became champions in athletics, weight throwing, judo and boxing. The Gallaghers are easily the most successful family in the history of the Community Games. In one particular year, five of the family, Kevin, Bernadette, Angela, Caroline and Paul, competed at the Community Games National Finals and each one of them came home to Donegal with either medals and/or certificates in athletics and judo. The success of his children made it inevitable that Hugh would be drawn back to compete again. In 1987, some 17 years after the accident and at an age when most men are reaching for their slippers, Hugh Gallagher reached for his trainers and began a new chapter as a master's athlete.

Wearing a special support jacket to brace his injured back, Hugh won the 16lb shot putt at the Donegal Championship in Lifford. Although he has gone on to win much more prestigious titles competing internationally, the '87 Donegal Championship that signaled his return to track and field is a very fond memory. Hugh was hooked on sport again and he has competed at national level every year since. Going from strength to strength since his return, Hugh has competed in a wide variety of master's track and field events including weight throwing, hammer, discus, javelin, long jump, triple jump, the 60m sprint and the 3k and 5k walk. He is far and away the most prolific athlete the nation has ever produced.

Hugh has donned the green jersey in European Masters Athletic Championships winning a string of gold and silver medals in Finland, Sweden, Germany, Denmark, Poland and Ireland. He represented Ireland in six World Masters Championships again taking gold and silver medals home to Donegal, from England, South Africa, Australia, Spain, Puerto Rico and Ireland.

Hammer throwing has a long history in Ireland. Competitive hammer throwing dates back at least 4,000 years to the ancient Tailteann Games where competitors threw a weight attached to a rope. In its evolution as a sport, hammer throwing entered a long phase in which the hammers were conventional workmen's hammers with wooden handles. It was a widely popular sport. A 16th century drawing shows King Henry VIII throwing a blacksmith's sledgehammer. Over the next few centuries the hammer returned to its roots and became a metal ball attached to a wire with a handle grip on one end. It became an Olympic event in 1900 and when Hugh Gallagher was a lad, Corkman Dr. Pat O'Callaghan was a gold medal winner for Ireland in Los Angeles and Berlin.

In August 2009, at the age of 85, Hugh took part in the world weight throwing championships in Hungary winning 7 gold and 2 silver medals. The international crowd took him to their hearts as the "Irish Warrior". Hugh himself has a real sense, not just of the personal pride in his unique achievements, but also of the shared recognition for Donegal and Ireland. The moment they hung the 7th gold medal around his neck will always resonate in that way. Later in the year, competing in Dunboyne, Hugh set a new world record for the 56lb shot putt and received a special cup to mark the event. He was subsequently inducted into the Irish weight throwers' Hall of Fame.

And what of the descendants of the Gallaghers who remained in Philadelphia? Hugh relates the story of how, a few years ago, a bus full of Gallaghers from the US arrived in Carrigart to trace their roots. As the long-absent Gallaghers set about getting re-connected, it transpired that athletic prowess is just as much part of the picture on the other side of the pond. In fact the page on the Gallagher Clan website that records the athletic successes of Hugh and daughter Rosemarie Gallagher also features Olympic medal winner at 800m, Kim Gallagher from Philadelphia!

There is a kind of mythical sense in which it is places that own people, in which the Gallaghers are as much a part of the Donegal landscape as its rocky blue hills.

A monster rock
Stood on our land
For a million years
Or more
We played in all its shadows

Hugh Gallagher wins V 90 at nationals in Tullamore 2014

When James Gallagher returned to Creevy in the 1880s, Donegal was not about to lose him for a second time. And so it was, two generations later with Hugh: evicted from his livelihood and good health, he landed back in Creevy barely able to walk, never mind work. Donegal gathered him up. The story is much broader than Hugh finding his feet again through the Community Games. Hugh's community activism extended into many other areas. He promoted a group water scheme that was the most successful of its time bringing running water to over 50 homes in the local area. He recognized the benefits of integrating a healthy life style with sporting endeavor for men and women, at a time when drinking and smoking were commonplace in sport. A lifelong non-drinker/smoker Hugh served as President of the Meevagh Pioneer Total Abstinence Association and started up an athletic competition for members.

Being chosen Donegal Person of the Year in 1996 is Hugh's most treasured accolade. Six hundred people attended the function at the Burlington Hotel in Dublin and, by all accounts, at least another hundred couldn't get tickets and were left outside. Hugh commented, "if I had known I would've got them in somehow". Lord Leitrim thought he owned the sticks and stones and people of Carrigart. Hugh Gallagher's sovereignty is of a spiritual kind: throughout his long life he wears Donegal as a second skin.

Major Achievements

World records in field events
Multiple Irish Masters champion
Multiple European Champion throws
Multiple world Champion throws
British Welsh Scottish champion
Donegal person of year 1996
Tadgh Lynch memorial award best Irish master athlete
Pensioner of year award
Donegal sports star master athlete 2
World champion Lyon Weight Throw

JOSEPH GOUGH

Date of Birth: 10/1/1953

An Expert in the Art and Science of Racing

By Michael Gygax

"An athlete cannot run with money in his pockets. He must run with hope in his heart and dreams in his head." – Emil Zatopek

Every athlete looks forward to the day they win their first race or set a personal best. For some, success comes as a juvenile, while others excel as senior. A select few come into their own when they move into the masters ranks. Such an athlete is Joe Gough.

Although Gough began running as an eleven year old when he joined his local club in Dungarvan, he didn't come into his own until he passed his 35th birthday. Around the same time, the Regional Sports Centre opened at Kilbarry and, supervised by his long time coach, Dick Murphy, Joe got into the routine of training six days a week, every week, year round. That routine has brought Joe many rewards, including multiple titles and records at provincial, national and international level.

Hubert Dreyfus, the American philosopher, argues that becoming adept at an art or science requires more than simply adhering to a set of rules. Human experience and shared social mores are other factors to be considered.

Knowledge and understanding generally come in five stages – novice, advanced beginner, competence, proficiency and expert. For Joe Gough, the progression from novice to expert took fifty years of training, experience and determination.

In his first year as a master in 1989, Joe took bronze in the Munster championships. A year later, he took the first of many Munster titles. Since that breakthrough, Joe has never lost an 800m race at Munster level. He had to wait a year before he won his first All-Ireland title and since then, he has amassed well over seventy titles – and counting – at national level.

Joe's first masters' international vest came in 1998, when, as an M45, he competed in the Russian Indoor Athletic Championships in Moscow winning his first international competition in a new Irish record time.

Since then, Joe has become a prolific competitor at European and world championships both indoors and outdoors, and has travelled to England, Scotland, Wales, France, Spain, Denmark, Sweden, Russia, Germany, Hungary, Puerto Rico, Poland, the USA and Italy for competitions.

In 2008, he made his regular trips to England, winning the British 400m and 800m titles outdoors and the 800m indoors. For the 400m, he clocked 58.56 seconds underlining his basic speed.

At the 2013 European Indoor Championships in San Sebastian, Spain, Joe won gold in the 800m and the 1500m and smashed the European record. It was the first time any Waterford athlete had broken a European track record.

A year later in early 2014, competing in the Leinster Indoors at the newly built Athlone Institute of Technology indoor arena, Joe broke the M60 world record for the 800m becoming the first athlete to set a world record in this state-of-the-art stadium. His time of 2 mins 14.06 secs broke the existing record of 2:14.23 held by Horace Grant of the USA.

That record launched an outstanding year for Joe. A total of 3,800 athletes from 58 countries had entered the World Master Indoor Athletics Championships in Budapest, Hungary, with Joe opting for the 800m and 1500m. Having previously won two world silver medals, Joe was going for gold - he would have regarded a third silver as a failure. After breaking the world record, he knew he was a "marked man" and a target for others. The American world outdoor record holder Nolan Shaeed was also in Joe's race and seen by many as the favourite.

Progressing through the heats and semi-finals, the battle was on for the medals. In the final, the American led at the bell and was ready to sprint for home over the final 200m lap. Joe had him in his sights and when he kicked past him, the gold was his. He had taken just 30 seconds to run the last 200m lap and his winning time was 2:15.08. For Joe, victory was the fulfillment of a life's dream.

Such was his achievement that the bronze medal he took in the 1500m two days later was almost overlooked. Winning the race was Joe's team mate Brian Lynch from County Louth who won the race in a world record time. For their achievements, Brian Lynch and Joe Gough could be seen as Ireland's version of Sebastian Coe and Steve Ovett.

Joe's winning ways continued in 2015 at the World Masters Championships in Lyon, France. On a great day for the Irish team, both Joe and City of Lisburn's Kelly Neely won gold in the 800m finals. His championships had started when he won

Joseph Gough

his heat comfortably in a time of 2:19.06. The semi-finals, held in 38 degrees heat, were not so straightforward. After a slow start, Gough was badly spiked as the tempo quickened and slipped back to third with 200m to go. He reclaimed the lead with 50m to go and won in 2:20.

So it was on to the final two days later at La Duchere Balmont, where Joe led for the first 600m against a field that included former Olympians and world champions. With 200m to go, Oleksandr Lysenko from Ukraine surged passed him only for Joe to regain the lead with 100m left. Now the finish line was in sight, and both the Uruguayan Omar Clok fand the defending champion Carlos Humberto Loiza Londona from Colombia gave it one last effort, before a big kick from Joe saw him cross the line for victory. His time was 2:15.9; second was Clok 2:16.89 and third Londana in 2:17.18.

Two days later, Joe was lining out in the fourth of five 1500m heats. In a tactical race, he secured the win and his place in the next round with a time of 4:53.65. It was the slowest heat of the round. In the final, Joe moved from eighth to third place in the final 300m finishing in 4:38.36 and smashing the Irish record by a whopping 13 seconds.

In March 2016, Joe was one of just eight athletes selected for a masters' M60 800m which took place at the World Indoor Championships in Portland Oregon. Joe went into the race as the fastest of the field with a time of 2:15.90. He surged to the front late in the race and entered the final straightaway with a narrow lead over Wilcox. With 7,000 fans screaming their lungs out, Joe literally fell over the line, just losing out to British athlete David Roy Wilcox, when his legs gave out. Wilcox was timed at 2:15.90 and Gough at 2:16.01. Third was Oleksandro Lysenko of Ukraine in 2:17.38. "I loved the

Joseph Gough

atmosphere," Gough said afterwards. "I was playing a bit to the crowd."

Gough was proud of his performance. "Going into the tape, I'd given everything, and I could hear the crowd shouting," he said. "So I'm happy, the crowd's happy, and I think Ireland's happy."

Next up were the European Masters Indoors in Ancona, Italy from March 29 to April 3. In the 800m final, Joe timed his effort to perfection tracking the leader until the bell and then moving to the front for a clear win. A few days later, he finished a close fourth in the 1500m, won by Brian Lynch, with just two seconds separating the top four.

So what's next for this masters of masters? One thing is certain: as long as there are barriers to be broken and medals to win, Joe Gough will be there.

Major achievements

Champion or Ireland 68 times
Champion of Northern Ireland
Champion of Wales
Champion of Scotland
Champion of Great Britain 9 times
Champion of Russia
Champion of Europe 7 times and European Record Holder
Double World Silver Medallist
World Champion and World Record Holder
Irish Master Athlete of the year
Lyon world champion 2015 800m 1500 M bronze
National records in the 200m, 400m, 800m and 1500m

PATRICIA GRIFFIN

Date of Birth: 5/3/1955

Putting Leitrim on the Map

Colin Griffin

"Children should be brought through the athletic process slowly. There should be no rush for underage success that comes with time, fun and perseverance"

Athletics has been a big part of my life for as long as I can remember. From an early age, everything in the family home revolved around athletics. My mother was an international athlete who represented Ireland on the track and over road and cross-country. Nearly every weekend there was a race on somewhere in the country. I travelled to most races with my parents. My mother won national titles from 800m up to half marathon. She represented Ireland at World Cross Country, Europa Cup, World Half Marathon, and World 15km Championships and World Marathon Cup. My father, Padraig Griffin, was president of Athletics Ireland (formerly BLE) from 1991-1994, team manager at 1972 and 1980 Olympic Games and also served as director of coaching in the 1970s and 1980s.

My mother was born in 1955 and grew up in the parish of Aughawillan just outside Ballinamore in county Leitrim. She was the second oldest of a family of seven. It was a strong sporting family with three of her brothers who played inter-county football with Leitrim. She experienced a tough upbringing as her father died when she was twelve and later on her older brother died tragically. Her first race was at the age of 11 when her late father brought her into Ballinamore Open Sports on his bike. From there her interest in athletics blossomed and she would go on to compete in races all over the country representing Ballinamore Athletic Club. My father, who founded Ballinamore Athletic Club in 1965, having moved to the town as a teacher; would be her coach.

Growing up in the 1980s and early 1990s, I learned firsthand what it was like to be a professional athlete and that "professionalism" in sporting terms was not about financial status. It was about applying oneself to do a job to the best of one's ability. Along with a demanding training programme, my mother also had a family of four to raise (Colin, Ronan, Niamh and Grainne). She would still train during her pregnancies – running every day until 2-3 weeks beforehand and then walking every day. Our neighbors probably thought she was mad!

She applied herself to her training and competition with a sense of purpose and attention to detail. She was very independent and not afraid to push the boundaries of what was the norm. She was tough and that was evident when she raced. One of my earliest memories was of her being stretchered off after a National cross-country championships in Killenaule in 1987 having exhausted herself. I think it was the same race that Sonia O'Sullivan won at the age of 17 to launch herself on the world-class stage.

I can remember the time she won her Dublin Mini-Marathon titles in 1988 and 1989 – two major milestones in her career. I spent the day being minded by my grandmother at home in Leitrim. When news came through that she won and was featured on the RTÉ news, I could sense the significance of her achievement. It was big news at home and she was a local hero. Her winning time in those years (33.57), compare strongly with winning times of recent years.

In those days there was no high performance system or "Carding Scheme". My mother had no government financial support but what I did notice was a good coaching structure at the time with regular national squad sessions. I remember being with my mother at regular squad training sessions in Dublin and she would undergo lactate testing, blood testing and biomechanical analysis. There were some occasional warm-weather training camps. Simple things were done well and there was a good high performance mindset among many coaches.

My mother had started her senior career as a 400m/800m runner in 1970s, moving to 5km/10km in the 1980s; in the 1990s she began to tackle the marathon. Her first marathon was in London in 1991 with an encouraging debut. She would then target her next marathon later that year in Chicago. But she embarked on a relatively innovative (as it was in Ireland at the time) modality by preparing with an altitude training camp. In August 1991, herself and a couple of other athletes traveled to Alamosa in Colorado for a four-week altitude training camp. In October she came 7th in a time of 2.42.36 at the Chicago Marathon. The following spring she ran 2.43 in London Marathon while 3 months pregnant with my sister Niamh. We used to joke that Niamh was the youngest person to have completed a marathon! It was very late in my mother's career when she moved up to the marathon, but it would seem that the marathon was perhaps her true forte. She also won the Belfast Marathon in 1995 in what was her last marathon.

I was inspired and intrigued by my mother's endurance exploits at the time – particularly the concepts of lactate testing, altitude training and endurance performance. She was also diligent when it came to strength and conditioning training. There was a big emphasis on plyometrics at the time, something her then coach at the time Joe Doonan was a huge advocate of. I watched her curiously performing bounding and medicine ball work in the back yard most days.

From an early age I began reading up about training methods, altitude training and asked my mother lots of questions. I always had a fascination for endurance events and as a young athlete I always strayed for the longer distances. When I was a junior I could not wait to do my first 20km. As a senior, 50km became my primary distance. I currently have my own altitude training company, the Altitude Centre Ireland, and lactate testing is something I've used as an athlete and now as a coach. There is little doubt that my interest and curiosity in my mother's exploits during her career most certainly developed my interests in coaching and physiology.

As a young athlete I was competitive as a runner, played gaelic football but also dabbled in the race walking event. When I was in the under 13 age group I prepared for the race walking event for the Community Games, qualifying for the national finals in Mosney. Without much specific preparation I finished 2nd and one clear memory I have, was my mother saying to me, "you have a future in this event". Those words stuck with me and at the age of 15 I began to specialize properly in the event and my career took off from there.

The one thing missing in my mother's career was to represent Ireland at the Olympic Games. She came close in the 10,000m in 1988 and the Marathon in 1992. I was very motivated during my own career to qualify for the Olympic Games and I was proud to qualify and represent Ireland at the 2008 and 2012 Games and have my parents there to watch me compete. Throughout my mother's career, family always took priority.

My youngest sister Grainne was born in 1996 and from then my mother's senior international career began to wind down. She still continued to compete at Masters level, representing Ireland internationally. She had always been involved in coaching in our club and took a great interest in passing on her knowledge and experience to the next generation. She was team coach to the Irish team for numerous international events and was team coach as part of a three-year preparation programme for the junior teams for the 1999 World Championships in Belfast. In recent years she has served as an Athletics Ireland official at national events and is a member of the Competition Committee.

Watching my mother train, compete and subsequently coach certainly inspired me and helped shape my own career path. Her attention to detail, passion and determination with which she applied herself, gave me an early in-

Patricia Griffin

sight into what it was like to be a professional athlete. In those innocent times growing up in the 1980s and early 1990s, my mother and those she worked with were ahead of their time in how they trained and prepared for competition. Being prepared to step into the unknown, innovate and back yourself along the way, has become a strong principle of mine as an athlete and now as a coach and businessman.

Senior: Best Time

Marathon: 2.41
Half Marathon: 74 approx.

Top Achievements

Irish Senior International
World Cross Country participant
7 Marathons under 2.50
Winner of Belfast City Marathon
National Champion
800, 3,000m, 5,000, 10,000km
15km, Half Marathon, 4 x 400m
Second Senior Pentathlon
1988/89 Winner Ladies Mini Marathon
Four children competing in athletes

Patricia competed well into her fifties in senior competition but never participated in Master's competition, as she was too busy coaching, doing administration work and managing Irish Junior teams. However, she runs every day as recreation.

FRANK HEARNS

Date of Birth: 23/3/1941

A Rich Heritage of Faith, Blessings and Genes

"No such thing as a hard training session, only weak men"

Surnames can tell us something of who our forebears were and what they were like, where they lived and what they achieved. They can also tell us something about ourselves; who we are and whether any of our genes can be traced to known ancestors who won sporting fame.

I had the wonderful blessing and privilege to have heard my father telling stories of my forebears, on the Hearns side of the family, until I was 52 years of age. My great grandfather Pat Hearns (1811-1882) was one of a long line of anglers on the river Moy in Ballina, Co. Mayo. Pat was famous for his skill in wielding the salmon rod and as a deft caster of a long line. Fame in angling circles earned him the sobriquet "King Pat" and his humble thatched dwelling "The Palace".

The following is an extract from an obituary in *The Field* dated 9 December 1882: "A fine old angler, and a man of mark as a fisherman, has gone to his rest, and hundreds of patrons and pupils in all parts of the world will hear with unaffected sorrow of the death of poor old Pat Hearns. We can in our minds eye see him now as we saw him once on a wild day on Lough Conn, when the waves were high and the spray broke over him perpetually, casting away without ceasing, and not regarding threatening weather an atom; for when he had a fishing companion to his mind he was keen as a razor, and no trouble or pain was too much. Let us hope that his place may be worthily supplied by his sons Frank, Mike and Jim who will carry on the business. Pat was seventy one and his end was peaceful."

His place was indeed worthily supplied by his three sons. While not quite acquiring the "royal" stature of their father they upheld the reputation of their forebears with the rod and the gun. Mike, the eldest of the surviving trio, had the reputation of being an unerring marksman. Frank came next and was described by Rev. J. Adams in the *Western People* as "a big burly fellow, who enjoyed the distinction of never striking a salmon with a tight line, but always from the reel". The same Rev. Adams proclaimed that Jim, the youngest of the trio, was one of the finest specimens, physically, of a young man that he had ever met, tall broad shouldered and with an ease and grace of movement as light as the fly falling on the water.

Jim Hearns (1850-1936) was my grandfather. Sadly, he passed to his eternal reward five years before I was born, and so I never knew him in person. However, I had the great good fortune to learn much about the legend that was "Daddy Jim" from my father, Richard (Dick) Hearns (1907-1993). Dad was an inveterate storyteller and enthralled me from an early age with accounts of his father's prowess as a sportsman.

My great grandfather, "King Pat", lived through The Great Famine of 1840s and my grandfather was born in 1850 at the end of the same tragic event. How they and their families survived this horrendous catastrophe has remained a mystery to me. Mayo suffered greatly and many inhabitants either died or emigrated. Was it the availability of fresh fish, clean water, wild fowl, rabbits and goat's milk that saved them? All were in plentiful supply along the River Moy and may account for the survival of my immediate ancestors.

Between reeling in salmon, tying flies and bagging mallard and rabbit "Daddy Jim" found time to father sixteen children. No idle "buachalín" my grandfather! One of these children was my father, Richard, who was always known as Dick. Whatever about my great grandfather and grandfather achieving fame as sportsmen, their achievements pale into insignificance when compared to their descendant. His life story alone is worth a complete book but I will try to shorten this account and keep it relevant to my subject.

Dad was born and grew up in Ballina. At the age of fourteen he sustained a serious injury to his spine when he fell from a horse-drawn cart. Following a three month stay in hospital the doctor advised his mother that he would always be weak and suited only to light work. His mother found employment for him in a local grocer's shop. Dad had a different idea. He had a burning ambition to have a physique like the legendary Charles Atlas and the fact that his contemporary fourteen year olds jeered him, calling him "grocer's boy, grocer's boy", only increased his determination to do something worthwhile with his life.

As a mere boy of fifteen he ran away from home and enlisted in the fledgling National Forces. Soon after completing his recruit training he was catapulted into the Civil War and, at one stage, as a unit scout, he entered his home town of Ballina on a bicycle ahead of his battalion. Luckily, the opposing Republican Forces retreated north across the Moy and so a firefight and possible death were avoided.

Following the end of the Civil War in May, 1923, Dad commenced a career of peacetime soldering which was to last five years. It was during this time that he began to discover the delights and challenges of sport. While serving as a corporal in the 6th Battalion in Galway in 1924, at the age of seventeen, he attended and passed the first ever P.E. Instructors' Course in the Curragh Training Camp. He recalled "always being hungry" while on the course. There was not much attention given to nutrition and hydration in 1924! Soon after returning to Galway he commenced his football career and while serving in the Military Police in Collins Barracks, Cork, in 1927, he won an All Army Football Championship with The Southern Command. The *Irish Press* correspondent in his "All in a Day's Sport" described this team as "one of the greatest Southern Command teams of all time".

On completion of his tour of duty in Oglaigh-na-hEireann he returned to Ballina where he played football with the local Stephenites Club and kept fit by using the facilities of the local boxing club. Much against his wishes he was twice persuaded to box for the club in charity tournaments. For the record he won both middleweight bouts.

Then in early 1928 Dick Hearns joined the Garda Siochana. Little did he imagine what lay ahead of him. The boxing instructor, Tommy Moloney, was quick to spot his fine physique, speed of hands and lightness of foot. With a little firm persuasion from the Deputy Commissioner, General W.R.E. Murphy, Dad was convinced he had a bright sporting future with the Garda Boxing Club. Having trained with such renowned champions as Matt Flanagan, Jack Driscoll , "Boy" Murphy, Jack Chase and a host of other famous members of the Club, Dad commenced his competitive boxing career. This career was to extend from 1928 to 1939. His achievements can only be summarised in this short story. His career record reads 197 bouts – 175 wins. Over 50 of these fights were at international level. Major titles included five Irish, one British ABA and one European Police title. The latter two titles were won in 1935 and in both cases Dad defeated Frenchman Roger Michelot. Ireland did not compete at The Olympic Games in 1936. Michelot won the Cruiser Weight Title. Dad cherished the honour of captaining the Irish team versus USA in Chicago in 1933.

The long time and greatly respected boxing correspondent of the *Irish Independent*, Arthur P. McWeeney, in a series on famous Irish boxers, described Dick Hearns as "the finest workman of them all. There was never anything impulsive about his performance in the ring. He gave the impression of ice-cool efficiency and though he could work himself up to a high pitch of aggression it was a calculated ferocity rather than a berserk fury."

Frank Hearns

The following postscript from the *Western People* in 1965 indicates how Dick Hearns maintained his fitness as he approached the end of his sixth decade: "Once described as a lion of the fold of boxing; hard as iron; active as a bee; Dick Hearns stepped out of the ring in Ballina last night after boxing three rounds of an exhibition with Paddy Goggins, amid thunderous applause. Supremely supple and scientific as in his active boxing career, Dick at 58 was making his last appearance in the ring".

Prior to winning his first Irish title in 1933, Dad won a Dublin County Football Championship with the Garda Club and two Connaught Championships with his native Mayo. At the age of 29 he trained the first Mayo team to win the Sam Maguire Cup in 1936.

Above all his achievements in sport I remember my Dad for his gentle manner, generosity and firm faith in his Christian beliefs. Like St. Paul, "He fought the good fight, he finished the course, he kept the faith".

There was no sporting history on our mother's side of the family.

For his children, Dick's act was always going to be hard to follow. I was the fourth child in the family. From as early as I can remember I admired his collection of gold medals and silver trophies. Dad encouraged us all to engage in sport but adamantly refused to let us box until we finished school. By the time we graduated from St. Vincent's C.B.S. all of us had majored in other sports.

It was a source of great disappointment to me not to be able to "make the grade" at primary school level either in football or athletics. Thankfully, that changed dramatically during my years in the secondary school. Five successful seasons with the football team climaxed with a Leinster Colleges Championship. With the encouragement and good coaching from the Christian Brothers my track record was crowned with a European Catholic Students Championship Gold Medal at 800m in Chambery, France in 1959. My time in that race was a record breaking 1-57.8

During the same period, under the watchful eye of Dublin City Harriers coach, Des Deloughry, my running career blossomed. Among many achievements at national level I had the good fortune, at fifteen years of age, to team up with Des, Sean O'Riordan and Chris Brady to win The National Senior Medley Relay in 1956 and at eighteen years to win the National Junior 800m in 1959.

In my final year at school I applied to several American universities for athletic scholarships. The Universities of California, South Carolina and Notre

Dame were interested provided my academic results and athletic performances were satisfactory. I qualified on both counts. Even on much reflection I cannot say how seriously I took the interest they showed in me, having had nobody to guide me through the process of weighing up the scholarship offers and other career choices open to me at home. However, I do know that my parents were not enamoured with the idea of my going to America. They suggested instead that I apply for a Cadetship in the Defence Forces and, to be totally honest, I found that to be a very acceptable alternative.

Had I gone to the States, a much different future would have beckoned me. I do not know what that future might have been but to this day I am curious as to how my athletic career would have progressed. At the age of 50, I was a world class master athlete. While I would not swap any of my life or the people I love, a part of me still wonders what I might have achieved in my 20s with the coaching I would have got in America.

I was successful in my bid to obtain a Cadetship in the Defence Forces and enlisted on the 25 January 1960. Although cadet training was not conducive to running good 400/800m races I did manage a silver medal in both events at the Defence Forces track and Field Championships in July of that year. The gold medalist was none other than Trooper Noël Carroll, soon to be an Olympian. I won a number of Defence Forces medals in the next three years and as 800m champion in 1963 I represented Ireland at the World Military Games in Brussels. There I ran a P.B. of 1.55 in reaching the final. As the season was ending I received a "hammer blow" to my ambitions as an athlete. A serious injury to my right knee, playing volleyball, necessitated a series of surgical procedures which effectively ended my career. It was a shattering experience and one which, yet again, leaves me wondering "what might have been"? As I matured I began to accept that God had his own plan for me and that obviously being an Olympian was not part of it.

In the next ten eyes I married Margaret and we adopted three children, Sarah, Clare and Richard. U.N. peacekeeping duties brought me to Cyprus, Israel, Palestine, Syria, Lebanon, Jordan and Egypt. All this time my fitness training was primarily carried out in the gym as even gentle jogging left my knee sore and uncomfortable.

In August 1975, Margaret, Sarah and I went on pilgrimage to Lourdes. While there I prayed for two blessings. The first was that we would get a sister for Sarah and the second was that my knee would heal properly and that I could return to serious running and improve and maintain my quality of life. On the Feast of the Assumption, 15th August, we received news that Sarah was about to have a sister. First blessing received.

Three generations of Hearns

On returning to the Command and Staff Course in the Military College at the end of August I ran one and a half miles on my first evening and while most of my body ached my knee was pain free next day. I persisted and eventually regained a standard of fitness which enabled me to compete on the track once again. In 1982 I began my master's career which was to be crowned with a Silver Medal at 800m in the M50 category at the World's Masters Championships in Turku, Finland in 1991. My time was 2-4.1, an Irish Masters' Record, which still stands at time of writing.

I treasure the many championship medals garnered over a master's career spanning 26 years. It is the privilege of having known and competed with my coach and training partner Noël Carroll, master athletes of the calibre of Sean Cowler. Jim McNamara, Jimmy O'Neill, Mags Greenan and a host of other great ladies and gentlemen that I value most of all.

As I close in on my "sere and yellow leaf", a time for remembering and reminiscing, I thank God for the countless blessings and good fortune bestowed on me throughout my life. As I reflect on the joys of my sporting endeavours I thank God for the genes that contributed to these joys, which I believe were passed on from King Pat, Daddy Jim and my legendary father Dick.

Top Achievements: Senior

All Army champion 1962

Major Achievements Master

800 metre British champion 1986/1988/1991/1992
4th 1986 Malmo European Championships
4th World Championships Turku 400m 55.3
National champion master 100m, 200m, 400m, 800m three times in same year

JIM HOGAN

28/5/1933 – 10/1/2015

All or Nothing

By P.J. Browne

"To live is the rarest thing in the world. Most people exist, that is all." – Oscar Wilde

"I have 7 sisters and 1 brother. Two live in the United States, Nora and Francis; there are two in England, Margaret and Josie. Mary lives in Ardpatrick, and Tess is back in Boherard Cross, Athlacca. Betty is living in Mayo now after living in England for years.

When I started out running, Betty used to come out and time my runs with an old wind up clock. I was doing something like 400 yards, 800 yards and she helped me quite a bit actually. My brother, Mickey Joe, never did any running at all. I'm pleased to note that they are all in good health and they are all keeping well. Mary is the eldest and I am the second eldest. My father died in 1976 and my mother died in 1984. They both lived into their 80s and may the Lord have mercy on their souls.

They had hard lives, and that's putting it mildly. Like all small farmers, they worked hard all their lives but it was very difficult to make a living in the 40s and 50s. My father and I used to cut a lot of hay for other people. We had three horses – there was no machinery then – and we cut for all the local farmers. We'd often be out at three in the morning with the three horses.

At lunch time we'd change horses to keep them somewhat rested and up to the work. T'was hard work, I'm telling you, but sure we were all in the same situation; the whole area had to work just as hard. A small farm might be all right in the summer with 15 or so cows, but in winter there was no money coming in. The main thing was to try and make enough money in the summer in order to see you through the winter. There would be winters where it was tight enough.

You can well imagine how my mother and father felt about my running. It just wasn't done; you'd be considered an oddity by neighbours and they'd be talking about you. I can't say I blame them for that. If the situation was different I'd have been laughing with them at the clown tearing around the place.

Of course all that changed dramatically when I won a national title. That must have given me some credibility and might have justified the madness. All I can say now, is thereafter, I wasn't as self-conscious about the training. I suppose winning a title made the running acceptable.

Tralee 1952

I began at cross-country in January of February of 1952. I was 4th in the County Limerick Novices Championship, and then I was 2nd in the junior and second again the senior, so I was improving all the time. I didn't go beyond county championship class until the track season. I started on the track in July, and I'm talking now about a track pegged out on grass, not the high tech jobs you see today.

In Tralee, I won an Irish championship: the 5 mile miles in 26 minutes dead. That was actually an Irish record then. I was 19 years of age. You could say that was my first significant breakthrough in Ireland. It was a very special day for me because my father made the journey specially to see me run. He enjoyed my win, and it was one of the proudest days for him to watch me win that title.

That title was more meaningful for him than my winning the Gold medal in the European Championships. You see that was something that could be talked about locally, An All-Ireland Championship. That would have impressed the local boys and there was great pride in being a national champion.

My father didn't see me compete a whole lot which is understandable. First of all, getting to a track event or championships wasn't easy. Then there was the work on the farm to consider. There was always work and more work and taking a day off had to be planned well in advance.

I was delighted that my mother and father were able to come up to Santry to see me run the Irish 6 mile championship. My brother Joe accompanied them. I'm glad to say that I ran well again even though conditions were very windy and cold. I lapped a very good field of Irish athletes including Bertie Messitt, so it was good occasion for all of us. By this time I was working and training in England. If I had stayed in Ireland (as an athlete) I would have wound up with nothing. I'd have achieved nothing, reaching a certain level of competence and probably packing it in as many lads did.

Pa McAuliffe is one athlete who comes to mind. He was a talented runner over the 400 and 800 distances, but he retired young. He was 23 when he gave it up, a bit early thought, but it does prove the point I just made about the benefits of leaving the country. When I started running in 1952, there was nobody doing it. We had a good club in Croom and there were also some very good runners in the Cappamore area – Paddy Carmody, Willie Daly.

We wasted a lot of time running in Ireland under the NACA. The officials were no help because you couldn't run outside the country. The one good thing about the NAIA was you had athletics every Sunday from May to September. You could go somewhere almost every Sunday and race, whereas under the AAU you didn't get as much competition except maybe in Dublin.

I still find it remarkable that we were able to run the distances we ran. I never ran more than 4 miles in any night's training, and that would include four or five fast quarter miles. I never actually trained for the distances I had been running. There was no distance work at all and I still won 10 and 15 mile championship races. I look back now and I think – Jesus how did we run it.

I should clear up one area of confusion here. I went to England in February 1960 to get work, nothing else. Actually I had given up athletics at the time. I hadn't run since August of 1959 and didn't start again until the April. And there's another reason which made it easy for me to leave the country. You had no jobs and the country was riddled with class distinction. I saw more class distinction in Ireland in the 1950s than any other country I've ever been to. And I travelled more than most I'd say, something in the region of 25 different countries.

When you came out of Church of a Sunday morning, the big farmers would stand around inside the wall. The small farmers and labourers would gather and stand across the street – they never, ever mixed. If you went to a social event and you were nicely dressed, they'd look at you as if to say why you are here. I experienced the full brunt of that snobbery in my time but I always had the last laugh especially at horse dos and the like. You see I knew the owners, the trainers and the jockeys and there was always a warm greeting.

You don't have that snobbery among genuine horse people no matter what their background. They accept you on your merits and never turn their back on you. Thanks be to God with more money in the country the days of looking down on a fella are long gone. Class distinction as we knew it is gone now which is a very good thing."

"An Irishman won a Gold Medal when the European Championships wound up yesterday, but he was the wrong one so to speak. Jim Hogan, the improbable Irishman carried the colours of his adopted country to a resounding success in the marathon. It was the ultimate in irony." (Tom Cryan, *Irish Independent.*

This was a defining, vindicating victory for Hogan whose career had been such a mix of dismal failure, unfilled promise and controversy. For Irish athletics, however, his achievement was an indictment of conniving officialdom. Hogan was in a class of his own by Irish standards, and was pointedly ignored by selectors even after a series of world-class performances prior to the championships.

To comprehend the magnitude of his achievement, one must consider this undercurrent of recurring insult and humiliation that he was subjected to. His desire for victory was given added impetus after a disappointing 1964 Olympic Games, and a hellish run in the Olympic Marathon.

Separated from the field with Bekele, a silver medal beckoned. With three miles left Hogan faltered and collapsed, totally dehydrated. He might have died without the medical assistance of the New Zealand support team. There was no Irish official to be found.

Hogan recalled that era recently: "I was within a few miles of a silver medal, and I kept going until I collapsed. I was not interested in finishing far down the field just to earn a few sympathetic cheers. It had to be all or nothing. I gambled and lost but I wasn't disappointed. I ran quite well as a complete novice. I learned a lot, and I thought, the next marathon I run I'll be ready for it.

"I had some super races all through 1965, at 3 miles, 10,000m but I felt that my best chance for success was the marathon, so I just trained for that distance. Gordon Pirie was always very helpful and influential."

Training for the Marathon

Hogan ran barefoot for the most part, especially track and cross-country. "Over three miles I'd be 30 seconds slower wearing shoes. My main run was a 15 miler in Chiswick with 3 big hills in it, and I would do that once a fortnight. I ran lot in RichmondPark but I never went farther than 15 miles if it was a hard run or a time trial. I'd sooner run a fast 15 than a slow 22 to keep the snap in my legs. Sunday was the 22- mile run with the lads, not fast at all.

For speed, I was doing 10 to 12 high intensity 500s on grass with a quick run back for the repeat. There was minimal rest between the reps. On the track I'd do 20x440 with a recovery of 110. I hit the quarters in 64 seconds with a 56 second jog. Each was completed in 2 minutes or less.

I once ran 30 of these with the same guidelines. It was intense quality training. Ten days before the marathon I ran the hilly course in 75 minutes and I knew if anybody wanted to beat me they'd have to be going really well. I tapered off and went to training camp outside the city.

I trained with Alan Simpson (miler) and he remarked on my fitness level. When you get to 18 miles, he said, you'll just wave then goodbye, and that's how it went. I made a break at 18 and got away unchallenged. Never had any

England won the World Cup in 1966. Later that summer, Limerick man Jim Hogan won the European Marathon Gold Medal, wearing an English vest. Budapest: 4 September 1966

worries, just kept going. I got a great reception when I entered the stadium and I could have gone faster if pushed." (2:20.04.6) I got a standing ovation from 50,000 in the stadium.

Representing England

I had a great time in England; I loved it. Never had an ounce of bother, and athletically I couldn't have done much without going there. It was brilliant. I got time off with pay to go to meets, and they picked me for attractive competitions in good climates.

I had a terrible time with the Irish officials. They gave me no f.....g chance. Never. They detested me because I was living in England, but they had to pick me for the big events because they had no one good enough. If you're getting a living in a country you should stand by it. I had no problem whatsoever wearing an English vest.

Basically, I was running for myself anyway. Poor auld Billy Morton sent me a telegram congratulating me. That was typical of the man; he was class was Billy. He was always very helpful to me. There was no comment or reaction from the f.....g Irish officials, but I knew the f....rs would be around come the next Olympics. A bad minded mean lot, to be honest.

Peers

David Bedford, Ron Clarke, and Ron Hill were the best runners I ever ran with. The best in England at the time was Ronnie Hill. He was the hardest man to beat in the country. If you beat Hill you'd nearly beat anybody. Clarke was the best; he was way ahead of them all. Jesus he was unbelievable. I trained with him in Australia. There was never an easy session, and nobody in the world could get near him in 1968.

Derek Clayton was the hardest trainer of all those blokes. Clarke told me that if you trained with Clayton for 3 weeks every day, your career would be finished.

Bedford, my old mate, he was a marvellous runner. I've seen him totally bollixed, flat out, and he still wouldn't give in. He should have won Gold in the 10000m. You could question his front running tactics I suppose. I'm absolutely convinced that if he stayed with the field for about 17 laps or so, and then made his move, nobody but nobody would have beaten him over the last 8 laps. I see him every year in London and he says to me, 'Christ Jimmy, I retired (23) before I became good.' Hogan is a member of the UK Milers Club and attends the London Marathon every year.

I know lads running 100 miles a week and they're never going to make it. If that kind of training wasn't improving my performance, I'd find something else to do. I very seldom raced unless I was right. I'd wait 8 or 10 weeks just to be right. I would never run a race just to make up numbers. Maybe athletes have gone soft. I ran the fastest time in the world for 6 miles in Paddington after working all day. We had 10 runners inside 28 minutes for a 6-mile race in White City.

Not much has changed on the Irish scene as far as the athletes are concerned. They took the money off (Mark) Carroll, which is f.....g disgraceful considering the times he has put up over various distances. They even tried to insult Sonia the same way and she has been our best athlete by far over a long period. There's a message there surely. Why the f...k would any athlete feel good about a shower of f.....s who are not interested in promoting the sport?"

For Hogan there are no regrets, no lingering bitterness. "I had a good career despite all the f.....g setbacks. I wish I'd had a faster (in the 50s) closing lap. That would have made a massive difference. There's a lot of money for successful athletes now, but what's money. I dislike people going around with a chip on their shoulder, saying oh if only we were running now. There's no good in that. It's gone and past."

After Mexico

I ran in 1969, just average running really and I retired the following year. It was an easy decision for me. Age was catching up with me and if I could't run to a decent competitive standard then I didn't want to be out there. I still ran and kept myself fairly fit but my racing days were over, or so I thought. With the advent of the Veterans Championships there were fellas coming out of the woodwork to try their luck, in most cases these were blokes who weren't good enough to go near open competition in their prime. I've nothing against Veterans Competition if that's what a bloke wants to do with his time. More luck to him. Before I made a comeback in 1983 I had massive doubts about whether or not it was worth the bother.

There was one factor that influenced me more than anything else, and that was my training. When I got back a measure of race fitness the training I did at the age of 50 was unbelievable. It was high quality and I was totally blown away by what I was able to do. Because of that I decided to give the Veterans scene a go and see what I could do with it. If you had told me in 1970 that I would be in serious training at the age of 50 I would have said you're completely off your game mate.

There was also the attraction of going to South America where the championships were to be held. There was a collection made up for me by many of my friends in the horse industry to help defray expenses, so I felt I had to go and honour their commitment to me. It still took me a while to get my head around the whole thing.

I had a lovely place to train in England about 1½ mile a circuit. I used to divide it up into 3 x 500m, 2 x 400 and I'd cover four laps. Therefore I'd wind up doing 12 x 500, 8 x 400; in total I was running over 6 miles inside of 41 minutes doing this interval training.

I went to America first of all and stayed in New York for 12 days. I went down to White Plains and I'd get to talking with the lads. They were primarily interested in what age group I was in. The training was going well and we'd be doing bunches of 400m laps in 70 secs no problem at all. I think being away for more than 10 years from competitive running gave me a renewed freshness. But it only lasted for 12 months, and then the injuries started due to the age factor. You can't trick your body when you get beyond a certain age, no matter what kind of training you're doing.

The White City

The White City was built for the 1908 London Olympics. It was the first of all Olympic stadia to be purpose built, and at the time it was the largest stadium in the world. Its capacity was 150,000 with 68,000 seated and 17,000 covered. After the Olympics it was used for track and field, greyhound racing and speedway. From 1932-1970 it was host to the AAA Championships, before Crystal Palace was built. The stadium was demolished in 1984 and the site is now home to BBC Radio Headquarters in Wood Lane.

'The White City was a marvellous place to run; it was out on its own. I loved running there; it had tradition and history and the atmosphere was special. I never ran a bad race in the White City; I had great success there. The

6 mile 3 AAAs was the next best race to the Olympics. The cream of English athletes was there. The odd out outsider, like Gamoudi raced there. The times were always fast I broke the Irish record there two or three times. I broke the British 10,000m record there; it was at least 75f degrees, very hot. I could always run much better when the weather was hot. I didn't mind the heat at all.

Breaking the British record there would have been one of my special memories. At 4 miles I was 16 seconds inside the record. The last 2 miles were very hard and I was 2 seconds inside the record. So you can see the fall off. Fergus Murray took me through the first 8 laps. After that I was on my own, so I was running against the clock, a very hard challenge.

The condition of the track was not always the best. I remember people getting blisters while wearing shoes. In Finland they rolled the tack before every top event. When I first went to England they used to do that at the White City but then they stopped rolling it. This was the case at the AAAs where the race went on after about four hours of competition and no one put a brush to it.

That was terribly unfair on the athletes and it could have been avoided. On the Continent the athlete's needs came first and that's as it should be. I'd get annoyed with the way they watered the track as well. They'd water the track on a Thursday for a Saturday meet but when the sun came down it turned the top inch of the cinder into dust. The right time to water the track would have been the morning of the race.

Even so, I have fond memories of the old stadium. I feel it was a privilege to have been able to compete there, and that some of my best performances took place on that track.

World Veteran Championships 1983

I was entered for the 5000m and the cross-country race. I won the 5000m and I looked at the cross-country race as a bonus if I won it. The weather was not in any way favorable to performing well. Conditions were brutal with temperatures 90f and above and 85% humidity. We ran four age groups together – over 40, over 45, over 50, over 55. I decided to run steady and sensibly (this wasn't the Olympics!) and come through, and if I had to I'd drop out. The course was over golf courses and that kind of terrain. As the race progressed, I just kept picking people off and ended up 3rd overall. I was beaten by two 40-year-olds.

There was a right bollix of a bloke called Maurice Morrell, Wirral AC, who was 2nd in the race and he refused to come to the rostrum for his medal. They had these showers set up in the trees and you stood under them to cool off after finishing. Morrell is standing next to me and I didn't know he finished 2nd and I says to him, "Jesus, Maurice, I ran 'em ragged didn't I?" He took offence to my remark. Then there was an American who got 3rd in the over 40 category and he finished behind me. We went down for the medals in the evening and he said to my best pal: "Jesus, man, a 50-year-old finished in front of me." Well I had to laugh. But it all came to an end shortly after that.

However, I did run in the Championships two years later in Rome. I had unfinished business with Mr. Morrell. I was unlucky in the 10000m because they mixed up the lap count, and they made me run an extra lap in the heats. I lapped everybody in the field and some of them twice but it didn't do me any good since Vets racing goes on time and I was already finished.

I won the British Veterans 5000m in Wolverhampton. Morrell was in this race also, and I said to myself. "I'll f…..g do you mate before this thing is finished." I had been waiting two years for a chance to race him. I sat on him all the time until 600 metres out, and then I blasted him out of it, f…..g destroyed him. I got immense satisfaction from that but I knew that was the end of my brief flirtation with the Veterans scene. I have no regrets about competing in those Championships but as I've said elsewhere, I have no great respect for that kind of competition, and even if the injuries didn't set in, it was next to impossible to get motivated and worked up about them. I'd had my time when I was younger and able to compete against the very best. Nothing could ever get near to that kind of experience, not for me anyway.

Running Barefoot

People have always asked me questions about running barefoot. I know I was the exception amongst the white runners certainly. With the high technology shoes and footwear to suit every surface I sometimes wonder if the manufacturers have gone over the top somewhat. I suppose the name of the game today is sales, money and sponsorship. I have no problem with any top athletes making as much as they can because they work hard for what they get and it's a relatively short career. You're only an injury away from being totally forgotten about.

I'm not sure of the advantages to anyone running barefoot bar me or a bloke called Bruce Tulloh perhaps. So I can't say I'd recommend it. But my times showed that I could always run faster barefoot. One year I ran all my races with spikes on and my times were diabolically slow compared to what I ran barefoot. I'll give examples to show this.

My best barefoot three miles was 13:19.6, with spikes it was 13:30; that 11 second difference is massive in a track race, like night and day. Over 6 miles, I ran 27:35 barefoot, but only 28:18 with spikes. How can you compare it? When I put spikes on I felt tied to the ground, and when I finished a race, I felt as though I hadn't run as hard as I could. I was fresh as a daisy ten minutes later.

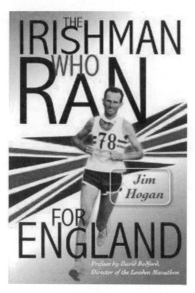

Jim Hogan

I taped my toes when I ran barefoot. I put on a piece of plaster the day before, so it would fit into the skin, and definitely stay on for 3 miles and usually for 6 unless the track was very bad. I had to wear spikes when it was muddy, though. I loved running in the White City, even though many times the track was well chewed up when it came to the middle distance events and that made racing a bit more of a challenge for all competitors.

I was first and foremost a track runner. Cross-country would have been second on the list for me. I never considered myself a marathon runner. It was a distance I came too late in my career and even though I was successful at it, at heart I was always a trackie, which is the essence of running really. By and large I was a front-runner. It was often a tremendous strain leading all alone, and I never had any help. I arranged with different blokes but they always backed out when the pressure was really on.

More to the point though, I was conscious of not having a good finish. This meant I had to try and take the finish out of the kickers by taking it out fast and staying there. I don't know why, but I was never able to run faster than 62 seconds for the last lap although a runner of my ability should have been able to do 60.

The Importance of Running

I liked running/racing provided I was doing it well. I never liked being beaten by blokes that I knew I could beat if I were running at my best. I didn't mind getting my arse kicked by good blokes that were running within a couple of seconds of my best time ever, but I wouldn't have been satisfied with losing to fellows running 13:50 and 13:55. I just couldn't take that. I suppose it has to do with the competitive instinct. I would rather be beaten in a fast race by class runners where I was taken to the limit than winning an event in a mediocre time. There was no satisfaction in that, no challenge or sense of achievement.

What I liked best in athletics was that feeling when I was running well. I think that's true of any committed athlete. I liked the traveling mind you and athletics took me to 25 different countries. The blokes I mixed with and competed against were good blokes – 99 per cent of them anyway.

Veteran Competition

I tried it a few times once I turned fifty but I packed it in quickly enough. Winning an age group made no sense to me, and you'd be up against fuckers who came late to running and thought they were Olympians with their attitude and fanaticism. I went to Puerto Rico and picked up like three Gold medals. I'm running the cross country race on a blistering hot and humid day, two to three minutes ahead of my nearest competitor, and I'm thinking to myself – "Hogan what the f..k are you doing out here beating nobody."

I could never get my head around the veteran scene. I have no time for it really and I get a bit disgusted when I see fellas my age out there competing. I have nothing against running to stay in shape and for health reasons. But I did my running when I was at my peak and anything after that was a let-down, a bit artificial to be honest. When I'm asked about my running career I do not include the veteran wins since they meant nothing to me personally. My running career effectively ended when I no longer felt good enough to race in open competition.

Major achievements
European 3 mile record 13.32
30 km world record 1.32.25
1966 European marathon champion
Tokyo Olympics [Ireland]
Mexico Olympics [England]
Best marathon 2.1922 [1966]
Best 10km 28.49.66 [1965]

MARY RYAN JENNINGS

Date of Birth: 18/2/1955

Catching Up with Mary

By Lindie Naughton

*"Dumbing down in our education system means that the
brightest and most dedicated may not be adequately challenged"*

Lindie Naughton chatted to Mary Jennings, a pal for many years since the
days when they both competed for UCD Athletics Club.

I come from a sporting family. As well as athletics, the sports enjoyed by
my siblings included boxing, squash, gymnastics, hurling, football and hockey.
From one sporting family, I moved to another – my husband Brian was a
former 800m international. All four children have competed with Dundrum
South Dublin Athletics Club. Kian and Emmet have represented Ireland at
mountain running, while Emmet has competed in three European Cross-
Country Championships and at the World Junior Track and Field Championships. Ryan and Emily did the sprints and jumps and all four have played
football and hurling (or camogie!) with Ballinteer St. John's GAA club. Emily,
from the age of 17 was playing on the senior women's team.

My father was a cyclist. He would have thought nothing of cycling with
his siblings all the way from their farm in Waterford to sports around the
country (such as Banteer) and then cycling home again with big silver cups
displayed on their bicycles. In those days, cycling and running events were
held together and I remember going to local sports in the People's Park in
Waterford where there was a slightly banked track. We – there were four girls
and four boys in our family – would compete in the races for the little children.
When I was quite young, I joined St Paul's Athletics Club for a few months.
The club was just starting. Then with my older sister Anne, I joined Waterford
Athletics Club. I think we were the first ever female members of the club. Shay
Fitzpatrick and Cyril O'Regan were among those competing at the time.

Frank Leahy, our first coach, mentored everyone in all disciplines in track and field. He believed that the full experience of diverse events led to a better fit of athlete and discipline. So we tried everything.

Fintan Walsh – "Mr Waterford Athletics" – was also a member of WAC at the time. Fintan has kept Waterford athletics going through the good times and bad – and the great times when Waterford men won six inter-county titles with teams that included Gerry Deegan, John Treacy, Ray Treacy and Brendan Quinn. He has been a radio and newspaper athletics correspondent for many years. Fintan is fantastic – his articles contain useful nuggets of advice and he reports on the performances of every Waterford athlete from the youngest juveniles to Olympic

Lindie Naughton and Mary Jennings –
The best of friends

medallists like the aforementioned John Treacy. He gives every athlete great encouragement and can be seen and heard commentating at every athletics event from one side of Waterford county to the other. I'd ring him after one of my own races and he'd insist on knowing all the details and how any other Waterford athletes had done.

There also was Paddy Burns and Martin Halley. They were totally dedicated to athletics. They did it for the pure joy of seeing athletes of all standards doing well. They travelled the country to events loving every minute of it.

I remember winning the Munster 4×100m with the WAC Ladies team due to the slickness of our baton passing. None of us were faster than members of the other teams, but, boy, had we practised our baton passing! I also remember competing in the triple jump at County and Munster level – this would be 40 years ago – before girls were banned from doing it. The International Authorities declared that it would "displace the womb"! It was to be the 1990s before it was revived.

I don't remember having any heroes or looking up to any athlete in particular, although I do remember Margaret Murphy from Ovens in County Cork – she won everything in Munster in those days and then went on to the nationals, winning there as well.

When I came to UCD, Jack Sweeney was my coach. My best event then would have been the 400m hurdles; my best time was 63 seconds. Jack was a great coach with a priceless turn of phrase.

After college I joined South Dublin AC for a very few years where Hayden Lewis was the coach. But my heart turned to home. At Waterford AC, there was a very good women's intermediate team led by Grainne Quinn (Brendan's brother) so I decided to lend my weight to it.

Athletics teaches you to cope with failure at a very young age without you even realising it. Now we are afraid to expose younger children to competition – the IRFU doesn't have finals for under 12's for instance. Young people are not allowed to experience failure in sport, thus depriving them of one of the biggest lessons life can provide.

A few years ago in athletics, there was an attempt to stop cross-country championship races in the younger age groups because of the perceived anguish in these age groups. The sight of children crying at the finish line was upsetting some people. Yet two minutes later, those same children would be laughing and joking – they were learning that their friends were still their friends and their parents still their parents, even if they hadn't triumphed.

Now when youngsters experience failure in their late teens, they can't cope and, in some extreme cases, what's their response? Suicide. I am not naive enough to suggest that running is the cure for suicide but it might and could help to ameliorate the problem.

We don't challenge our children enough in case they fail. If not fully challenged, children will never achieve their optimum potential. As a teacher, it worries me that we are dumbing down our education system so that those at the bottom won't fail. The result? Mediocrity.

Also, health and safety are issues that need to be addressed. I was in Germany on a school trip a few years ago and seven and eight year olds were given little saws and were off cutting enough wood for a barbecue. They were also enjoying climbing trees during break time. Can you see that happening in Ireland? Our children are wrapped in cotton wool and mollycoddled. We are not encouraging them to develop in a natural and organic way.

In my life outside athletics, I'm a teacher at Willow Park in Dublin. I love Irish and the Irish culture that I teach. I'm not so fond of the amount of paperwork and administration the job involves these days - as is happening in a lot of professions these days. A number of teachers are leaving the profession because the paperwork is sapping their energy and detracting from the job which they really love to do, which is to teach.

If I was sports minister, I'd make one PE class a day mandatory for every child in the schools system from junior infants to Leaving Cert. and as with

GAA pitches, I would also have tracks and indoor athletics facilities within reach of everyone. In the smallest of country villages in rural Ireland, you will find a football pitch. Whatever you may think of the GAA, they had a vision that went way beyond simply seeing boys and girls playing football and hurling. So can we have an athletics track beside every GAA pitch in the country?

Mary Ryan Jennings

My proudest moment? I'm not sure about that, they are so many things that you feel pleased about but proud? I'm not sure even what the word "proud" means. I don't like seeing the arrogant way some athletes behave when they win. They show no respect for the others in the race. I've told my own children that if they ever behave like that I'll disown them! My four children make me proud. I am more nervous for them if they are racing or competing because I can't do anything. For myself, I would feel pleased after a good run – that's all. Pleased.

When I have my hundred marathons done (Mary had reached 99 at the time of writing, May 2014, but a fracture in her foot meant she was "resting"), I'll start aiming for 200. I want to get 100 done while I am still competitive, not crawling around. Most of my marathons I've completed in under 3 hours 30 minutes – ten were under three hours. My best was 2:51 in 1988. I had two at 3 hours 50 minutes. In one, in Connemara, I hadn't recovered from a 'flu and in the other, in Clonakilty, I pulled a calf muscle. Every marathon is a different adventure – you can never be sure what will happen.

My biggest regret in athletics is that no one advised me to move on to the longer distances earlier in my career. I started running marathons in my 30's – too late, in my view. If I had started in my 20's, I think I would have run in low 2 hours 40 minute times. But then women didn't do long distances until quite recently and we didn't know a lot about marathon training. I improved for five or six years before the children arrived, but after the children, I didn't improve at all.

On race day, I fall out of bed, put on my gear and stagger out the door to do a 10-minute run. I then have gluten free toast (I was diagnosed coeliac after the birth of our second child), a cup of coffee and start drinking – water if it's a short race, Hi5 if it's longer.

I then get dressed for competition – everything on – because that way I don't forget anything essential!

I never learned to drive because I had so many accidents when I drove a moped as a student. Later, I signed up for ten lessons and got a dreadful teacher, who terrified me and put me off for life. I walk most places, and the marathon community is fantastic at making sure that no-one goes home alone after a race.

When I reach 75, I hope I'm not much different to what I am now. A bit greyer perhaps. In my head, I still feel about 30 – it's everyone around me that's getting older! Not me. It's amazing when you're running and feeling good, you still think you're running at 6.30 minute pace – even when your watch would tell you its closer to nine minutes.

Achievements

Five National Senior Marathon titles
Two World Mountain Running World Cups (Wales, Austria)
A World Marathon Cup (selected with two others)
Numerous British and Irish Masters' Cross-Countries
Team silver 10km cross-country, World Masters' Championships, Gateshead;
103 marathons completed
3 senior Internationals – 1 marathon, 2 mountain running
14 times on team for Masters International Cross Country, team medals each time
including gold 3 times
82 National Masters titles across track and field, indoors, outdoors, cross-country
and road (also 50 silver, 26 bronze)
Team silver cross-country (4th individual) World Masters Championships

Mary broke her foot in April 2014 and was told she may not run again. She had it in plaster for 6 weeks and a further 3 weeks on crutches, but 2 weeks later, on 28 June, ran her 100th marathon in Waterford. Since then has run 3 more marathons finishing 5th woman overall in the Longford Marathon, second in her age category in Dublin City Marathon 2014 and winning her category in Clonakilty.

ADAM JONES
Date of Birth: 19/2/1943

King of Athletics and Ace of Many Trades

By Zoë Melling

"It's never too late to start and always too soon to finish".

It's a bitterly cold winter's morning in a park on the outskirts of Dublin, and a lone figure is standing shivering in a T-shirt. His fellow volunteers are all swathed in warm fleeces, hats, gloves and scarves, although not all have arrived equipped for the chilly conditions. Despite his notorious dislike of cold weather, Adam Jones has stripped off several layers of clothing without a moment's hesitation to ensure no one else has to suffer any discomfort. This man would literally give you the shirt off his back. Since rising shortly after dawn, Adam has driven halfway round the county to collect athletes in need of a lift, fielded numerous phone calls from panic-stricken competitors who have lost their singlet, spikes or nerve, and averted more than one calamity in his usual calm, collected and capable manner. By the time the day's competition commences, he has uttered his catchphrase "don't worry, it's not a problem" countless times, and as always when Adam is in charge, everything runs like clockwork.

Nearly as renowned for his coaching achievements as his considerable talent as an athlete, Adam is a master of multi-tasking, and has been jokingly referred to as a "master puppeteer". His uncanny ability to simultaneously monitor the training progress of the myriad athletes in his charge with eagle-eyed precision while in the midst of his own session has caught out many a newcomer labouring under the mistaken impression that a momentary lapse of discipline might go unnoticed! Every spare moment in Adam's busy life is devoted to the pursuit of athletics, and despite his hectic schedule he gives his time willingly and generously, without seeking recognition or reward for his efforts. His generosity and selfless concern for others didn't escape the attention of the judges who awarded him the inaugural AAI Coach of the Year

Adam Jones

Award in 2007. This was a great honour which recognised his tireless commitment to the sport, his perseverance and patience, and his inclusive approach in encouraging athletes of all abilities – often helping them achieve goals well beyond what they thought possible.

Like many top runners Adam came from a farming background, growing up in Castlemaine in County Kerry. He participated in several sports at school including athletics, and despite not having trained as a runner, one sports day he managed to beat boys two years older than himself to win the one mile event on a 200m grass track. Although he didn't match the sub four minute mile record which had recently been broken by Roger Bannister, it was an indication of greater things to come. Adam's upbringing was of the "school of hard knocks" variety, with a "character building" stint at boarding school and no third level education until over 40 years later when he graduated with a Bachelor of Science Degree in Exercise and Health Fitness from the University of Limerick at the age of 72. In the intervening years he settled in Rathfarnham, raised two children, and has had a successful career in business which spans over fifty years and is still ongoing.

A relative latecomer to athletics, Adam started running in earnest during the height of the running boom in the early eighties, at age 38. His philosophy is "it's never too late to start and always too soon to finish". Unless of course he's clocking another PB or breaking records in his age category! He started slowly, initially going on short runs with his children Tarah and Glenn before school in the mornings, then graduating to longer runs with Glenn when he began playing rugby at a competitive level and needed to build up his fitness. One evening in 1981 when Adam was out running he met a friend who was training for the Dublin Marathon. He decided he might as well join him, and as he says, the rest is history. He recalls that when he came home and told his children he planned to run the marathon they had a great laugh. However it wasn't long before the laugher turned to cheers, and then tears of pride as their father demonstrated his formidable talent over the distance.

After his first marathon attempt which he describes as a "disaster" in which he slowed to a walk for much of the second half, he decided to have another go and ran a time of 3.03 on a hilly course in Galway in the spring of 1982. Having reached the age of 40 he was then considered a "real" master or veteran as they were more commonly known at the time. He was not affiliated with a registered club during the early years of running. He and a group of training partners then joined Rathfarnham Athletics Club which was at that time juvenile only. They established the senior section which was later merged with Walkinstown Social and Athletics Club to become Rathfarnham WSAF AC.

Among Adam's many notable achievements as a masters athlete are winning the National Masters Cross Country Championships in Dungarvan against a high quality field at age 50. He also scored on the winning club team and Dublin County team that day, and his trio of gold medals was probably the first time anyone in the M50 category had achieved this. At the time he was being coached by Murt Coleman, also an athlete of considerable stature. In the 1993 Dublin marathon which was won by John Treacy Adam finished first over 50 in a time of 2.34, and the following spring at age 51 he went to London and ran 2.32 despite a very difficult first seven miles when he considered pulling out. A year later he again won the over 50 category in Rotterdam in a time of 2.36. He racked up many other outstanding performances at home and abroad, including a bronze team medal in Oregon when representing Ireland in the over 45 category and team silver in the Toronto Half Marathon in later years.

Adam's most memorable race was his first attempt at the 10k distance in the inaugural Streets of Dublin 10k in 1981 which was won by Eamonn Coghlan, in which he finished in under 36 minutes, much to the disbelief of all his friends. His biggest disappointment was finishing fourth in the World Championship Marathon in Brisbane in a time of 2.46, which he says is the worst possible position in a championship event. The course was difficult and poorly stewarded, resulting in him taking a wrong turn and running an extra half mile at 23 miles.

In his late 60s a series of injuries forced Adam to take a break from competitive running, and now his focus is on coaching and contributing to the enjoyment and success of others. He says one of the highlights of his involvement in athletics is all the positive people he has met along the way. He doesn't regret a minute of his experience and intends to continue as long as he is able. His advice for young athletes is that patience and hard work will bring rewards but it is also important to enjoy the journey. With his degree framed and on the mantelpiece alongside his extensive collection of medals, and a treasure trove of super-master medals and records waiting to be unearthed, who knows which direction Adam's travels will take him next. One thing is for sure – anyone currently competing in the M70 category would be well advised to stay on their toes and watch their back!

Major Achievements
Developing athletics in Rathfarnham Athletics club
National master cross country O /50 Dungarvan
Won individual, club, county gold
Dublin City Marathon 1994- First O/50 2.34
Fastest marathon in world O/50 London 1995 – 2.32
At 59 years of age ran 2.46 in Brisbane 4th world championships M 55
Multiple team medals competing for Ireland in world championships
Team Gold Ireland in Japan, Silver in Toronto, Bronze in Oregon

PADRAIG KEANE
5/1/1952 – 26/1/2016

Keep it Country

By Peter McDermot

"Demise of poor running in Europe is down to bad coaching"

"Elvis may have had his Blue Suede Shoes but I had my brown suede shoes and I won several road races wearing them. Sure back then, I couldn't afford running shoes." Padraig Keane is reflecting on his long career, a career which saw him become one of the top distance runners in Ireland and a ferocious competitor, especially in cross-country. "Keep it country" was one of Padraig's favourite expressions – and he wasn't talking about music. "When the leaves turned golden brown and the mud started flying I relished the prospect of racing over the country."

It all started for Padraig one Sunday in October 1967. He had come back from Mass in his native Ballinlough when another young man knocked on his door and said, "Hello there!" It was Frank Greally and he wanted Padraig to run for Ballyhaunis A.C. in the Mayo Youths 'Cross-Country Championships. They were a man down as Greally's great friend, Pat Cribben, had decided to compete in the Connacht boxing championships that day instead of running the race. Padraig cycled to Ballyhaunis, 6 miles away, was picked up by Mick Nestor and brought to Hollymount for the race. He had never even seen a cross-country race before; he had seen some of the Tokyo Olympics on television three years earlier but knew nothing about cross-country. In spite of that, Padraig finished second, his team won Gold and Padraig returned from his first race with two medals. He was bitten by the incurable bug. Afterwards he and his new team mates travelled to Ballina to support Cribben. They created such a cacophony of cheering that the M.C. threatened to have them thrown out of the hall.

He started training then, aimlessly as he would admit. "I'd just go out and run six miles as hard and as fast as I could", he remembers, "and if I met a car I'd jump over the wall because if they saw me they'd think I was mad. Luckily there weren't too many cars around in those days". A couple of years later, BLE organised an athletics' seminar in UCG and Padraig was invited. He remembers going for a run with the group of elite athletes who after a while started to pick up the pace. Padraig found himself beside Irish Senior champion, Matt Murphy, who told him to slow down and ignore the guys who were racing it up front. "Racing is racing and training is training" is a lesson that Padraig learned that day and he always remembered it. A firm believer in long slow distance as a method of proper conditioning, Padraig believes that there are too many young athletes today who try to jump to a level that they are not ready for without first having laid this solid foundation in conditioning. As a result of this lesson, Padraig himself was never injured: he is also a firm believer in the efficacy of stretching after training when the muscles are warm and pliant – not before.

In 1970 Padraig went to Manchester to look for work and joined Sale Harriers. He was a member of the Sale team which won a 100 mile relay. Each member of the team ran 1 mile (no athlete could run more than one leg) and they averaged 4:57. On Saturday afternoons, if he wasn't racing, Padraig would go to either Old Trafford or Maine Road to watch the team in red or blue. He still has an abiding love for United to this day.

On returning to Ireland he decided to head for Dublin with the intention of joining his friend Greally in the all-powerful Donore Harriers. There was, however, one slight problem: Padraig didn't know where Donore were located. Frank told him he'd ring him to let him know where to go. "I'm still waiting for that call." A work colleague told him that he knew a man who ran and he would put him in touch. Padraig was picked up the following Saturday at an appointed spot by this man, who turned out to be the legendary coach, Laro Byrne. The latter told him that he was on his way to a race in Santry and invited him to come along. He also told Padraig that if he didn't like his club, called Clonliffe Harriers, he would personally bring him to Donore.

Padraig lined up for the 4 mile cross-country club race in Santry Woods. He found himself surrounded by legends and Olympians: Frank Murphy , Danny McDaid, Des McCormack, Tom Gregan, Paddy Marley, George Mc-Intyre, to name just half a dozen. They were all Irish internationals but Padraig finished third in this exalted company. As a result of the warm welcome he received, he decided there and then to join Clonliffe.

Under the direction of Laro, Padraig made rapid progress. In February 1971 he won the National Junior Cross-Country championships leaving one Eamonn Coghlan a hundred metres in his wake. He represented Ireland in the International C.C. Championships in San Sebastian. The following season he was the hot favourite for the National Intermediate title but finished second after a tactical error. A couple of months later he lined up to defend his National Junior title but, surprisingly, could finish only third. Padraig, however, had his eye on a much bigger prize and two weeks later lined up for the National Senior Championship. He ran a stormer and came home sixth, nailing down his place on the Irish team for the World Cross in Cambridge while still a junior .He was joined on the team by his old friend, Frank Greally. He remembers that race in Cambridge being won by the legendary Gaston Roelants, the 1964 Olympic Steeplechase champion. It was to be the first of three senior world cross-country championships in which he would compete.

Donore continued to dominate Irish distance running for the next three years. But in the 1975-76 season, the Clonliffe captain, Christy Brady, knew that he had a young squad capable of toppling the champions. Christy knew that you could win big even "with kids" and he put his trust in the youthful Padraig Keane, Jerry Kiernan, "Young" Frank Murphy and Gerry Finnegan ("the toughest athlete I ever ran against" according to Padraig). Padraig and the rest of that team had enormous respect for Captain Christy (Brady, not the horse) and, on a historic day in Ballinasloe in February 1976, they toppled the eight–in-a-row winning team of Donore to take the National title for the first time. Padraig had a narrow escape from being killed in a car crash only a week before the race; indeed he was still combing broken glass out of his hair the night before but a little thing like that never stopped Padraig!

He won his first National Senior Gold medal on that occasion as a scoring member of that Clonliffe team and he followed it the next year with gold.

He always sang the praises of Christy Brady; he considered Christy to have been a very knowledgeable coach and shrewd psychologist, long before sports psychologists (or "witch doctors" as Padraig called them) were heard of. There was a huge mutual respect between the two men. He recalls being a bold boy on one occasion and having had a "few scoops too many" on the night before an important road relay. Despite feeling rotten up to an hour before he

Padraig, no 82, leads out the Quinlan Cup in Tullamore

was due to race he knew, as soon as he started to warm up, that he was "going to have a good one". And so it proved to be: he smashed the course record and opened up a 90 second gap on the second runner. He was rewarded by the "biggest bear hug I ever got in my life" from a delighted Christy!

Padraig continued to be an absolute stalwart for Clonliffe, winning his third National Senior gold medal in 1982 and amassing an amazing total of 15 Dublin Senior Team Gold medals over a twenty year period.

In the late seventies, he joined the Irish Army and was stationed in the Curragh. The army was assembling an elite athletic squad at the time and Padraig revelled in this new environment. He fondly remembers the great athletes who trained with him over the plains of Kildare during this phase of his career: Brendan Downey, Paddy Murphy, Brian Keeney and Paul Delaney. "They were all great guys and bloody tough runners". The highlight of this period was when he represented Ireland in the World Military Games in the marathon and finished 2nd in 2:22. Padraig could now add a world championship medal to his huge collection of Dublin and National medals. Imagine his disappointment then when, on his return, instead of being congratulated and feted by the army he was reprimanded by a sergeant-major because beer bottles and cigarette butts were found in his quarters. Padraig tried to point out that he couldn't possibly be the culprit: he had been away all week at the Championships, he never smoked and he certainly wasn't drinking before a World Championships. But an unreasonable authoritarian figure would not listen and told Padraig he had no right to speak in his defence. Feeling disillusioned, Padraig decided to leave the army shortly afterwards.

Padraig continued to run as a veteran or master athlete. He was the hot favourite to win the National Vets. title in 1991. But his old friend and rival, Jim

Clonliffe cross country team, 1984

McGlynn of Donore (who had also ran for Clonliffe for some time), stuck to him like a leech and outsprinted him in the home straight. Padraig afterwards said that he "felt like Long John Silver throughout the race and McGlynn was the parrot on my shoulder!"

He missed the next year through illness and it was feared that he might have missed his chance as younger men moved up to the master's category. But in 1994; Padraig was a convincing winner of the National Vets. Title thereby completing a remarkable collection of medals: he had now won National medals at Junior, Intermediate, Senior and Masters Level.

He was always a deep and original thinker. Thirty years ago he was advocating cold water baths (*not* ice water) long before the sports scientists started recommending the same. Interesting to note that the experts are now also saying that cold water is as effective as ice water and no longer approve of the more extreme form of this type of recovery therapy. "In the early summer we used to run in our bare feet in the Trinity playing fields. (This was long before bare-foot running and minimalist shoes became a fad.) "It hardened our feet for the track" and with a cinder track in Santry that turned to concrete in the summer hard feet were a necessity.

Many years ago, Padraig got a motion passed at the Clonliffe AGM proposing that cross-country running be restored as an Olympic sport. He now gets a wry sense of satisfaction that after all those years, and having had his motion passed through a labyrinthine process, the IAAF recently recommended to the IOC that cross-country should, indeed, be reinstated as an Olympic sport.

Padraig was saddened by the near demise of the National Senior Cross-country Championships. Once, the highlight of the season and the most coveted prize in Irish distance running, it has become a poor imitation of its former self. He believeed that it should be elevated to its former status by holding it before Christmas and that it, not the Inter-Counties, should be the trial for the European Championships.

He also had a revolutionary proposal for rejuvenating the National senior Track and Field Championships. Dismayed by the fact that heats are no longer necessary in many events and that only three or four competitors take part in others, he proposed that a prize fund of €1 million per annum should be set up for these championships with the winner of each event taking home up to €5,000 with a sliding scale down to €750 for last place. "The battle just to make finals would be ferocious because the athletes would know that just making the final would result in a minimum of €750."

Padraig would finance this bold idea by placing a levy of €1 on every competitor in the multitude of road races that take place all over the country every weekend, plus a €5 levy on each permit granted by the A.A.I to local race promoters.

He also bemoaned the performance of our top athletes in major track championships. He noted that back in the 70s, 80s and 90s we were getting athletes into finals and, indeed, winning medals. In spite of a much vaunted superior coaching regime, that is no longer happening. "Are they gone soft?", he wondered, and also questioned the fact that they have so many "experts" advising them.

Padraig always baffled these experts with pertinent questions. He bemoaned the lack of common sense. "Common sense is not a very common commodity, in fact C.S has been replaced by B.S."

Padraig usually held court in the Clonliffe bar on Sunday afternoons. He engaged in vociferous debates (or even heated arguments) with all and sundry on every topic under the sun. But no matter how hard hitting the exchanges may have been, Padraig always keep his opponent's vocal chords lubricated with a creamy pint or two.

"He was a man who never held a grudge" may well be Padraig's epitaph.

Major Achievements
4th National senior cross country
4th senior 10,000km
2nd World Military Games Marathon 2.22
National Master cross country champion
Marathon 2.22
Half Marathon 66 min
20 miles junior 1.44.48 Clonliffe 20
20 miles senior 1.41 Clonliffe 20

Fr. Liam Kelleher

Date of Birth: 29/12/1944

The Prophet

By Michael Gygax

Fr Liam Kelleher has been involved in Irish athletics for close to forty years. Born and raised in Cork he shares some of the characteristics with Colm O Connell, the man who has been responsible for the emergence of Kenyan athletes on the international circuit and the coach to David Rudisha the London Olympic 800,meter champion and world record holder. Liam and Colm are both Munster men, are friends, each life is absorbed by athletics which embodies for each the mainstay contact with youth and community forms their unique form of community and pastoral work. They share an attitude, that anything is possible if you work hard and persist. Where Colm has gained international fame working in Kenya with thoroughbreds, Liam has stayed at home, currently working with children in the local National school in the parish of Cobh where he has been recently posted as a priest. He always appreciates the benefits of fitness; he was appalled at the lack of exercise and potential obesity epidemic lurking in the background in primary schools. Liam took the bulls by the horns and decided to do something about it, so he approached the local primary school and set up his school of athletic excellence.

Liam for most of the past decade and a half seems to have been quiet, maybe he too had gone away. Those immersed in Gaelic football, knows that a switch in sport brought great success to women's football in CORK. He started with under 14 years girls and each match played their opposition off the pitch winning every championship by a cricket score and each year progressed in ability winning every match with consummate ease. Fr Liam Kelleher has that *je ne sais pas* factor. He brings an intangible genius which develops sporting greatness. A maverick true and true, organizations and sporting bodies one would imagine should be embracing his presence with great appreciation, often are threatened by his dynamism, independent thinking, non-compromising commitment to the people he serves and his extra ordinary work ethic.

This has often left him working outside athletic clubs which has developed a strategy of working in schools and feeding local clubs with his protégés.

I had heard that Liam was back into the athletic scene with a bang and he had initiated "an athletic school of excellence". I rang him up and he immediately invited me to stay as long as I like and observe participate engage as much or as little as I pleased. I had met Liam in the past and had known him by reputation as an extra ordinary individual who could move mountains. While reading *The Perfect Distance - Ovett and Coe: The Record-Breaking Rivalry* by Pat Butcher last Christmas, I was surprised to find Liam Kelleher eulogized by the author over five pages in this award winning publication. Liam had secured Steve Ovett, Eamonn Coghlan, John Treacy, John Walker and a world class field to run in the back arse of a mountain slope called Tulleylease, with a population of only 100 people in 1979. Building a track there, raising funds to do so against all the odds made Liam nearly a cult mythological figure in the early eighties. Ovett an Olympic champion 800 meter 1980 and multiple world record holder was considered an enigmatic figure by the world's press because of his reluctance to give interviews and his showboating on the track made him a loathed and loved figure in equal measure.

His participation in Tulleylease turning down big payments from other international meets and refusal to take any money from Liam for participation, showed a real appreciation and esteem that Ovett held Liam. Going through memorabilia in Liam's house, a Christmas card is signed "To Liam, love from Steve and Rachel" which dates back to 1979. Liam's enthusiasm, love of people, generosity and noble work had obviously struck a chord with Steve Ovett. When I visited the local primary school where he coaches I tried to work out what makes Liam so universally popular and effective with his charges. The results shows he has the Midas touch and he knows athletics inside out. Every person he deals with whether they are six, sixteen or sixty he engages them in a way where he is fully present with them, makes them feel important, imbues a sense confidence that anything is possible. After running sixty-five children off for trials for a cross country race a week later, he takes two five euro notes out of his pocket, a reward for a new course record over 600m. He has very limited recreational space but that does not deter him despite some crowding in the short 250, meter track marked out by cones. Liam only has this short circuit for potentially 700 pupils. Everyone who is there wants to be there and Liam keeps order by gentle persuasion, that to mess is to be sent back to class.

Observing Liam in action is to realize that excellence is achieved by daily engagement with children, coaching there every day. This is his priority in a hectic schedule. His love of sport is engaged with religious zealotry, but the motivation is his love of seeing people fulfill their potential. His methods are simple. The older children take responsibility warming up the group, so the children take ownership of the sessions are taught fundamental lessons in personal training before they reach secondary school. The friendship and comradeship between the children is enhanced through their participation in sport, team and individual. It great fun and a joy to be around. Liam has encouraged some parents and friends to help him out, which builds a cohesive and powerful training program. One of the parents is a Polish lady, a national high jump champion, who lends her time and expertise in the technical event, jumps and hurdles. The children when asked, "what does the school of excellence mean to them" and they say, "to be the best we can be".

Being with Liam feels likes a rolling snowball gaining down a hill, fueled by a dynamo. He is fully present but never stops. He often starts the day with Morning Prayer as he says mass in Cobh Cathedral, usually in under 20, minutes. Breakfast consists of porridge bread, tea and a host of plant supplements he takes in the morning to give him extra staying power and energy. His day consists of saying a funeral mass, attending a cremation, attendance at a football match for the school, a two hour coaching session, office work entering children into races, a short visit to a coffee morning for cancer, dinner and then he works for four hours till 3.30 am in the morning writing articles for the Cobh newspaper, country and western music blares from his computer into the early hours of the morning, periodically he takes a break to check sport results on sky sport.

A person's home speaks volumes of its inhabitant's tastes, history, habits and lifestyle. Liam's house is situated on the grounds of the magnificent Cobh Cathedral overlooking Cobh Harbor. Internally Liam's house is a curiosity box of athletic history, human rights and religion. Quotations from Martin Luther King greets you in his hallway. His kitchen displays photos of the greatest moments in Irish and international athletics. Sky sports is tuned into a whole world wide range of sport. Upstairs, Liam has a history of Irish and international in the form of books, pamphlets, posters and magazines. For over a decade Liam published marathon magazine a high quality athletic magazine. He was the pro for ble the old athletic national body for over twelve years. He was also the team manager for many Irish teams at major games for over two decades. His home is a museum of athletics history. When I snuggled up for the night I noticed that sports memorabilia were embroidered onto the duvet, one with the words "the world's greatest coach". A book on Martin Luther King graced his bookshelf, written by his wife, has a personal message from the same good lady to Liam, " With warm wishes for your success in helping to create a more just and peaceful society", Coretta Scott King.

Fr. Liam Kelleher

On one occasion recently after an afternoon coaching, Liam took off to Cobh golf course for some recreation. He was pleased with himself that great progress being made in the coaching session. Liam thrives when he is busy. On a roll, so to speak he ends up with twenty four points for nine holes, excellence begets excellence. Golf has been part of Liam's fund raising exploits historically. He holds the distinction of holding a world record of the number of golf holes played in one day, 252 holes, in Charville golf course back on Saturday, 25 June 1983. That is fourteen rounds of golf! Starting at four am, a golfing record was interrupted briefly as he rushed off to say mass, only to return to take a world record. He played with the same ball the whole day. On another occasion he fundraised by running around a 400m track for 35 miles.

Liam tries to avoid negative people and naysayers. As Liam walks down a street he meets a former pupil, enquires about his fitness and wellbeing. How are you getting on? Liam is aware that he is not only their teacher but for him a very important presence as their priest and spiritual guide, a representative of a church that often is seen to have lost the common touch. A young boy comes over to Liam after a training session and whispers to him that his gran died the night before and his mother wants him to say the funeral mass. For Liam Kelleher athletics has been his passion and through coaching and development of children he fulfils his pastoral role as a priest in a dynamic and meaningful way.

Liam came to Cobh, the former home of Sonia O'Sullivan, arguably Ireland's greatest track athlete, two years ago after a gap of fifteen years coaching athletics. He had become disillusioned with the elite end of sport which he believes had become corrupt and awash with performance enhancing chemicals.

Once upon a time Liam coached an athlete named Anita Philpot. Her claim to fame was that it took Sonia a couple of years before she could beat her. During this time Liam was in the other camp, coach to her one time nemesis. Liam smiles as he was later manager on many teams Sonia was on subsequently and feels special pleasure in having the honor of baptizing her two children. Is it not ironic that the priest whose nickname is "galloping Jesus" finds himself posted in Sonia's home town. Maybe he will produce some champions but what is not in doubt is that he will improve the quality of the lives of the children he coaches as they navigate their way through life, better equipped having met and worked with Liam.

In religion class the children were asked could they name three prophets. Not surprisingly they mentioned mother Teresa, Gandhi and father Liam. At least the young ones appreciate a prophet in his own land.

Major Achievemements

252 holes of golf played in the same day or 14 rounds of golf
Charleville Golf Course, 25 the June 1983
Played with 1 club – a five iron – all on foot

MURT KELLY

Date of Birth: 1/4/1948

Home-grown Strong Men

By Kieran Kelly

"Accept responsibility for your life. Know that it is you who will get you where you want to go, no one else." – Les Brown

Late 1960s rural Ireland was not a place for those looking for an easy life. A lifestyle dominated by agriculture resulted in many long labour intensive duties which unintentionally moulded and sculpted men into readymade athletes. With the little down time that was afforded, local men would test their strength against neighbouring parishes strongest in events such as tug-of-war, weight events such as the 56lbs for distance, shot putt and the discus. Murty's Father Joe and neighbour Nixey Comerford lived for these events at the weekends. The weekly trip in a packed Hillman Huskey van, and the common love of sport was what hooked Murty to competing. Running was also popular at sports days and Murty's brother Jimmy still competes in Vet events. But it was the weight events that drew the big crowds at sports days in Portlaoise and Ballinee, Carlow and commanded the big prizes. Kitchen clocks, a set of drinking glasses and bathroom scales were the gold medal equivalent and paraded as proud on the back of trailers prior to presentation to the victor.

With work scarce and money even more, like many Irish at the time in the mid-60s, Murty headed for London with the few bob he had, his love of sport and a strong work ethic to match. This is where he enhanced his chosen weight events such as the shot and discus at the local athletic club, the Croyden Harriers. Labourer's jobs on building sites during the week only feed

Murt Kelly

the appetite to compete in the weekly Wednesday night league meets in club grounds across England. A convoy of cars crammed with athletes would leave Croyden Harries on a quest for honours new.

Brow Rangers AC was founded in 1970 by the previously mentioned Nixey Comerford and Murty's older brother Jimmy. The Kelly family home was based on top of Coolcullan hill, Coan, which was one of the highest spots in county Kilkenny. As the Kelly name is popular in this area, Murty's family was known as the "Kellys from the Brow" and became the base of Brow Rangers AC. Jimmy Kelly was a fan of the weight events but was better known for his speed for sprinting and jumping events where he still competes competitively today as a proud masters athlete. Most of the Kelly Family and neighbouring family members have competed for this proud club at all levels from juvenile to masters which is steeped in the weight event tradition and is well known for its development of weight throwing athletes both male and female. Murty and his son Joe now look after the running of the club while still competing and developing the clubs juvenile athletes.

Murty returned from England in 1974 and lives in Kilkenny to the present day. Murty arrived at the masters stage of his career in 1988 when 40 years and over was counted as a masters. With athletics and his fellow Irish athletes, he has travelled and competed the world over. He has competed as a senior and masters athlete representing Ireland in such countries as Spain, Italy, Finland, Australia, Scotland, Wales, England and Portugal. His medal haul from over the years is quite extensive and unique.

Murty and his wife Rose have a family of three boys, Joe, Sean and Kieran. These boys like their father were heavily influenced by a family tradition of sport but mainly weight throwing. As children growing up, not a weekend would go by that they were not piled into a car, usually not fit for long journeys, along with their fellow club members and brought to the far corners of the country competing proudly in the blue and white of the club. All have competed at all levels for the Brow Rangers and each have a number of All Ireland medals to name but a few to their names. All are still involved in the club looking after the next generation of athletes.

The true competitor that he is, Murty has recently got a second hip replacement so as to extend his masters career and continue competing at a strong level, much to the bemusement of his surgeon. Lucky for him, his surgeon has a back ground in sport and understands the madness totally.

Achievements
Multiple national senior champion shot putt/discus
Multiple master champion age category shot putt/discus
Scottish/Welshe/Northern Irish national master champion in age category
1978 silver medal- 5 nations senior championships held in Portugal

CHRISTINE KENNEDY (BOYLE)
Date of Birth: 29/12/1954

New Frontiers

By Lindie Naughton and Joe Conway

"Do not regret growing older. It is a privilege denied to many."
– author unknown

Emily Dowling's victory in the 1981 Dublin City Marathon impressed many an Irish runner, nobody more than Galway native Christine Kennedy who was watching on television.

"I was inspired when I saw Emily Dowling win the marathon. I was not a runner prior to that. I was so intrigued by the idea," Kennedy said. "This is a married woman with two small children – just like me – that could win such a race. From that day forward, I felt that I needed to win that race."

At the age of 27, Christine Kennedy was late convert to running. After watching Emily's victory, Kennedy told her husband and family that she planned not just to complete the marathon but to win it some day. They thought she was joking. "I was so hurt that I decided to start training. It took me five years to win the Dublin Marathon and I haven't looked back since," Kennedy said.

Although Kennedy won the National Cross-Country title in 1989, she has always been a marathon runner, clocking 3 hrs 31 mins for her first one in 1982. Less than three years after she started training, she broke three hours for the first time when she won the Galway Marathon in 2:56.19. In 1984, she won her first Irish marathon title with a time of 2:49.46 in Clonmel – it was only the fourth time women were allowed to run the race. Two years later, in 1986, Kennedy finished second in Dublin with a time of 2:49.34. A year later, she finished 24th in the marathon at the World Athletics Championships in Rome, clocking 2:45.47. In 1989, she produced her best result at the World Cross Country when she finished 33rd in Stavanger, Norway.

Kennedy's breakthrough came in 1990, when at last she won Dublin in 2:41.27. "The first time I won it I was hero in my village of Corofin. They had bonfires blazing and it was just a spectacular surprise when I got back home."

A year later, she repeated that win in Dublin this time in 2 hrs 35 mins 56 secs, also taking the Irish title and hoping to impress the Olympic selectors. Her time was all the more remarkable because only a month earlier, she had run 2:35.05 at Berlin. That time was just five seconds off the qualification mark for the Barcelona Olympics.

After stretches in France and England, Kennedy and her family had moved to California in 1990. She finished second in the 1993 Big Sur Marathon in 2:46.30 aged 38; much later, she was to win age-group titles in the race in 2005 and 2006. That came after a long break from the sport between 2000 and 2005 because of a herniated disc in her low back; she returned to racing when she ran a time of 3:06.35 at the 2005 Big Sur Marathon.

In 2009, Kennedy ran the 30th anniversary Dublin Marathon with her 30-year-old daughter and her sisters Phyllis Browne and Mary Doyle. Running in the colours of Galway City Harriers, the sisters won the over 50 team award, although Christine, battling her recurring back injury, struggled to finish in 3:20.21. Since then she has become – arguably – the most consistent female master athlete in the world.

She has set new standards for older women in athletics. In 2010, she set a W55 world record for the marathon when she ran 2:51.40 in the St George Marathon Utah. A year later, when the World Masters Track and Field Championships took place in Sacramento, Kennedy defied broiling temperatures to win the W55 5000m and the marathon.

Christine Kennedy (Boyle)

"Part of the reason I ran so well is that I heard so much about the American Kathryn Martin and that she was unbeatable. I wanted to see if I could beat this girl. I had not run a 5000 on the track in years," says Kennedy. With two laps to go in the 5000m, Kennedy made her move. "I heard somebody say, 'Kennedy, you are going too soon,' and I thought, "no I am not," said Kennedy who raced home in 19:36:55 ahead of Martin's 19:58.74.

In the marathon, her time of 3:00:48 saw her not only winning the W55 title but finishing third overall. Kennedy dominated American master's track and road races in 2011, winning the 5K, 10K, and 15K road championships. and taking the 2011 USA T/F Masters Athlete of the Year award for her achievements. So far, she is the only woman aged 57 or older to break three hours for the marathon.

"Masters level running has changed so much. There is great respect for masters. When I go to a race, I raise the bar very high. I don't just look at my age group. I look at the overall masters group," Kennedy said.

"I know so many runners who live in the past and don't make adjustments physically or mentally for their age. They end up injured and not racing. I try to dwell in the present and recognise the limitations placed on me by age."

So how does she do it? Coach Tom McGlynn has been a key part of her progression. She had spent much of her running career self-coached. "We all think we can train ourselves but I realised that I needed a coach. It makes you more accountable. I am now back doing two track workouts a week. Also, running with younger girls and guys has really changed everything for me," said Kennedy.

Kennedy logs 80 to 85 miles a week — about ten miles less than from 1987 to 1990 when she made three word cross-country teams, also winning the 19190 Irish national cross-country title and placing third in the British cross-country championships.

Her training includes track workouts like 12 x 400m in 85 seconds with 60 seconds recovery; tempo runs (6:30-6:50 pace) on trails and road and long runs of 20 to 22 miles. Add in a flexibility program and cross-training as well as regular visits to a chiropractor, and there you have it.

"Just because a person is over 55 doesn't mean she can't get out on the track and do some speed work. I love the feel of doing speed work. Running has made me who I am and I don't want to lose that, and I hope I can inspire some women to keep running as they get older."

Kennedy is co-owner of the Athletic Performance store in Los Gatos, California, and her training environment is ideal for running with moderate year-round temperatures and a network of hilly running trails. As well as that, the age-grading system used in American athletics along with related prizes have helped fund Kennedy's travel to national events in the USA.

With over 50 marathons to her credit, Kennedy is a five-time Boston Marathon finisher, winning the 55-59 division three times and posting the best age-graded score in every marathon she's run since age-grading was introduced. In 2014, aged 59, her best run of the year came at the Boston Marathon when she finished in 2:56:17 – almost twelve minutes ahead of the next woman in her age-group. It was her third age group win in Boston and her fastest time – in 2009, aged 54, she finished in 2:56.32 and a year later, ran 2:57.17.

Kennedy is arguably the most consistent female master runner in the world. A time of 2:59.39 clocked at the Twin Cities Marathon on 5 October 2014 meant that 59-year-old Christine Kennedy was the oldest woman ever to break three hours in a certified marathon. Kennedy finished 30th woman and first over 55 by 26 minutes, despite suffering from a cold.

"One thing that motivates me is that right now my competition is Joan Benoit Samuelson. She›s three years younger than I am. Rumor has it that when (Samuelson) turns 60 (in 2017), she wants to break three hours. My goal is to run a 2:55," says Kennedy. Samuelson, the first ever female Olympic marathon champion in 1984, ran 2 hrs 52 mins in the Boston Marathon a few weeks before her 57th birthday.

Major Achievements

Three-time World Cross Country participant for Ireland
(1987, 1989 and 1990)
IAAF World Championship Marathon participant for Ireland (24th in 1987)
World Masters Champion in 5000 and marathon for USA (55-59 age group)
2011 USATF Masters Athlete of the Year
Only woman 57 or older to break three hours for the marathon – and she's now done it four times since turning 57 (2:58:37 – Twin Cities Marathon 2012; 2:55:01 – Boston Marathon 2013; 2:56:04 – Chicago Marathon 2013; and 2:57:44 – Boston Marathon 2014).
Member of the Jesse Owens Hall of Fame, she was inducted before an audience of 1,000 people in St. Louis, Missouri, in 2011.

JERRY KIERNAN

Date of Birth: 31/5/1953

Reflections on an Olympic Marathon

By Dr. Eamonn Delahunt

"Every day, running is an important part of my day"

The publication of *A Golden Era* provides a marvelous opportunity to write a piece entitled "Reflections on an Olympic Marathon". This piece chronicles the experiences of Jerry Kiernan, a figurehead of Irish cross-country, track and road running, in his build up to and participation in the 1984 Summer Olympic Games marathon. The information garnered for this piece was acquired by way of interview with Jerry. Uniquely, thirty years on from his participation in the 1984 Summer Olympic Games, the interview was undertaken on the outskirts of the University College Dublin campus in Belfield, whilst Jerry was coaching a session for four of his current athletes scheduled to participate in the 2014 Rotterdam marathon (13 April 2014); the date of which very nearly coincides with Jerry's Olympic marathon trial (22 April 1984), albeit over thirty years later.

Eight years on from narrowly missing out on the qualification time for the 1976 Summer Olympic Games in the 1500 meters, the realization of the potential for qualification for the 1984 Summer Olympic Games became a reality. This epiphany was actualized when Jerry won the 1982 Dublin Marathon in a time of 2.13.45. Interestingly, this time remained a Dublin Marathon record winning time for a further 22 years. Following on from his win in the 1982 Dublin Marathon, preparations for qualification for the 1984 Summer Olympic Games began in earnest with close oversight from his coach at the time Brendan O'Shea. Training was loosely based on the famed principles of New Zealand athletics coach Arthur Lydiard, with an average mileage per week of 110-120 miles, and typically included 5-6 miles in the morning, with 10-12 miles being run each evening.

In his preparations for qualification for the 1984 Summer Olympic Games, 1983 was a particularly fruitful year on the roads for Jerry. Times that he recorded included 27.01 for 6 miles (Castleisland, County Kerry), 46.15 for 10 miles (Bandon, County Cork) and 75.14 for 25km (County Limerick). A particular regret harbored by Jerry was the decision not to partake in the marathon at the 1983 World Athletics Championships in Helsinki, as considering his imperious performance on the roads in Ireland in 1983 he is adamant that a medal at these Championships was a categorical possibility. The marathon at the 1983 World Athletics Championships was won by the Australian athlete Rob de Castella, a runner whom Jerry would compete against one year later at the 1984 Summer Olympic Games, with de Castella placing 5th.

Bolstered by winning the 1984 National Senior Inter-Clubs Cross Country Championships, Jerry was supremely confident prior to the National Olympic marathon trial. The trial race was incorporated into the Cork City Marathon, a race also incorporating the National Marathon Championships and took place on Easter Monday, 22 April 1984. For Jerry, the only serious competitive threat was that posed by Raheny Shamrock athlete Dick Hooper, who had won the National Marathon Championships title on four previous occasions (1978, 1980, 1981 and 1982). Jerry emerged as the victor in this duel in a time of 2.14.30, with Dick Hooper placing second in a time of 2.14.39. Following the race Jerry was sensationally disqualified for apparently being in breach of IAAF rules governing sports brand advertising. However, Jerry does recall the magnanimity and humility displayed by Dick Hooper, who offered Jerry his gold medal after the race. The issue regarding selection for the Irish team for the 1984 Summer Olympic Games was later resolved, but to this day Jerry remains adamant that he would not have been selected, should he not have won the trial. Interestingly, Jerry is the only person to win both the National Senior Inter-Clubs Cross Country Championship and National Marathon Championship titles in the same year. However, regrettably when one consults the official results of the 1984 National Marathon Championships, it will be noted that Dick Hooper is listed as the winner, due to Jerry's aforementioned disqualification.

The 1984 Summer Olympic Games were hosted in Los Angeles, California, with the men's marathon taking place on Sunday, 12 August 1984. In preparation, Jerry self-funded a six week preparation and acclimatization camp in San Diego. His training regime during this six week acclimatization camp did not differ to that which he had completed during a particularly clement summer in Dublin. However, whilst in San Diego his full capacities could be dedicated to running, rest and mental preparation. So professional was his preparation that he did not attend the Opening Ceremony and had no incli-

Jerry Kiernan

nation to base himself in the Athlete's Village at the University of California. His sole objective was to run and compete with the best marathon runners in the world.

The men's marathon started at 5.00 pm local time, with a total of 107 competitors from 59 countries. Ireland was represented by three athletes, John Treacy, Jerry Kieran and Dick Hooper. The starting line-up featured the leading international marathon runners of the time, including Carlos Lopes (Portugal), the 1984 World Cross Country Champion; Rob de Castella (Australia), marathon gold medalist at the 1983 World Athletics Championships and marathon world record holder (Fukuoka Marathon, 1981, 2.08.18); Juma Ikangaa (Tanzania), winner of the 1984 Tokyo Marathon; Rod Dixon (Australia), winner of the 1983 New York City Marathon; Toshihiko Seko (Japan), winner of the 1983 Tokyo Marathon and 1983 Fukuoka Marathon; and Alberto Salazar, winner of the 1982 Boston Marathon and 1982 New York City Marathon.

The marathon course started on the track at the Santa Monica City College, with the athletes initially running two laps before proceeding onto the streets of Santa Monica, and ultimately finishing at the LA Coliseum. For Jerry, these two laps of the track were completed at 5 min/mile pace, allowing him to settle into a comfortable early rhythm. Jerry completed the first 10 miles in a time of 50.04; with the next 10 miles being completed in a time of 49.48. However, from the 20 mile mark Jerry experienced cramping sensations in his calves, ultimately limiting his capacity to continue at 5 min/mile pace. For Jerry, this was not his first experience of these cramping sensations. This was a problem that had been prevalent for a number of years, with Jerry experiencing similar sensations during the 1982 Dublin Marathon.

Muscle cramps, otherwise scientifically known as Exercise Associated Muscle Cramps, are one of the most common medical conditions that necessitate medical attention following endurance events. Muscle cramps are associated with a painful, irregular, involuntary contraction of the affected muscles that occur during or immediately following exercise. The first reports of muscle cramps associated with physical activity were reported from laborers working in mines in hot, humid conditions more than 100 years ago. In these reports it was noted that muscle cramps were not only prevalent in the heat but were also associated with profuse sweating. As such these early anecdotal reports led to the development of the "electrolyte depletion" and "dehydration" theories for the onset of muscle cramps. However, recent scientific research has refuted these two phenomena as being the primary factors associated with the onset of muscle cramps. It has been conclusively shown that athletes incurring muscle cramps do not have low sodium or chloride concentrations in their blood during exercise. Moreover, as dehydration is a systemic problem, it is simply not plausible that localized muscle cramps could be caused by dehydration.

More recently a novel hypothesis has been suggested that "altered neuromuscular control" as a result of the development of muscle fatigue may be the primary factor that is associated with the development of muscle cramps. The development of muscle fatigue resulting in "altered neuromuscular control" as a cause for muscle cramps was originally proposed in 1996 at an international symposium on "muscle fatigue". The primary observation that led to the development of the "altered neuromuscular control" theory for muscle cramps came from results of a descriptive cross-sectional epidemiological study that was conducted in the early 1990s. In this study, 1383 marathon runners responded to a questionnaire on muscle cramps. Of these runners, 26% reported a past history of muscle cramps. The majority (60%) of this group of runners with a previous history of muscle cramps indicated that "sensations" of muscle fatigue were always associated with, and preceded, the onset of their muscle cramping. Consequently, this seemingly incidental finding prompted an in-depth review of the possible mechanisms that may link the development of muscle fatigue to the onset of muscle cramps.

The onset of muscle fatigue causes a disruption of the functioning of peripheral muscle receptors, ultimately manifesting in sustained and prolonged activity of motor neuron control at the spinal level. This prolonged and sustained activity of motor neuron control presents as muscle fasciculation, and as such is characteristic of the painful, spasmodic, involuntary contraction of skeletal muscle associated with muscle cramps. Recent observations in the scientific literature have suggested that athletes who perform at a higher intensity compared to previous performances are more likely to develop muscle cramps. Could this have been the case with Jerry in the 1984 Summer Olympic Games? The answer could easily be "perhaps". With recent advances in sports and exercise science, high performance athletes now have a range of support structures available to them, which were not commonplace in the 1980s. Such athletes have access to exercise physiologists, and strength and conditioning personnel who can provide highly individualized support services to these athletes with the ultimate aim of optimizing the athletes' performance. Furthermore, sports medicine physicians and Chartered physiotherapists are more easily accessible now than they were in the 1980s. For the high performance athlete, recent

Jerry Kiernan

trends in sports and exercise science and medicine emphasize the identification of risk factors for injury and physiological constraints to optimal performance. Intrinsic risk factors for injuries include those unique physiological characteristics of the athlete, which may predispose him/her to injury. Most importantly, intrinsic risk factors such as decreased muscle strength, inadequate flexibility or decreased muscle endurance are largely modifiable. Specific interventions can be designed and implemented to minimize the chance of these intrinsic risk factors precipitating the onset of injury. So, when considering Jerry's problems with muscle cramping it is plausible that if such sports and exercise science and medicine support structures were in-place he may not have experienced these ongoing muscle cramps.

Jerry crossed the line in the LA Coliseum in a time of 2.12.20, placing 9th overall. The race was won by Carlos Lopez in a time of 2.09.21, a time which remained an Olympic marathon record until 2008.

For Jerry a top 10 place in the Olympic marathon afforded him an overarching feeling of self-worth. His primary objective was to run and compete with the best marathon runners in the world. Unquestionably, he achieved this. Reflecting on his Olympic Marathon experienced Jerry conceded that it meant "everything" to him. In recent times, Jerry has turned his attention to coaching and now supports a number of athletes with intentions of Olympic Games participation.

Major Achievements

9th Olympic Games Marathon Los Angelus
Two times winner of Dublin City Marathon
Sub Four minute miler
Former Irish record Holder 3km
National Cross Country Champion
National Senior Cross country champion 1984
Winner of Inter County Cross Country
National Marathon Champion
First Irishman to break 8 minutes for 3KM track
10km National champion
Silver 10km behind John Treacy

Senior: Best Time

Marathon: 2.12
Half Marathon: 62 min.

BOBBY KING

Date of Birth: 20/8/1945

Bobby, High King of Race Walking

By Michael Gygax

"Nenagh Athletic track allowed me to break the world record over 3 km indoors over 65. Gratitude to those who allowed indoor athletics thrives when no other indoor track existed in this country."

There are few certainties in life, dying being one, success and failure being part of the same process another and Bobby King being at a race meeting whether in Punchertown, Leopardstown, Ballybrittas or Cheltenham at the time of the races. It is a near certainty that he is present at the national cross country or national track and field championships each year, every year, that is, if he is not away, competing himself at an international competition. He is often glued to the television set, if not at the actual track meeting, is fond of

Bobby King

a flutter whether it is a race between equine thoroughbreds or an ass and a donkey racing. It is a matter of speculation whether the bookie or Bobby is in the black after a lifetime of gamesmanship. What is not in doubt is that Bobby King has dominated master race walking over the past twenty years nationally and internationally. I'm sure that the bookies are clued into his success and they have him on their blacklist, all bets off Bobby, if he is racing.

Bobby King a small frame of a man, some believe that he has all the qualities to make the finest of jockeys, him being the most athletic and competitive of men. He loves telling yarns, singing and celebrating winning, sometimes commiserating losing. Bobby is one Ireland's most successful master's athletes but does not fit into the stereotypical image of top class athlete, early to bed, serious, devoid of fun with a neurotic sense of perfectionism. It is his sense of humour, certain irreverence with regard to his own athletic greatness, are very endearing qualities that makes him an intriguing character to be around, and good company. He is known to stay up to the early hours of the morning, take a tipple or two, and land at major competition the next day, one would imagine worse for wear, but history has revealed with a knack of getting the best out of himself, usually finishing on the highest branch of the podium.

Bobby has learned his art around the roads, fields and tracks of Meath and Kildare. He has this rare ability to lock himself into a rhythm which leaves most of his competitors gasping, things may not always be perfect, weather, training or wellbeing, but Bobby can tune into that place psychologists call the zone. This has been nurtured by five decades of training, usually after a hard day's work on the buildings. He has seen boom and bust, and experienced highs and lows; he has engaged the lads on the building sites with stories, jokes and songs through thick and thin. The banter and the fun keeps lads going through the harsh winter months, as the work itself knocks the corner off the ego. Bobby has learned that to hold onto success, fortune or failure too tightly, is to get stuck in the mud.

Working on the building with every nationality, creed, age, you learn to understand human nature and at a glance he sees and understands the person in front of him. He weighs up the field of a race with certain guile and off he trots. We are only as good as out last race and at the time of racing it is of the highest importance but when the race is over, he knows it is only sport. He has proven himself to be a wizard at winning; some might say he often acts the clown but Bobby is nobody's fool. Maybe it is this attitude that has allowed him to compete at the highest level most of his life without letting the pressure gets to him. When there was no attachment to past glories or future competition, then there was no pressure.

Bobby has lived through a time of great change politically, culturally and socially. In his lifetime competing, the world has been turned upside down and inside out. To survive one has to learn to adapt. The fall of Berlin Wall has changed the face of Europe politically and thankfully the cold war is no more. He remembers athletics own cold war, when the NACA and BLE were bitter and competing organisations, running Irish athletics. He remembers the Business Houses athletic association emerging as a force attracting inter firm competition in the 1980s and two rival associations' memberships could compete against each other for the first time. Being part of Dunboyne whose early allegiance was with NACA, he could not compete internationally much of his senior years when he was a runner. Our history tells of a time when protestant and catholic, nationalist and unionist, upper and lower classes did not integrate, but all those walls are now crumbling which have been greatly assisted in people's involvement in sport and other cultural events. When master's athletics emerged as a force on the Irish athletic landscape, there were many objectors and naysayers. Bobby tended to pay little attention to these tensions and tended to get on with training, working, fluttering and tippling. Like a chameleon, he himself changed from being a very good club runner to being the highest calibre international walk champion. If one wants to excel, one need to know thyself, take responsibility of one owns destiny, adapt to a changing landscape and be flexible.

Bobby's earliest memories of competing is winning Meath Junior Cross country championships after joining the local club in his native village of Dunboyne, a club co-founded by his father. One of four children, he was the only one of his siblings to compete in athletics. Mileage was never difficult for him and he routinely trained over one hundred and twenty miles per week. Most evenings after eight or nine hours work, lifting bricks and engaging in masonry, he would run fifteen to twenty miles. He nearly always trained on his own. Even today, a year short of his seventieth birthday, his shortest run is seventy minutes and he often trains for over two hours. He went on to run 2.28 for a marathon but would be known to compete in multi events if a local sports meeting was being held. Bobby would race from one hundred meters to a marathon.

Bobby King and Michael Gygax

The NACA and BLE masters came together for the first time in 1990, and Bobby celebrated Irish athletics velvet revolution by winning a very unusual double national championship, the 5000m walk and 5000m running track championship. Despite making some progress in the walking event, he became frustrated and was about to give up this discipline, when Con Harty a walking coach from Civil Service Athletic club convinced him to stick at it and he would coach him to become an international champion, and that is exactly what happened. He would not let Bobby train if he was ill, and drilled him in technique.

Bobby has certainly been king of walking is Ireland and he has a golden career from 1992 to 2011 when he has amassed fifteen podium finishes in the European championships and fourteen in the world track field and road championships, breaking the world record in his age category on one occasion. Many of his rivals were former Olympians, an indication of the strength of the opposition. International competition has been his passport to travel and he has tripped all over Europe and the world, freewheeling from the Northern chimes of Norway, Sweden and Finland to Spain, France, Belgium, Germany, Italy and Austria to Puerto Rico, South Africa and Australia.

In 2011 Bobby won five titles at European level, 3000m and 5000m in Ghent Belgium and 10000m in Tinville in France, plus a team gold and silver for Ireland. He cites not being nominated for master athlete of the year by the Master's Association of Ireland, as one his biggest disappointments. Ever year three people are nominated and one is chosen, as master of the year. The Irish masters are replete with extraordinary champions, who have excelled on the world stage and competition to for "master of the year" is an accolade highly prized.

He moved to Kilcock after getting married nearly thirty years ago and is a co-founding member of St. Cocas Athletic club. Bobby likes to back a winner. He is involved in training and coaching, so it is more than likely that his expertise and nurturing is developing a stable of excellence. He can spot talent a mile off and has teamed up with his close friend and former European 1500m champion Gerry Robinson, coaching youngsters in race walking at St. Cocas Athletic club. He is now well retired from the building game and spends his days developing young talent He has a group of fourteen ,sixteen and seventeen year olds, a group he has nurtured for the past four years, all of whom have won national titles at school and inter club level. His four children were school champion race walkers. He tends to see the long range forecast and thinks in most cases it is ill advised to have young athletes training twice per day or even every day. They are like young saplings and need care and attention. I am competing for over fifty years and there is no reason why these young kids cannot continue competing well into their adult life.

Bobby keeps fit by running or walking every day, so he maintains a very high level of activity. A year off his seventieth birthday his is still breaking twenty one minutes for 5km. He achieved so much in international competition, he has taken a break and is back running and will compete at national level in his chosen events. Meanwhile Bernie O'Callaghan, John McMullen and John Lennon, men who have been part of Irish winning teams with Bobby can compete at national level for race walking spoils, an event that Bobby has dominated for so long.

Thanks to Sean Conroy for gathering some information used in the article.

Major Achievements
Senior: Best Time
Marathon: 2.28
Half Marathon: 68 min. approx.
Master European Championships

Walking Personal Bests
3km- 1992 - 12.24
5km - 1994 - 20.55 All O/45
10km - 1993 - 42.05
20km - 1993 - 130.5

MAEVE KYLE
Date of Birth: 6/10/1928

A Historical Figure

By Malcolm McCausland

"Those who do not remember the past are condemned to repeat it." – George Santayana

Once in a lifetime someone comes along who is like a shining light on a dark night. Such a person is Maeve Kyle. The Kilkenny native was not just a pioneer in athletics but in life. She broke down barriers for women whose place in Ireland was solidly in the home until late in the twentieth century. Maeve was controversially the first Irish woman to go to the Olympics when she appeared at the 1956 Games in Melbourne. She later went on to compete at 1960 Olympics in Rome and the subsequent celebration in Tokyo four years later.

The 1964 Summer Games were the first Olympics to be held in Asia. Tokyo had been awarded the 1940 Summer Olympics but had seen the honor withdrawn when Japan invaded China, before being cancelled because of World War II. It also marked the first time that South Africa was excluded from taking part on account of its apartheid system in sport. It was also where the Paralympics first made its debut.

The Games are remembered for a 800m/1500m double by Kiwi Peter Snell and native American Billy Mills was a shock winner of the 10,000m. Another US athlete, Bob Hayes, won the 100m in a world record 10.0 seconds. The late great Abebe Bikila became the first man to win the marathon on two occasions. These Games saw the debut of an experimental fully automatic electronic timing system and was the first to be telecast internationally without the need for tapes to be flown overseas.

Maeve was celebrating her 36th birthday the very day she arrived in Tokyo, 6 October 1964, and was well into what is now the Masters' F35 age group. It was to be a momentous week of competition for her culminating in semi-final places in both the 400m and 800m. A remarkable achievement given she had only taken up the latter distance after the Rome Olympics four years earlier.

The Irish woman opened with a heat of the 400m on Thursday, October 15, easily taking fourth of the five automatic qualifying places n 55.4 seconds. However, the following day she failed to make it past the semi-finals with a 55.3 timing in seventh place. After a days rest, she was back on the track on Sunday for the first round heats of the 800m. Despite the residue of fatigue from the 400m, she was able to secure the fifth and final automatic qualifying spot in the second race of three in a time of 2:11.3.

The next day, in the semi-finals, she continued her unfortunate knack of drawing either the eventual winner or fastest in the World. On this occasion she had both Ann Packer, who was to go to take the gold medal in a world record 2:01.1, as well as New Zealander Marise Chamberlain who filled the minor podium spot in the final. It was one race too many for the brave Ballymena AC athlete who struggled home eighth in 2:12.9 behind Chamberlain who won in 2:04.6.

"I should have been in both the 400m and 800m finals. I was running very well that summer, and defeated most of the girls who were in Japan for the Games – but I had to qualify too often," she said.

Maeve Kyle

That was not to be her swansong on the international stage. She went to Dortmund for the European Indoor Championships two years later and took a bronze medal in the 400m. After being overlooked for Commonwealth Games in 1962 and 1966, she was included in Northern Ireland's team for Edinburgh in 1970 where she helped the sprint relay squad to reach the final, setting a NI record and also qualified for the individual 400m final. All that at almost 42 years of age!

Maeve Esther Enid Kyle was born in Kilkenny on October 6, 1938. It was a remarkable year in Ireland's history with Fianna Fáil winning a majority in the national elections for the first time; Britain handed back the Treaty Ports under the Anglo-Irish Agreement. Douglas Hyde was selected unanimously by the two political parties to serve as the first president of the state but lost his status as patron of the GAA after attending an international soccer match.

She was born into what many would regard as a privileged family. Her father Carrodus Gilbert Shankey was headmaster of Kilkenny College and her grandfather William Thrift was Provost of Trinity College. Her great uncle Harry Thrift was an Irish 440 yards champion, cricketer, cyclist but his real claim to fame was a rugby winger who won 18 caps for Ireland, including one against New Zealand the first time the All-Blacks came to Dublin in 1905.

It was quite normal for her father to have a round of golf with three different bishops at the weekends and play tennis with the Duke of Ormonde. He also met Edward VII who had Kilkenny connections and was a frequent visitor to the castle when the Duke lived in Kilkenny. Growing up in a predominately Catholic town posed no problems for the Shankey family. Maeve recalls being an avid Kilkenny hurling fan and even cycling to Croke Park to see the Cats in action.

"I was given a good grounding in education and also in sport. I met so many distinguished people when I was so young I thought that was the way everybody lived. Bishop Connor, Bishop Day or Bishop Phair played golf with my father on a Saturday. They were the best of friends, all coming from various religious persuasions. There was a special ecumenical spirit around Kilkenny in those early years, long before the word became fashionable."

After attending Kilkenny College, Maeve was enrolled in 1938 as a 9-year-old into Alexandra College in Dublin. It was situated then in Earlsfort Terrace before moving in the 1980s to its present location in Milltown. But she did not start as a boarder until four years later. In the interim, she stayed with her grandparents in a huge house at the bottom of Grafton Street and was met off the train each evening by their butler.

Although there was no competitive hockey in Kilkenny, Maeve had been taught the skills well and she shone at the sport at Victoria. In 1946, she was a member of the Alexandra team that won the Schools' Cup against Muckross. She would also have appeared in the final the previous year but was ruled out after waking up on the day of the match with mumps!

As a 14-year-old she had the distinction of playing along side her mother in a South-East team in the Inter-Provincial Tournament which admittedly was low-key in those days. And at 17, and while still a student at Alexandra, she was included in an Irish selection in a match against Leinster. There was no international scene at the time due to the war.

After that it was on to Trinity College where she continued to excel at hockey. In 1947, she was called up to play for Ireland and three years later she was in the Ireland team that won its first Triple Crown title. She

Maeve Kyle

was also included in the first women's team to play at Wembley Stadium, and in front of 40,000 screaming spectators, against England.

Maeve's introduction to athletics came almost by chance. She was playing for Pembroke Wanderers before joining Crusaders AC who used the same Serpentine Avenue ground. The hockey girls were persuaded to take part in a tournament at Lansdowne Road in 1948. She had no formal athletics training until this point but ran in the 110 yards and won the high jump.

She trained all summer under the tutelage of Crusaders coach Joe O'Keefe before going to Belfast to compete in the RUC Coronation Sports at Ravenhill. She won both the 80 and 220 yards races. It was her first serious attempt at sprinting; women did not compete at distances longer than 220 yards at the time. The 400m would not appear on the Olympic schedule for another 16 years while the 800m was included in the 1960 Rome programme but only on an experimental basis.

The most influential figure in her life did appear until some years later when she met Sean Kyle on a blind date after a hockey international in Belfast. That was 7 March 1953 – a day that was to change her life. It was love at first sight and kicked off a whirlwind romance that led to a marriage ceremony in St. Mary's Parish Church in Howth the following February.

Maeve moved north after the wedding and competed regularly in Northern Ireland sprint events. She won the NI 400m titles every year from 1959 to

1970. She clocked 59.0 seconds in 1959, 57.7 the following year, 56.6 in 1964 and even in her swansong year 1970 she was timed at 56.4 seconds!

Women's athletics flourished in the North during the fifties with Thelma Hopkins setting a world record in the high jump and taking an Olympic silver medal in the event at the 1956 Melbourne Olympics as part of the British team. Mary Peters was cutting her teeth in the sport and was also coached by Sean in her formative days and right up until age 22.

It was much different in the newly founded Republic of Ireland. Fanny Blankers-Koen's four gold medals in the 1948 London Olympics had proven to be the inspiration for woman all over the world to take part in sport. But not so south of the border where the Catholic Church still exerted undue influence in matters of society.

Dr. John Charles McQuaid, the then Catholic Archbishop of Dublin, disapproved of allowing "young women to compete in cycling and athletics in mixed public sports". The Archbishop felt that it was unbecoming of young women to "display themselves before the public gaze."

Maeve's selection for the 1956 Olympic Games was also not without controversy. Conservative Ireland was very much against a wife and mother, Maeve's daughter Shauna had arrived by then, going off to the other side of the world to take part in a sporting event leaving the family to fend for itself. The cost of the trip, £200, was also prohibitive – a small fortune in the mid-1950s.

"Ireland was a difficult place back then for women participating in sport," says Maeve. "So, when I was young and married with a child, people in conservative Ireland did not believe I should be running around the world leaving my husband and children. But my family did not take any notice and thought the letters written to the papers were hilarious. I grew up with a belief I was perfectly entitled to do what the boys were doing."

Maeve failed to get beyond the opening heats in Melbourne. She was sixth in the first round of the 100m and fifth in the heats of the 200m. But her participation ensured a place in Irish sporting history – the first Irish woman to compete in the Olympics. She had also paved the way for more women to take part not just in sport but in politics and society as well. It was a major advance in a country heavily influenced, some would say dominated, by the Catholic Church.

"Before that married women did not work," explains Maeve. "It was felt that a women's place was in the home – in the kitchen – full stop – end of story. But things were changing. Females like me were beginning to emerge and compete on a regular basis. Looking back on it, I am quite certain there were people who felt this was the way to show we were moving forward."

RTÉ/ Irish Sports Council Hall of Fame in 2008, Maeve and Sean

She did not get through he first rounds either in Rome four years later. "I just wasn't fast enough on the sprints." At this time the International Olympic Council introduced two new distances for women, 400m and the 800m.

"To me the 400 is the greatest event of the lot. You have to stay in your own lane. You've got to think. You can't sprint the whole way. You've got to judge and you've got to not be influenced by the people either side of you. Those are all serious challenges, both mentally and physically."

Maeve was selected for a fourth Olympics when she was one of the team managers in Sydney in 2000. Further honours were to follow. She was bestowed the Lifetime Achievement Award at the 2006 Coaching Awards in London in recognition of her work with athletes at the Ballymena and Antrim Athletics Club.

Earlier in 2006 she was one of 10 players who were first to be installed into Irish hockey's Hall of Fame and to cap an incredible career, she was appointed Officer of the Order of the British Empire (OBE) in the 2008 New Year Honours.

Fact file

Hockey, 58 Irish caps.
Athletiics, Olympics: 1956, 1960, 1964, 2000 (as Ireland team manager)

Awards

1953 + 1959 World All Star Hockey team
1999 UK Coach of the Year (Athletics)

2004 Ballymena Borough Hall of Fame
2005 Ulster Athletic Association Hall of Fame
2006 Honorary doctorate from the University of Ulster.
2006 Lifetime Achievement Award at UK Coaching Awards in London.
2006 Irish hockey's Top 10 Hall of Fame.
2007 Independent Newspapers' Hall of Fame
2008 OBE.
2008: RTÉ/The Irish Sports Council's Hall of Fame.
2008: UK Athletics Club of the Year for the Ballymena and Antrim Athletics Club.
2009: Belfast Telegraph/Sport NI Hall of Fame
2010: Trinity College (DUCAC) Hall of Fame

Best times
100yds 10.8 secs 1964
200m 24.4 secs 1060
400m 54.5 secs 1964
800m 2.10.7 1962

Maeve was on the inaugural international steering committee that set up the world masters' championship competition, the first competitions held in Toronto in 1975. She won multiple world championships over 100, 200 and 400 meters most notably in Sweden in 1977 and Hanover in 1979.

BRIAN LYNCH
Date of Birth: 14/01/1954

The World Record in His Hands

By Caoimhe Lynch

"Every dog has his day"

I'll never forget how surprised I was to find out Brian Lynch, my dad, started running at such a late age. It was only when I sat down to work on this project with him that I realised it wasn't until he was 45 years old. He turned 60 this year, which means he's been out running the roads for the past 15 years. I would have been 7 years old when he first started, but I honestly can't remember a time when my Dad wasn't running.

Brian was born on the 14th of January in Dundalk. Growing up he was an avid football player and spent the majority of his late teens and twenties engrossed in the sport. It wasn't until much later in life that he realised his passion for athletics.

When he was 45 years old he ran his first race. It was a local 2 mile race around Seatown. No one in the running community knew who Brian Lynch was. And when he was first to cross the line, no one was more surprised than him. He described how he didn't feel nervous before the race because didn't expect anything. "I was running for myself, not for a club, I ran to see how I compared amongst more experienced runners, I was delighted but also extremely surprised when I won."

Brian ran the race in a time of 10.25. He remembers the awards ceremony where he got to choose from a selection of prizes. He chose a little girls bag for his niece who was three at the time. He was approached by a few of the other runners who asked him to join a running club to which he replied, "I'll think about it".

Brian didn't give it too much thought as he continued running solo for the next three years. He felt he had proved to himself what he had set out to prove and continued training on his own.

He began training in a football pitch owned by a local secondary school and it was here that he first met Michael Jordan and Eamonn McMahon. They were members of Dundalk's local running club "The North East Runners" or NERDs. They invited Brian to do a few laps around the pitch with him and eventually convinced him to join the club. A couple of months after joining the NERDs he began competing in local 5ks. It wasn't long after that he decided to try his hand at a cross country. "It was a disaster," is how he described it. "It was lashing rain and I didn't tie my running spikes properly." The fields were located just outside Dundalk, in Kilkerly, and were water logged from the downpour.

Every time Brian ran into a patch of mud one of his shoes would come off his feet and be absorbed into the ground. He distinctly remembers crossing the finish line with one shoe on and one shoe off. "I got so fed up that eventually I just carried one of my spikes, I even walked across the finish line."

Despite his less than enjoyable first experience, Brian continued to run cross countries and competed in 3 or 4 more before returning to 5ks when he was 50. He noticed his times were improving week by week. He was now running them in around 18.30, which was half a minute quicker than he had been running them originally.

His fellow athletes also noticed the difference and encouraged him to compete at a higher level. Eamonn McMahon pulled him aside after a training session one day and told him he should think about running in the national

Brian Lynch

master's track and field championships, held annually in Tullamore.

In the summer of 2004, Brian made his first trip down to Tullamore to compete in the 800m O50. It was his first time to run on a track. Brian led for most of the race and got involved in a terrific battle in the final 100 metres with two other athletes. With a time of 2.23, he edged ahead to claim the gold medal with only a half a second separating the top three finishers.

Still being described by fellow runners as a newcomer to athletics, he also went on that year to win the O50 in the Dunshaughlin 10k with a time of 39.11. According to Brian, that 10k nearly gave way to early retirement. After a gruelling race he found himself in a sprint finish with a younger athlete. Not one to give up without a fight, Brian powered across the finishing line finding himself in a heap beside his younger competitor. To this day he maintains he was first to cross the line, his fellow NERDs however still say he was beaten by an inch. It wasn't until he realised he had come first in his age category and was handed an envelope with €50 in it that he soon decided to come out of what his fellow NERDs described as the "shortest retirement ever".

Brian returned to Tullamore in 2005 with his sights set on gold again. He ran in both the 800m and 1500m that year placing 2nd place and 1st place respectively. He got two personal bests that August with a time of 2.09 for the 800m and 4.39 in the 1500. Brian also ran in the national masters indoors in January of that year. He travelled to Nenagh for the first time and placed 2nd in the 800m and 1st in the 1500.

In the years that followed Brian continued to travel to Nenagh and Tullamore picking up more gold and silver medals along the way. In 2010 he broke his first national record for the 1500m at the Louth County championships with a time of 4.32. Later that year he won Louth master athlete of year. He received the Deirdre Mc Grath trophy which is presented to the athlete of the meet or performance of the year in track and field. Brian went on to break his record in Tullamore that year with a time of 4.31.63 in the 1500m.

In 2013 Brian broke the national record for O55 in the 1500m once again. He travelled to Drogheda where he smashed the record with a time of 4.29.49. Brian has fond memories of the day as he was competing alongside fellow NERDs. "It's one thing competing against people from other clubs, but when

Brian Lynch's World Record

you're racing against your own club members it doesn't matter where you come in the race once you beat them. It's just the way it is amongst the NERDs, healthy competition and great craic is what it's all about."

In 2014 Brian started off the year strongly when he broke two national records in Athlone. At the end of January he ran the 1500m in the Irish Masters Indoor Championships breaking the national record. A couple of weeks later in the same venue he ran in the O60 3000m, breaking the national record in a time of 9.52.

In February Brian travelled to Athlone once again to compete in the Connaught indoor senior championships. He was running alongside athletes less than half his age in the 1500m and described how he felt slightly out of place. "They were all so young, I felt like a Granddad. It was the fear of being last that pushed me on to break the world record."

The following month Brian travelled to Budapest to compete in the World Masters Indoors Championships. He ran the 1500m in 4.26.62, breaking his own world record and winning a gold medal for Ireland. On the day of the race Brian made the decision to run from the front. "I wanted to break the field up from the start, I didn't want there to be any rhythm in the race, I didn't want anybody sitting on my shoulder and thankfully it worked," he said.

Joe Gough, a fellow Irish athlete, also ran in the race that day. He crossed the line in third place and the two Irishmen stood on the podium side by side when they were receiving their medals. Brian describes receiving the medal as the pinnacle of his career. "After all my years of hard work and training I felt in that moment it had all lead up to this, it's something I will never forget."

Brian's training intensified in the months running up to the Worlds. He trained relentlessly 5 days a week, dedicating two of these days to hill work. He would spend one session a week solely training on a running track, alternating between 200m, 300m and 400m.

At 60 years of age, my Dad is running the fastest times of his career and is showing no signs of slowing down anytime soon. Running is something he loves to do and he describes the adrenaline rush experienced during races as what pushes him to keep going. He plans to travel to the Europeans in Poland in 2015 where he hopes to bring home a medal. He also has his sights set on the 2015 World Championships in Lyon where he hopes to hold on to his title. I am extremely proud of everything my Dad has achieved so far and I know he still has a lot to give to Irish Masters Athletics.

Major Achievements
1500m World Champion V 60 1,500 M V 60
European 1500m and 3000m Champion European Indoor Championship,
Ancona, Italy 2016

DANNY MCDAID
Date of Birth: 4/8/1941

The Flying Postman

By Michael Gygax and Bernie O'Callaghan

"I do not do draws"

Athletics has thrown up many larger than life characters like Pablo Nurmi, "The Flying Finn", Don Thompson, "The Mighty Mouse", John Joe Barry, "The Ballinacurra Hare", Dave Wattle, "The Man with the Cap" and in Donegal we had our own Danny McDaid, "The Flying Postman." Danny's exploits have made him a larger than life character, known the world over, but those of us who know him well will know him as a very modest and deeply private individual.

Danny was born in Glenswilly outside Letterkenny on 4 August 1941. As a young man along with his brothers, Neily and Frankie, Danny developed an interest in running. This interest was no doubt fuelled by tales of the exploits of another Glenswilly man Cyril O'Boyle who had won several athletics titles in cross-country and track events in the early 1950s before being forced to immigrate to Scotland to seek work. The three McDaid brothers made their own piece of athletics history by winning the team event in the National Marathon with all three scoring.

Danny joined Cranford Athletic club in 1964 and under the leadership of Eamonn Giles he was soon wearing the mantle of Ulster Novice Champion.

Like so many of his countymen Danny had to move to Dublin to get work and he was soon wearing the black and amber of Clonliffe Harriers and developing under the expert eye of coach Lar O'Beine. Danny won his first Irish title in 1968 when he won the BLE two mile title in Drogheda. The following year he gained the first of his nine full international vests in the International Cross-Country Championships. Danny had the honour of captaining his country from at the World Cross-Country Championships from 1975 to 1981.

I remember that day so well, an occasion etched on my memory for time immemorial, Danny McDaid's head bobbing up and down, only seeing his white cap, and working his way through a world class field, in the mud of Limerick Racecourse in 1979 to the roars of encouragement and near disbelief of the crowds in the stand. Danny, a postman in and from Donegal, reputedly did his training delivering his post in double quick time in the Donegal countryside. If John Treacy was becoming an athletic legend by winning his second World Cross-Country Championships in two years, Danny McDaid, who captained the Irish team that finished second to the old enemy Britain that day, was the toast of the ordinary man in the street and the ordinary club runner. By finishing eleventh, at the age of thirty-eight, Danny's performance questioned the conventional wisdom that athletes hit their peak at twenty-six and were by and large beyond their sell by date at thirty. Carlos Lopes of Portugal, himself a former World Cross-Country champion, demonstrated to John Treacy and the world that one can be an Olympic champion nearing 40 years when he won the Olympic Marathon in Los Angeles five years later. Such was the depth of talent that day in the Irish team that Neil Cusack, the 1974 Boston Marathon champion and former American Cross-Country champion, failed to make the team, on his own turf in Limerick, one of his biggest athletic disappointments. Eamonn Coghlan, who made the team, failed to let his legs do the talking as the ground was unsuitable to his stride pattern – Limerick being a mud bath – did not score, but nevertheless the team members attribute their fine run partly to Coghlan, whose gift of the gab and magnetic personality had inspired them to run out of their collective skin.

Danny's athletic career started at the relatively late age of twenty-four years of age, and it was his engagement with FCA that ignited his interest in

Danny McDaid

athletic competition. It was Captain Hunt of the western command who had a great love of athletics and had the whole platoon training for the all army championships. This included his three pals, Patsy McGonagle, Paddy Marley, Hugo Duggan and of course Danny. At one stage he managed to win the army Cross-Country Championship. Danny prides himself on cross-country running above all else.

In 1967 the three lads set off to Dublin to seek fame and fortune. They all established themselves as fine athletes in Clonliffe Harriers and found relative fortune on the national athletic circuit. Fortune was more difficult to acquire as the work days were long and the work hard on various building sites in Dublin. Danny's fortune improved when he got a job working for contract cleaners, driving a van from one city location to the next. Although the job was tough, it was a great improvement on the drill of a labourer on a building sites shovelling cement and allowed him systemize his training better. In another twist of faith Danny was laid off in April 1972 due to "restructuring" in the business. This allowed him time to train full time, something he took advantage of as he qualified for his first Olympic Games in Munich, finishing third 2.17 in the trials behind Donnie Walshe 2.15 and Dessie McGann 2.16. The Munich Olympics is infamously known for Israeli athletes being apprehended and held hostage by Black September movement and subsequently stormed by paratroopers, only for all the perpetrators and victims being killed.

Danny and his teammates held their breath while the organizers made a decision whether the games should be cancelled. After a day of mourning, the games went ahead. Danny remembers the amount and quality of food available, which he consumed with great relish at the Olympic Village. Unemployment freed up time for training and recovery but created financial problems that often left Danny with inadequate nutrition. Danny's first Olympics performance was poor by his own high standards, something he attributes to being a novice at the time. The dole was a pittance, subsistence rations, to add insult to injury his payment was suspended for four weeks when he was away in Munich, the official line being he "was not available for work" while representing his country in the Olympic Games.

After Munich Danny secured a job driving a van for Philips Electrical, in October 1972, unemployment fortunately ended. In 1973 he moved jobs to become a postman, initially in Dublin. He worked what is known as a double shift, starting at 7.30 am and finishing at 11.00 am. Walking and tripping up and down five flights of stairs in Dublin's corporation flatland was his warm-up to an athletic session of seven to eight miles, which he did after his morning's work. His second shift started at three and usually finished around seven, another warm up to his evening fourteen or fifteen mile runs. In 1974 he got a transfer to his native Donegal where he continued to train usually clocking up 140 miles per week and racing every second week end.

Danny McDaid leading the pack at Santry Stadium

This diligence brought him to winning a 2.13 marathon in Limerick which was the qualifier for Montreal Games. He was accompanied by Jim McNamara and Neil Cusack. Determined to excel, he took leave from work and stayed with a friend in Boston where he trained for Montreal for a month before the games. Like many an athlete before and since, the extra training and preparation for a major games led to injury and a poor performance ensued. A week after the games he got married to Cathleen and subsequently they had 4 children together.

Danny continued to run, compete and race on regular bases. As a 46-year-old, he broke 30 minutes five times for 10 km on the road. Such was the depth of competition in Ireland in 1985 that he never won any of these races. He remembers Neil Cusack, Roy Dooney, John O'Toole, Gerry Deegan, Ray Treacy, Dick Hooper, Jim McGlynn, David Taylor, Liam O'Brien, Gerry Kiernan, Seamus Lea, Paddy Murphy raced each other, week in week out on a circuit of road races, all hard uncompromising athletes in the heat of competition.

Danny McDaid, now in his seventy third year, is deeply immersed in athletic administration and coaching in his native Letterkenny in County Donegal. He still runs four to five miles daily and had recently bought a bicycle and spins off regularly on two hour trips. The Danny McDaid stadium in Letterkenny bears witness to the affection and esteem the Donegal people hold Danny, an affirmation of one of Donegal's great sportsmen, a career that spanned three decades that brought Danny to two Olympic Games, a 2 hr. 13 min. marathon and what many Irish people remember him for, eleventh place in the World Cross-Country in 1979, an occasion that saw Irish cross-country running reach its pinnacle.

Danny McDaid in his forties preceded the official hosting of masters competition but as you see from the above, Danny was Ireland's first world class veteran before masters international athletics became established sport.

However he did win the National Masters Cross-Country title in snow and icy conditions in Navan in a fine time of 23.03, from P.J. Fagan 23.50 and John Buckley who had won world championships in his age category the previous year 24.05, proving that the domestic masters scene exhibits world class performances. He took his foot off the competitive pedal at forty-seven and spent more time with his family.

He has won many races and shares with John Treacy the distinction of never winning a National Cross-Country championship. He was second to Gerry Deegan in 1979, the trial for the World Cross-Country, but remarkably beat him in Limerick. John Treacy affirmed his performance after the race as being the most exceptional run of anybody in the field considering his credentials and age.

At fifty-three Danny ran a 10km race in 33.30 but was not taking it seriously. The veteran athletic scene had not taken root when Danny had tied up his competitive socks. Speaking to Danny you get the impression that he has had his day, enjoyed every battle and now it is about the youth. He likes to promote an international meet that the stadium named in his honour hosts each July. He speaks with satisfaction about the great life he has had with his wife and children. He speaks enthusiastically about Mark English, a fellow Donegal man, a bronze medallist in the European 800m. "He has the greatest racing brain in Europe over 800m," he enthuses. "I know all the family well and they is great people, all high achievers. He will go far."

Neil Cusack tells a story of Danny when they were both racing in Sweden. Danny pulled away from the field and Neil caught up with him. There was nobody else in sight. Neil whispered to Danny, let's come in together, joint first. Danny didn't flinch. On the line, Danny dipped. He looked over at the disgusted Cusack. "I do not do draws."

Major Achievements

Two Olympic games
11th world cross country, Silver medal world x country
All army cross country champion
Five times less than 30 minutes aged 46
For 10km at 46 years cross country titles from 1967 to 1987
Scoring member of the Irish team in the CISM (World Military Sports Council)
In Fermoy on St Patrick's Day 1979 when the team also won silver medals
Two European Championships
Nine World Cross-Country Championships
Four BLE National Major Marathon Titles
Two BLE Inter-County Cross-Country Titles
BLE 15 mile title, BLE two mile title
National Master's champion cross country 1986

JOHN MACDERMOTT

Date of Birth: 12/3/44

Getting Quicker with Age

"It is not that I'm so smart. But I stay with the questions much longer." – Albert Einstein

For as long as I can remember I have been a runner. When I was a kid growing up in Boyle, County Roscommon I remember my older brother and others would tell me to slow down and stop running here there and everywhere. I ran to the shop, I ran to school, I ran to the park to play football. I continued to run all my life. Why did I run? The simple and obvious answer is that I liked to and now as I approach my 70th birthday I still do.

My first experience of competitive running was at local sports when I was 7. I won a few prizes. The next sports day I remember was when I was 9 and to my great disappointment I only won medals. I never quite lost that negative feeling about medals. The joy of running and competing is the buzz for me.

In my teens there were few opportunities to take up athletics, so my main sport and love was Gaelic football. I made the county minor team two years running and also represented the county at under 21 levels. I won championships with my home club Boyle and with the Dublin club Clanna Gael when I was a student at UCD. I continued to play football into my early thirties.

Athletics did not become important to me until I went to UCD in 1962. I joined the athletic club in my first year. I thought I was a sprinter but soon learned I was a second or two short! My first experience of hurdles came at the UCD sports day when I competed in the 400 meters hurdles. I am sure my time was poor but I knew I had found my event even if I was not the classic long and lanky hurdler type. I enjoyed my time in UCD athletic club winning some inter-varsity events and also winning the national 4 by 400 relay on one occasion. I had the honour of captaining the club in my final year.

While in UCD I qualified for the Irish team in 400 hurdles for European cups and travelled to Iceland for the 1970 cup.

153

John MacDermott

By 1970 I was married to Marie, my soul mate, working in Sligo and had two beautiful daughters. I still managed to win the 400 hurdles in the national championships that year. That was my last individual national competition until I started competing as a master in the early 2000s. Those middle years were devoted to the more important task of supporting a family of six while developing a career with the youth organisation Foroige.

However I continued to run and keep fit in those middle years and competed in some local events like the famous warriors run in Strandhill and local superstar's events. I did compete once on the track, when I was about 40 years, in an interclub event for Sligo athletics club as they had no one to do the hurdles.

I did not keep in touch with national athletics and was not even aware of Masters running until around the year 2000 when someone suggested I should compete in the National Masters Championships. I competed in my first National Championship in 2001 when I got a mixture of first, second and third place in both indoor and outdoor 60m, 200m and 400m events. I enjoyed the experience very much and the results were good enough to motivate me to do better. Over the next few years I won the national 400 meters a number of times.

What amazed me was that the wonderful energizing feeling you get from being on the track and competing was just the same as it ever was. The same anticipation, the same exuberant exhilaration of sprinting at full speed, the same joy of competing – everything the same until you check the stop watch!! Most people never sprint once they leave their teens.

I am very consciously grateful that I can fully experience this feeling. I am blessed to have been able to achieve appropriate fitness for this level of exertion and I am doubly blessed that I have no joint problems or other aches and pains. Genes play a part and clearly there is an element of luck involved as to survive a lifetime of sport, especially playing football, without injury is very fortunate.

There is however another factor that effects health and wellness. The new science of epigenetics is now establishing that one's lifestyle is very significant in determining one's health, rate of aging and performance. What you eat, toxins you are exposed to, and how you exercise etc. determines what genes are activated or turned off.

I have studied this area extensively over the last 20 years and I have developed science based personalised training methods and balanced nutrition diet and life style. I strongly believe what I eat and the supplements I take have contributed to my health and wellness. This health has allowed me to train hard and remain energetic and injury free. It is this combination that has enabled me to hold back the effect of aging, on my speed and power, more than would be predicted. Looking at my times below quite clearly me was not at world standards in my youth or in my first years in masters.

In the 1960s my best times of 50 secs for 400 and 54 secs for 400 hurdles was not close to world standard. It is true I had no coaching and my training was very amateurish. Even in my first years of masters running my times were still not near world standard.

Why have I maintained or even bettered my times over the last 10 or twelve years when my competitors have slowed relatively more? An experiment of one is not scientific proof but the fact is that I now can expect to be in the medals at world or European Events in Decathlon, Pentathlon, 400 and 300 hurdles. However I always try to remember that I don't control all the factors of my health and fitness. I give thanks to the universe.

After a number of years just doing the Irish Nationals I gradually became more interested in competing. In 2006 someone again suggested I should compete in the World Masters. I thank this "someone" also for giving me the necessary push.

During a walk on the beach with my wife I suggested that we travel to the World Masters in 2007 if it was taking place some place exciting. Italy was pleasing to both of us so it was decided we would travel. I came 11th in the 300 hurdles in my first competitive hurdles race in many years.

So from this gradual entry into masters running I am now a fully committed Masters competitor. I started competing in the UK as preparation for European and World Events as the National Masters Championships did

John MacDermott

not feature hurdles or decathlon events. I have won the UK 300 hurdles for the last three years and won the UK 400 last year.

In 2011 I took up decathlon and I've won the UK decathlon also for the last three years. For the first time in my life I am now getting coaching from excellent coaches David, Paul and Eamon in Donegal Town for which I am very grateful. I find trying to become proficient in field events, especially the pole vault, is an exciting new adventure for me. In the 2012 European championships I got 3rd in the decathlon and 2nd in the 300 hurdles. After achieving reasonable success nationally and internationally I now feel it is realistic to aim for world and European gold in the coming years!

Recognition is nice – we all have an ego – and winning races is very satisfying but these are not my main motivations. If no one knew I ran I would still do it because I enjoy it. An equal motivation is the desire to achieve the maximum state of fitness that I can. A recognition that health and fitness are not necessarily the same motivates me to continue to study health and the role nutrition and supplementation play. My desire is to get as near, as I can, to achieving optimum health and fitness by having optimum nutrition.

John MacDermott www.selfhealingscience.com

Results and Irish records– 2012 to 2014

M65 Indoor- 400 metres 64.36 sec. Irish record set Athlone 2013
Pentathlon 2999 points - Irish record set at UK indoor pentathlon January 2014
1000 metres 3 min 44.20 sec Irish record set during the UK indoor Pentathlon 2014
60 metres hurdles 11.66 sec. Irish record set during the UK indoor Pentathlon 2014
M65 Outdoor-Decathlon - 5931pts. Irish record set European Decatathlon held on
17 august 2012 in Zittau Germany. Got 3rd
100 metres hurdles M65 19.02 sec Irish record set during the European Decatathlon
Pole vault M 65 2.30 metres Irish record set during the European Decatathlon 2012
300 metres hurdles 49.96 sec. Irish record set at the European championships - Got
2nd Ranked world no. 2 2012
M70 Indoor- 200M M70 time 29.27 sec. Irish record set in Irish championships
Athlone 2014 Won
400 Metres M70 time 64.8 sec. Irish record set at the Irish indoor Athlone 2014

Pentathlon 3793 pts. Irish record set at world indoor in Budapest 2014 Got 3rd
Long jump M70 4.13 m - Irish record set during the World indoor pentathlon 2014
M70 Outdoor 200M- 29.03 sec. – Irish record set at the Irish championships
Tullamore 2014 Won
400M- 1.04.69 sec. – Irish record set at the European championships in Izmir
Turkey 2014 Won - Ranked world No. 2
300M hurdles - 49.77 sec Irish record set in the European championships in Izmir
Turkey 2014. Won - Ranked world No. 1
80M hurdles, 14.45 sec. – Irish record set at the UK decathlon Birmingham, 2014
Pole vault, 2.20 meters – Irish record set at the UK decathlon, Birmingham. 2014.
High jump - 1.21 metres – Irish record set at the UK decathlon, Birmingham, 2014.
Decathlon - 6988 points – Irish record set at the UK decathlon, Birmingham Sep.
14, Won 4th year in row

JIM MCDONAGH
4/2/1924 – 13/9/2008

Shufflin' Mac: An Aristocrat of the Running Spirit
By Ian O'Riordan

"Chewing too long makes life bitter"

Late September, 2008, the first day of a long-overdue holiday, and I intended spending every waking minute of it free of all talk and thoughts about running. But more important things first: because that evening, I headed to Loughrea for their running seminar and the annual five-mile road race.

The good people at Loughrea Athletic Club were making it a weekend celebration as part of their 40th anniversary and were kind enough to invite me along. Truth is they had a lot to celebrate, and the one enormous pity is that Jim McDonagh wasn't there to share in it.

Loughrea has always been one of Galway's hurling strongholds, with a fairly strong running tradition too. McDonagh was born there on 24 February 1924, and sure enough started out as a hurler, then turned to cycling, and after a brief spell as a motorcycle stunt rider, later made his name as a runner – and no ordinary runner at that. If the definition of greatness takes age and height into account then McDonagh is one of the great Irish runners not just forgotten but never really known.

Over the years, the Loughrea road race attracted some of the great distance runners of the world. Brendan Foster won there in 1976 and 1977, and 30 years ago this weekend, another Briton, Mike McLeod, just got the better of a certain Sebastian Coe.

There was no race in 1979 as it clashed with the Pope's visit to Galway, but still the tradition continued, and eight years ago the race was made famous again for the clash of Sonia O'Sullivan and Paula Radcliffe.

McDonagh never won there – at least I don't think so – but then five miles was always way too short for him. With McDonagh, the longer the race the better he became, and in America, where he spent a large part of his life, he was almost unbeatable at any distance upwards of the marathon.

It took McDonagh a while to realise this talent. He was 29 when he left Loughrea and sailed for America aboard the converted troopship the MV Georgic, and at that stage his sporting endeavours were over. On his first night in New York he went to an Irish gathering and met a woman from Kinvara named Helen, and they soon married. McDonagh found work in construction and for the next 10 years that was the only exercise he got.

On his 40th birthday, Helen finally commented on his increasing weight. McDonagh stood 5ft 5in in his shoes, and since his teenage years had weighed a little over eight stone. By then he was over 10 stone, his growing fondness for American beer being part of the problem. McDonagh realised himself something had to be done.

"I was 40 years and three months old when I took up my running," he later recalled in an *Irish Runner* interview. "They all told me that I should get my head examined. I started off walking and then jogging and eventually I got to running and that was that."

McDonagh soon rediscovered his competitive instincts and on his morning runs into Manhattan would race the school buses along the concourses towards 56th Street: "They were my stopwatch, and I used to beat the bus all the way down." This coincided with the burgeoning marathon scene in New York and after a few months of this regime McDonagh entered the 1964 Yonkers Marathon, finishing eighth in 2:58:30. It was all the encouragement he needed. Now a US citizen, McDonagh aimed higher, and longer.

In 1966, the father of American ultra-distance running, Ted Corbitt, organised the first US National 50-Mile championship, partly because he would be fancied to win. The race took place around Clove Lake Park on Staten Island, and while Corbitt led up to 40 miles, McDonagh eased past with his short, choppy stride to win in 5:52.28. The New York press quickly christened him "Shufflin' Mac" given his deceptively quick stride, and aged 42, his best was yet to come.

In June of 1967 the US National Marathon championship and Pan American Games trial took place in Holyoke, Massachusetts, on a freakishly hot day. So hot, in fact, practically the entire field dropped out before 20 miles. Leading at that point was Boston's Tom Lardis, and while victory seemed to be his, he then had a horrifying premonition he was about to collapse, describing it as a "flash of doom". He stopped there and then on the road, determined he wouldn't die to win the race.

Only McDonagh and Midwesterner Ron Daws made it to the finish the day; Daws first in 2:40:07, and McDonagh second in 2:43:42. The race was soon

Jim McDonagh

dubbed the "Holyoke Massacre" although that didn't put McDonagh off; he returned to Holyoke and won there in 1968, 1969 and 1970.

One of the many myths that developed out of that race was that McDonagh drank 36 beers the night before to ensure he was well hydrated. Years later, he neither denied nor confirmed that: "I'd drink a good few alright. Coors beer was great if you were running a race the next day. You'd only sweat it out very slowly. You could drink a lot of them and it'd only do you good."

There'd been a lot of talk that week about Lance Armstrong returning to competitive cycling at age 37 (little did we realise what was really going on). Still, McDonagh could teach him a thing or two: in 1970, aged 46, he improved his marathon best to 2:28:49 in Boston, and in 1972, aged 48, ran 2:42:34 to finish seventh in New York. His prize that day was a gold wristwatch, which he promptly gave to Helen to make up for losing her wristwatch during the 1969 Boston Marathon – despite retracing over a mile of the race in an effort to find it.

In 1984 McDonagh and his wife returned to Ireland and purchased a beautiful farm at Larch Hill, about two miles outside Loughrea. McDonagh continued to run marathons with remarkable ease (including Dublin, six times), until one day he was up a tree on his farm cutting branches with a chainsaw, and fell. In trying to avoid the chainsaw, he landed directly on his hip – and for obvious reasons "Shufflin' Mac" was never the same again.

He later settled at Newtown, Kylebrack, close to where he was born. Earlier this summer, Helen was driving out of the house, with her husband in the passenger seat, when another car hit them from the side. McDonagh took the brunt of the impact. He spent several weeks in Ballinasloe hospital with only two things next to his bed: a picture of Helen and the trophy he'd won three times at Holyoke.

McDonagh appeared to be making a slow recovery when he died not long afterwards, 13 September 2008, at the age of 84. I never met him and I'm sorry I didn't. McDonagh was an aristocrat of the running spirit and had a colossal character to go with it. It should be only a matter of time before Loughrea gives him a permanent monument to ensure he's no longer forgotten but also forever known.

Major Achievements
In 1972, Jim finished in 7th place in the NY Marathon in 2 hours 42 minutes 34 seconds when he was 48 years old.
In 1967 he was selected on the US marathon team for the Pan-American Games. His best marathon time was 2 hours 29 minutes 8 seconds in Boston in 1969 (when he was 45 years old!)

MARTIN McEVILLY
Date of Birth: 8/7/1948

Excellence is Contagious

"Intense rivalry makes great champions"

Martin McEvilly lives life quietly on a small holding near Oughterard in County Galway, supporting six cows. There was also a clutch of hens until the fox got them. Now over the pension age, Martin still works for himself as a builder on small jobs. His wife Mary works in a nursing home.

He speaks slowly, pausing between sentences and economical with words. Despite a decade and a half spent in England, his Galway accent remains intact without a trace of a London in it.

Like most athletes, Martin's body is getting stiffer with age; he jokes that his ankles and hips are in need of some 3-in-one oil. The landscape around his house is bare; few trees grow here and the land is rocky and infertile. When winter closes in, the mornings and evenings are dark and the wind coming off the Atlantic coast would cut you in two. Yet it is here that he has trained daily for nearly three decades – mostly on his own. There are few people around, and even fewer athletes.

Martin McEvilly

Some Sundays, Martin take the trip into Galway city, a distance of twenty miles, to join his team mates in Galway City Harriers for a long run, usually of twenty miles. Down the years, this ritual has turned Martin into a top class Irish master athlete, a world champion who has won numerous titles for track and cross-country, both nationally and internationally.

A big influences on the young Martin was his cousin Mick Molloy, a towering figure in Galway and Irish athletics. Mick won national titles at a variety of events, including cross-country and marathon. He ran at the 1968 Olympic Games in Mexico while still a relative novice and later finished 13th in the marathon at the European Championships in Athens. In 1974, he broke the world record for 30 miles on the track at Walton-on-Thames near London.

Mick ate, slept, ran, worked and did little else, routinely running 120-150 miles per week, first with a small club called Derrydonnell AC (documented by Michael Rice in his book *In Their Bare Feet*) and later with the newly formed Oughterard AC. Martin still receives a warm welcome from his cousin when he visits him at his house three miles away, although Mick no longer runs.

Life in Connemara during the 1950s and 1960s makes the current period of austerity seem like a picnic. Roads were poor, amenities basic and life could be gloomy, particularly in the winter. Martin's education was founded on the four "Rs" - reading, writing, arithmetic and religion. Priests were all powerful and the Irish were seen as poor but special – a chosen people saved by its faith. The lack of industry in the country meant that jobs were few and the traditional small farm was no longer able to provide an income for the large families typical of the time. Things were bleak enough for Martin growing up; he never went hungry but rarely felt full. With the country in the depths of depression and few jobs on offer, up to 80% of the population in Connemara emigrated, mainly to England – the old enemy, but in this case, economic salvation.

Martin was one of them. After leaving school at fourteen and learning his trade with a local builder, he took the boat to London seeking work on the buildings. He immediately joined two athletic clubs, Shaftesbury Harriers and Heron Hill Harriers. Training consisted of sessions on Tuesday and Thursday evening; on other days, he ran to and from work, leaving the house at 7.30 am and often returning at 7.00 pm. Although he was young, strong and full of energy, he feels that he probably overdid it. "If I had worked less and rested more, my performances might have been better," he says.

Despite the "no blacks, no Irish" ethos of the time, Martin never experienced an iota of anti-Irish feeling during his decade and a half in London. He was welcomed with open arms wherever he went and enjoyed the English hospitality. Saturday was racing day, followed by a meal, drinks and a night out with friends at a club, bar or disco. He loved this social side of sport in London – something he feels is largely missing in the Irish athletic scene. Sunday was always a long run, usually twenty miles in less than two hours with a good group of lads.

He had arrived in London during a golden period of British athletics. One of his club mates and training partners was David Bedford, a man renowned for his long mileage, reputedly training up to 200 miles per week and his distinctive red headband and luxuriant moustache. Bedford never won an international title, but on 30 June 1973, set a world record of 27 minutes 30.8 seconds for 10,000m.

Gothenburg in Sweden holds special memories for Martin. Travelling with a group of athletes from Heron Hill, he won a cross country race there in the 1980s and a year later, was invited back to run a marathon, with all expenses paid. Now aged 28, he trained extra hard for the race, and ran out of his skin to win the race in a personal best 2 hours 16 minutes. In his own inimitable manner, he understates this achievement: "It was not a big deal. Sure, there were lots of people running faster than that in the company I kept in England."

One of these was Ron Hill, a European and Commonwealth champion with a marathon best running of 2 hours 9 minutes 26 seconds – a time rarely run in the 1970s and only bettered by a handful of British athletes since. Ron became a European and Commonwealth champion and held world records over 10 miles (47.02), 15 miles (72.48), and 25km (75.22). Today he has the distinction of running every day since 1964; he has not missed a day's running in over fifty years.

Then there was Ian Thompson who, as a total outsider, entered the 1973 national marathon to make up the club team, only to win in 2 hours 12 minutes 40 seconds. A year later, he clocked 2:08.34 for victory in the Common-

Martin McEvilly

wealth Championships in Christchurch, only 39 seconds off the then world record. He went on a year later to win the European marathon in Rome.

Brendan Foster, another man lining up in the same races as Martin, was a mainstay of the British team, running in three Olympic games, with the highlight a 10,000m bronze over in Montreal 1976. At home, he set a world record of 7 minutes 35.1 seconds for 3000m in his native Gateshead, a feat witnessed by Martin.

Another world record holder was Dave Moorcroft who ran 13 minutes 00.41 seconds for 5000m at Oslo's Bislett Stadium in 1982. When he turned 40, Moorcroft returned to racing aiming to become the first master to break the four minute mile. His best effort was a time of 4:02.53, set in Belfast in 1993. It left the way open for Eamon Coghlan who became the first M40 to break the four-minute barrier a year later.

Biggest stars of them all were Sebastian Coe and Steve Ovett who provided the highlight of the Moscow Olympics in 1980. It was at these games that Ovett unexpectedly beat Coe in the 800m, only to have Coe return a few days later and win the 1500m. In 1979, thirteen Britons broke four minutes for the mile – success begat success but all too soon, this golden era ended.

Martin rarely ran track during his senior years, although he finished third in the national steeplechase championships Irish championships while living in England. He looks back on his days in England as among his happiest. In 1983, he returned to Galway after the death of his mother to look after his father, who was in failing health. It was not an easy transition: dark days of unemployment followed. One bright light in a grey world was his racing and training with his old comrades in Galway City Harriers.

Martin was a witness to and part of a great tradition that trained and developed champions. He was certainly in the athletic garden when it was in full bloom and felt this exuberance. As the years progressed, Brian Geraghty, his GCH club mate, suggested to Martin that he compete in master's competitions. This he done with rare distinction, accumulating numerous national titles, as well as a European title specialising in the Steeplechase – best of them all – a world title in San Sebastian in 2005.

He continues to compete, taking silver for the steeple chase at the World Masters in the summer of 2015 when he was just pipped for the gold.

There has been an odd snippet in local newspapers and the *Irish Runner* magazine, but no great fuss or media attention, just a lot of personal pride. Martin believes that intense rivalry creates great champions and he looks back on his days in England as probably his happiest days, when the British were the best in the world at middle and long distance running – an excellence that has proven contagious as Martin himself has demonstrated winning a number of European and World Championships in his age category.

Master Road Times
Half Marathon 83 min. Age V60

Top achievements: Senior
3rd National steeple Chase
Marathon: 2.16
Competing national masters t/f 2014

MICHAEL McGARRY
Date of Birth: 1/12/1932

The Joy of Throwing

"A mind is like a parachute. It doesn't work if it is not open."
– Frank Zappa

I was born and reared on a farm in the parish of Bornacoola, County Leitrim, a parish that straddles the Leitrim/Longford border and is separated from County Roscommon by the river Shannon.

From my earliest years, I was madly interested in sport – running and jumping and particularly football. We played with rag balls, air balls, sponge balls or whatever was available. I can still remember getting my first real football when I was about ten years old and it got a lot of use. On Sunday afternoons, impromptu matches took place and most of the local lads took part. Those matches were often chaotic but, in time, we learned the rudiments of kicking, catching and free taking, while the rules of the game were gradually learned and even more gradually adhered to.

Life was austere; there was a lot of work to do on the farm and food was short, with rationing taking place not just during the war years but for a time after. When I was about ten, I did "messages" – going to neighbours' houses or the local shop or bringing food and drink to men working in the fields or on the bog.

From the age of eleven, I went to fairs with my father. This involved getting up at about three o'clock in the morning and driving cattle to either Mohill (six miles) or Longford (ten miles). Later I "graduated" to the heavier jobs of pitching hay, wheeling heavily laden turf barrows, cutting turf with a slane and – the most hated job of all – weeding potatoes or other vegetables.

On Sundays, it was football all afternoon, with large number of young men and boys involved and play only stopping when hunger drove us home. I played football with the parish under 12 and under 14 teams and finally, at the age of 15, was selected for the minor team. The training built strong bone and muscles and aided agility.

In September 1947, at the age of fourteen and a half, I went to Colaiste Einde in Taylor's, Hill, Galway as a boarder. Most of the students were from the Gaeltacht areas of Donegal and the only English spoken was in the English class. As a result, even the non-Gaeltacht students became fluent speakers. Life was tough and the discipline strict but the school was no worse than other boarding schools of the period and teaching standards were high.

I was there for four years – two years to Inter Cert and then two more to Leaving Cert, which was unusual, since most people left after the Inter Cert. In my first year, I was selected for the college's junior football team and also for the a 4 x 100 yards relay team.

Holidays, especially summer holidays, were cherished, with plenty of football, handball and fishing for entertainment after the work was done on the farm. During my first summer holidays, I played with the parish minor football team, getting as far as a semi-final in a county tournament. Back at school, I was centre half back on the junior football team and also represented the college in the shot putt, 100m, and 4 x 100 yards relay in the Connaught Colleges Athletic Championship. I won the shot putt and went on to compete in the All Irelands in Dublin where I was outclassed.

My interest in athletics was growing and I would scan the ads in the local newspapers for sports meeting, where, if there was no clash with a football match, I would compete in the sprints and the high jump. On offer were money prizes, usually either five or ten shillings. Coming home on Sunday evening with a pound in winnings was a source of pride.

During my third summer holidays from Colaiste Einde, I played with the Bornacoola minor football team that – at last! – won the County Championship. I was selected for the Leitrim minors, but although we had a good team, we lost by two points to Mayo, who went on to win the All Ireland.

In athletics, four senior athletes from my school were selected for the Connacht team competing at the All Ireland Colleges Championships at the Iveagh Grounds, Dublin. In the shot putt, I was competing without any great hopes after my experience at junior level two years earlier. During the warm-up throws, however, I realised that I had a very good chance of winning. Unfortunately I was disqualified for some rule breach.

After leaving school in 1951 came two years of teacher training at St. Patrick's Training College, Drumcondra, Dublin. There I played for the college senior football team in tournaments against other colleges as well as in the Duke Cup, an interfaculty competition held in UCD but also including Trinity College teams. In the St Patrick's athletic championship of 1953, I won shot putt and the 100 yards, which was the most prized event.

After graduating in 1953, I got a teaching job in St Mary's CBS, Mullingar, and then won my first Leitrim Senior Football Championship medal with Bornacoola and was selected at centre half back on the Leitrim Senior football team; a significant year indeed. The group of young players who started playing football at underage level with Bornacoola had finally come good. After success at minor and junior level, the team went on to win three senior county titles in the 1950s. I continued playing senior football with Leitrim until 1958.

In 1955, I was offered a job at Oatlands College in Mount Merrion and, after I moved to Dublin, joined Clanna Gael turning out for a senior team that included many well-known county footballers, not only from Dublin but from all over the country.

After I retired from football in 1961, I did no organised sport for over ten years. My only physical pastime was swimming year round for many years at the famous Forty Foot, in Sandycove. By the 1970s, overweight and concerned about my fitness, I took up tennis and joined a weights throwing and weight lifting club. At the club, the trainer club advised us all to do some running and so I began to run on the roads, mainly at night. I also joined the Castle Handball Club and competed for a number of years.

By this stage, I had a wife and children and on our annual holidays in Salthill, Galway, I would run around the western part of Galway city, a distance of over six miles and found it very enjoyable. As I began to run longer and longer distances, I took part in many 5k and 10k fun runs. I decided to enter the Dublin Marathon and at the age of 51, finished my first marathon in 4 hours 15 minutes. I subsequently ran five more Dublin Marathons, one of them in 3 hours 59 minutes.

Towards the end of the 1980s I decided it was time to give up road running. I had done an awful lot of it over the previous fifteen years and, being almost 15 stone in weight, didn't have the ideal build for such activity.

One day, I came across the results from the Irish Veterans Track and Field Championships in the *Irish Independent*'s sports pages. I hadn't known that such a

Michael McGarry

competition existed and immediately checked the result of the shot in my age group. I decided I would compete the following year. Because I hadn't picked up a shot since 1953, it took a bit of practice. In 1989, I duly won the event in Santry. Two years later, I won both shot and discus and came second in the hammer. I was now enjoying the competition very much. It opened up a whole new vista for me adding a new dimension to my life.

In 1993, I travelled to Newcastle to compete in the British Masters Championships for the first time. Although both numbers and standards were higher than in Ireland, I took silver in both shot and discus and bronze in the hammer. From then on, like many other Irish competitors, I competed almost every year in the British Championships in successive age groups from over 60 to over 75. I managed to win the shot nine times, the discus thirteen times and was placed second or third in the hammer eight times.

I competed in three European Veteran Championships: Athens in the M60 age group, Italy in the M70 age group and Aarhus, Denmark in the M75 age group. My best performance was in the shot putt in Athens, where there were 38 competitors. I scraped into the final in tenth place and, with my final throws, improved to seventh. Those who came 4th to 8th got a replica medal (and a certificate!); a nice memento but not, unfortunately, a real medal.

In recent years, I have been plagued by a shoulder injury. I did not compete at all in 2013 but was persuaded by friends in 2014 to go to Tullamore for the Irish Championships. There I won the hammer and came second in the discus.

As well as the national championships, the Irish Weight Throwers Association has held independent championships over a number of years. These championships have included a variety of throwing events, including throwing several different hammers of various weights; the brick, the rock, and the weight for distance and over the bar, and many more. Although I was quite successful in those competitions, my favourite memories are of an event I never won: the weight for height. In this, I came up against Eddie Mulcahy from Sneem who has been almost unbeatable at national or international level for a long number of years. I usually finished second but always found it a most enjoyable experience.

My best event was probably the Greek discus in the M60 age group. During one particular year (I can't remember which one), I had a throw of 22m; the best in Europe that year was 23m.

In summing up, the twenty-five years spent competing in veterans weight throwing have been among the most enjoyable of my life. I have liked every aspect of it: the travel, the new places visited, the friendships formed, the changing room banter and, of course, the competing. Getting a medal was a bonus, winning an added bonus and setting a new record a double bonus. There is a great camaraderie among throwers everywhere. Throwers are very supportive of each other and competitions, while always keenly contested, are pleasant and enjoyable experiences.

Let me finish by quoting the late an t-Athair Peadar O Laoire who at the end of his autobiography wrote, "*Gurb shin mo sceal go n-uige seo*" ("That is my story so far").

Note: I have just read the article on Hugh Gallagher's career, as a weight thrower and as a worker. I wish to offer him my congratulations on all his achievements. He has been even more successful than I had previously known. As well as weight throwing, Hugh and I have something else in common. I too worked (during three summer holidays) on the hydroelectric schemes in Scotland, once on a high dam in Pitlochry and twice in a tunnel at Ben Lowers over Lough Tay.

Major Achievements
23 years of pleasure competing
18 shot putt titles
Irish shot, discus, hammer age category records
British champion shot and discus
British age category shot putt record

DOROTHY McLENNAN

Date of Birth: 11/9/1935

A Granny's World

*"Look back on the past with gratitude, the present with
enthusiasm, the future with confidence"*

It all started in 1984 when I saw an old boy (probably only in his 70s) finish the London Marathon. If he could do a marathon at that age, well so could I, me being a mere 49 years at the time.

By June of that year, I had run the first Dublin Women's Mini-Marathon and by October, completed my first of 22 marathons. My best time was in Dublin with 3 hours 40 minutes when running in the over 50 age group. The most notable one was Berlin – the year The Wall came down. We were there a matter of weeks before it all happened.

When we went abroad for championships, I never did the marathon since it was much too hot; instead I did the 5000m. Now I was pretty useless at that distance, which must have been obvious to the lovely Jim Fanning. "Why don't you girls try one of these new athletic events for women like hammer throwing, triple jump or pole vault?" he suggested to my twin sister Sheila and me. These events were new to senior women never mind veterans.

Sheila and I had a think about this and both of us immediately fancied pole vaulting, but where to get started? Fortunately, my youngest son Stephen was a member of Heathrow gymnastics club and in his group was a boy whose father was a pole vault coach and, yippee, was willing to let me have a go. So it was that Chris Jousiffe became my coach for about fifteen years.

As Chris himself would say, he had a head full of brown hair when I joined the group but by the time he retired he had very little grey hair left. Nothing to do with me I'm sure! I loved pole vaulting from the start and still do. In about 1992, I realised that gymnastics could be a great asset to my pole vaulting so I joined an adult class at Woking Gymnastics Club where my daughter Vanessa and son Stephen were then training. Although my gymnastics improved, I am not so sure about the pole vaulting but, what the heck, I really enjoyed

169

Dorothy McLennan

it and competed in the annual British Gymnastics Veteran Artistic Championships for twenty years. For the last four of those years, I also competed in their Sports Acro champs. Yes, I usually got gold, but then there were not that many 70-year-old grannies competing; in fact, I was competing against 50 and 60-year-olds where I got age bonus points. So you see there are advantages in being over 40!

It was through gymnastics that I was chosen to be a volunteer at the 2012 London Olympics. I was involved in the ceremonies team from February 2012 right up to the closing ceremony of the Paralympics and enjoyed every moment of all those months of travelling to the other end of the world (Stratford) – it did seem like that at times. It was a never-to-be-forgotten experience and even though I was absolutely shattered by the end of it all, I wouldn't have missed it for the world. All that time I never missed a training session.

I never travelled further than Liverpool for gymnastics competitions but, when it came to veteran athletics, that was a different matter. There is a whole big world out there waiting to be enjoyed by all you veterans. My athletics has brought me all over Europe and all over the world including South Africa, Japan, Australia and the USA. It has brought me to places I would never have had the opportunity to visit. Not alone that, but you are with like-minded people, meeting old and making new friends along the way, it was brilliant. I have won over twenty gold medals all over Europe and the world; that's apart from the golds won in Ireland or the UK.

Of all those medals, the one that gave me the most satisfaction was the gold I won for the heptathlon in Potsdam, Poland with a total of 3554 points. When I started, pole vaulting was a new event for women. My best height was 2.10m at a women's Southern League match in Kingston-on-Thames on 18 August 1996. My best height indoors was 2.05m (then a world record) in Eskilstuna, Sweden on 3 March 2005. I have held quite a few world and European records, all of which have probably been bettered by now.

A little over a year ago, our pole vault coach – by now my son Stephen – and I (reluctantly) agreed that it might be the right time to stop pole vaulting. Well, I had a fall, not a bad one, and my son felt he would be hold himself responsible if I had a worse fall. So what was I going to do instead? We hit on sprinting, well, wouldn't any 78-year-old take up sprinting instead of doing housework? Easy decision! It has to be said that the pole vault group includes sprinting as part of their training so it wasn't that much of a change.

Coach Stephen, with mum Dorothy

So now I am a sprinter with large "L" plates. From here on we will have to wait and see where the road leads me but one thing is certain, I ain't finished yet.

Sean McMullen

Date of Birth: 5/3/1946

In Search of a Long-lost Race Walking Medal

"Associate with those who will make a better man of you. Welcome those whom yourself can improve. Men learn while they teach."

The St. John Bosco Athletic club was formed in Donegal Town in 1959 and as a thirteen year old I was one of the inaugural members and subsequently enjoyed many training sessions and long runs around the town on crisp, frosty, moonlit nights with the other members of the fledgling club. Many years later when I again took up distance running as a hobby the greatest motivational moment, when pounding the roads around Mullingar on long distance runs in preparation for marathons, was the delirious feeling I enjoyed after completing sixteen laps of Tyrconnell Park on a very wet June Sunday morning. However, the greatest achievement of my short athletic career with St. John Bosco was not in running but rather in race-walking and this took place in the said Tyrconnell Park during the first major athletic event organised by the club in 1960. This was a major sports event in which many of the leading senior and juvenile athletes of that time in Ulster took part. As a fourteen year old with little or no knowledge of the intricate technique of race-walking I managed to place third in an under sixteen race-walk and was presented with a bronze medal by Johnny Caldwell (RIP) the then Bantamweight champion of the world and former Olympic bronze medallist at Melbourne in 1956.

This was the first medal I had ever won at anything and proudly carried it around in my trouser pocket taking it out at regular and frequent intervals to admire and treasure it. The following day was a Monday and on the school summer holidays I spent the day helping my father to mend fencing on our farm with the medal in my trouser pocket. Disaster struck at the end of the day when my father decided we had done enough work and to my horror there was no medal in my pocket or anywhere else that could be scanned by the human eye. The search for the medal continued until darkness fell and continued each day for weeks, months and years but was never to be found again leaving a totally distraught budding young race-walking champion.

Shortly afterwards Gaelic football took over as the main sporting activity and remained so for the next sixteen years until I retired as a long-standing member of Ballymun – Kickhams Junior team and again went running to keep fit in St. Annes Park, Raheny and subsequently became challenged by the Dublin Marathon which I completed in 1981 and on seven further occasions and also the Belfast marathon (2) and New York and Capetown, South Africa (35 miles) in 2004.

During all this time I was oblivious to the existence of competitions for veteran/masters athletes. It was only in February 2001 at the prompting of Bobby Begley that I first discovered and took part in a master's competition at the age of 55. My maiden voyage as a masters athlete was at Tymon Park, Dublin in the National Veterans Cross Country in 2001 where I finished 4th in the over 55 category. My first national masters medal came as a gold medal in the 3000m indoor run at Nenagh in 2002.

In preparation for the Two Oceans 35 mile marathon in Capetown in 2004 I was reading advice given by a number of well-known leading American distance runners, most notably Jeff Galloway which advice advocated walking breaks to be incorporated into long distance races. As a consequence I began practising race-walking as part of my long training runs but I must admit I did not do a great job of incorporating them into the Two Oceans Marathon.

Bernie O'Callahan, Bobby King, Sean McMullen

However, this practice did have the unanticipated consequence of setting me out on a new athletic career (or rather got me back on the track which I had strayed from as a fourteen year old).

I entered my first race walking event at the National Masters Indoors in Nenagh in 2004 and reclaimed that long lost Bronze Medal in the over 55 3000m race walk. This was to be followed by a number of silver race walking medals over the following years but never a gold one due to the misfortune of being in the same age group as Bobby King former World and European Champion.

My first National Gold Race Walking Medal did not come until 2007 (indoors) when a few months age difference meant Bobby had moved to the over 60s. Since then I have accumulated a dozen or so more National Gold Race Walking medals. I have also had the good fortune in between to get four National Senior Championship Race Walking medals being one silver and two bronze in the 30 km and one silver in 2013 in the 20km in St. Anne's Park, Raheny.

The first international event I entered and completed in was the European Indoors in San Sebastian in 2003 when I competed in the 3000m run. Pat Bonass also competed in the same event. In 2004 I entered and completed in my first international race walk at the outdoor track and field in Aarhus, Denmark in. In 2005 I competed in the European Indoors in Eskilstuna, Sweden in 3000m on track and finished 5th (Bobby King finished 3rd) and also finished 5th in 10km on road. Also in 2005 I entered the European Non Stadia in Monte Gordo, Portugal but had to withdraw after one lap in 10km race-walk with a hamstring tear. In 2006 I took part in my first World Championship being the 2nd ever World Indoor Championship which was held in Lilnz, Austria. I suffered my only disqualification at International level in the 3000m track walk (Bobby King taking silver) and I finished 7th in the 10km road walk.

My first European success came at the 2007 European Indoors in Helsinki where I got two bronze medals in the 3000m track walk (Bobby taking silver) and 5km Road Walk (gold going to Bobby). Also in 2007 I finished 5th place in both the 10km and 30km Road Walks at the European Non-Stadia Championships in Regensburg, German

In 2008 at the European Masters Games held in Malmo, Sweden I won double bronze in the 5000m Track Walk and 20km Road Walk. In 2009 I took part in the World Masters Games in Sydney, Australia finishing 5th in both the 5000, Track Walk (in which 7 of the 16 starters were disqualified) and the 10 km Road Walk. In 2010 in my final year as an over 60 I finished 8th in both the 5000m Track Walk and 20km Road Walk in the European Track and Field in Hungary.

The year 2011 was a very successful one yielding 5 European medals and a 4th place finish in the World 20km in Sacramento USA. The European silvers were firstly (3) at the Indoors Ghent In the 3000m track (Bobby was 1st) and 5000m road (Bobby 1st) and team silver (along with Bobby and Bernie O'Callaghan).

Secondly at the European Non-Stadia at Thionville, Yutz France came silver in 30km and team silver in 10km over 45 (with Pat Murphy and Bobby). 2012 was the highpoint at the World Indoors in Jyvaskyla Finland with silvers in 3000m Track Walk and 10km Road Walk. In the same year at the European Outdoor Track and Field I won silver in the 20km Road Walk and bronze in the 5000m Track Walk. A bronze medal followed at the 2013 European Indoors in the 5km road walk and also finishing 4th in the 3000m Track Walk.

To date I have two world silver, six European silver and five European Bronze Medals but the search goes on unabated to find those elusive European and World Gold.

While medals represent pleasant reminders of joyous moments in International competition the continuing desire to take part in these competitions is about much more than pieces of metal. The atmosphere, the camaraderie and friendships formed with athletes from other countries is equally as important as winning medals. I would instance two examples of my many experiences in this regard.

At Hradeck nad Nisou in the Czech Republic after finishing 2nd in the European 20km and totally exhausted I sat on a wall at the side of the road with my wife Veronica. I was after having a ding dong battle with the German Peter Schumm who took the bronze medal and much to my surprise and delight I saw emerging through the crowd at the side of the road Peter holding two large tankards of beer, one of which he handed to me and we both sat on the wall drinking Peter's beer. Again at the European Indoors in San Sebastian while sitting watching the action Peter sat down beside me and pulled out a bottle of wine from his kit bag and asked me to pass it on to Veronica as a thank you for some photos which she had sent to him.

Secondly, Walter Brandenburg for Switzerland never misses any European or World Championships and has been competing for many years before my first International Championship in 2003 but Walter has never won a medal of any colour and is unlikely to do so. Never the less, he is one of the most enthusiastic and generous of all competitors. He has taken many videos of medal ceremonies in which I was on the podium and emailed them to me. Every time I meet him and his wife he is always in joyous and humorous mood and is extremely uplifting in his mood.

These are just two examples of the kind, generous and fun-loving type of fellow athletes one encounters at these championships and always leaves me with a feeling that I cannot wait for the next championship.

Author's Note: After years of competing and missing out on the elusive gold championship medal, john succeeded three times in becoming a European champion in 2016 over 3km, 5km and 30km.

JIM MCNAMARA
17/4/1939 - 10 March 2016

Born to Run

By Jim Kelly

"There is something magical about running; after a certain distance, it transcends the body. Then a bit further, it transcends the mind. A bit further yet, and what you have before you, laid bare, is the soul." – Kristin Armstrong

"Pain is temporary, pride is forever"

In March 2016, Jim McNamara, known to his many friends in athletics as "Jim Mac" lost his final battle with illness. He had made his mark, first as a senior athlete then as a master and finally – and perhaps most significantly – as a coach with his beloved Donore Harriers.

In the heyday of the club, when it won seventeen consecutive national cross-country titles, Jim was part of the winning team nine times. When the Europa Cup came to Santry in the 1960s, he added a win in the steeplechase to his collection. By then he was running marathons and and represented Ireland at the Budapest European Games in 1966, where the late Jim Hogan, a Limerick man running for Britain, won the marathon ahead of him.

The pinnacle of his senior career came in April, 1976 when he qualified for the Montreal Olympics by finishing second to Danny McDaid in 2:14.57 at the National Championships in Limerick. In Montreal, McNamara finished 39th in 2:24.57, three places ahead of McDaid.

At masters level, Jim came into his own. He won eleven gold, five silver and four bronze medals at European and World Masters Championships at the 1500m, 5000m and 10,000m distances as well as one 10,000m cross-country medal.

Jim McNamara was born in London on 17 April 1939 - just before World War II broke out. His family soon returned to their native Cabra in Dublin where Jim was to remain for the rest of his life. Growing up on Broombridge Road, his next door neighbours were the Tracey family, with Eddie Tracey, a boxer, destined, like Jim, became an Olympian. Tracey was one of several international boxers from the same road, among them Paddy Maguire and the Murphy brothers – Frank, Tony and Tommy.

In Cabra, sport was at the heart of the community and, as well as boxers, it was no surprise that the area produced a succession of international and League of Ireland soccer players, as well as GAA men. High expectations when it came to sport were a defining characteristic of the neighbourhood.

Jim's first taste of athletics came at St Mary's National School where, like many a youngster, he id some sprinting and hurdles. As a boy, he played football with Naomh Fionnbarra and like many Cabra sportsmen, trained in Nephin Park, known locally as "The Bogies". After Pope John Paul II's helicopter landed there in 1979, the park was re-named John Paul Park.

For young Cabra lads with an interest in sport, boxing was hard to avoid and Jim joined the St Francis boxing club, founded by Larry, Tommy and Paddy Duignan and Paddy McGlynn, and based in Chapelizod. In his teens, Jim had his first brush with serious illness when he contracted tuberculosis and rheumatic fever and was hospitalised for months. When he recovered, he resolved to become physically and mentally strong; an attitude which was to

Jim McNamara

shape his running career. When a breakaway group from the boxing club decided to form a running club, Jim's destiny was decided. A runner he would be and a runner he became; as indeed did his brother, who would also make the Irish cross-country team.

In 1958, Jim won the Dublin Novice championship in the Phoenix Park. Before the race, he attended his sister's wedding and went to the reception at the Maples Hotel in Glasnevin. From there he was collected by car and brought to the race. After his win, he promptly returned to the wedding reception where he could celebrate not only the wedding but also his first significant victory as an athlete.

With work hard to find in Ireland, Jim moved to London in 1959 where he joined Thames Valley Harriers, running with them for two or three seasons. At the end of 1962, he returned to Ireland and to racing. It was not an auspicious homecoming – when he turned up in the Phoenix Park, all ready to run the St Stephen's Day 10-mile handicap, he was told he could not run because he was not a member of Donore Harriers. So furious was he that he decided that he was not going to join Donore AC.

As good fortune would have it, a few days later he went training in the Phoenix Park, where Harry Gorman, that great Donore stalwart, met him and persuaded him to join the club. What followed was over fifty years of service with one of the oldest clubs in Ireland. It wasn't uninterrupted: when Jim lived in Coolock for a few years, he joined the local club Raheny Shamrock. This lead to Liam Moggan, former athlete, coach and commentator, winning a silver national road relay medal when both were on a Raheny Shamrock AC team. Jim was always a good man to have on your team.

With Donore, Jim began his running career in earnest under the guidance of unassuming coach Eddie Hogan. Eddie's only tool when he monitored his athletes was the watch and Jim thrived under his practical and supportive regime; a regime he would later adopt when coaching the Donore women's teams.

Jim's training included ten-mile runs that took in the fearsome climb at Knockmaroon Hill, Chapelizod followed by 40 × 200m sprints. The cinder track known as the "trotting" track in Raheny at the old St Vincent's GAA club was the venue for his speed work. Contrary to what is now standard, he never bothered with stretching routines and recalled that there was little recourse to physiotherapy by runners before the early 1970s.

On summer Sundays, Jim would run fifteen miles in the morning and if Dublin were playing, would then go to Madigan's pub for several pints before taking up duty on Hill 16.

Balancing work, family and training is always a challenge, particularly for an elite runner. During Jim's senior career, the working week was five and a half day. So he would run to and from work and squeeze in extra training during the lunch break. Significantly he had the full support of his family. Although disappointed to miss out on the 1968 and 1972 Olympics marathon qualification he was not deterred, joining the Raheny Olympian Pat Hooper on the notorious Hill of Howth sessions. When he qualified for the Montreal Olympics, it was in front of his wife Betty, his mother and father and several friends. Later he was to present his Olympic jacket to Naomh Fionnbarra GAA Club where it is now on display.

A big tragedy for Jim was the sad loss of his wife Betty, aged only 40, to cancer His family rallied around, with his mother caring for his sons James and Shane and his sister looking after his daughter when he went back to work and continued his running. He also coached athletics at St Declan's, the local secondary college where his son was a pupil.

New challenges awaited when Jim moved into the masters ranks. In 1979, when 40, he ran under 51 minutes for the Frank Duffy 10-mile race in the Phoenix Park. Another remarkable feat was running a half marathon in 68 minutes when over 45. In 1984, he won three gold medals at the European Masters championship in London. He was rewarded as the athlete of the games another unique distinction for an Irish sportsperson. That year he ran a world age best of 14:47.8 for 5000m taking 8.6 seconds off the record. In 1989, he set a world over 50 record of 31:51.40 for 10,000m and also ran at the Worlds Masters in Eugene, Oregon, USA enjoying the superb facilities.

Jim liked an occasional alcoholic drink and never felt it affected his career; such an opinion was common among runners in those times. However Eddie Hogan was of the view that he would have been a better runner had he abstained from alcohol. Interestingly, Jim never drank water when he ran.

In the 1990s, Jim found a new lease of life when he began coaching the Donore women's running section of Donore AC. Over the years, he has coached women of all standards up to seven days a week and ensured that the club puts out teams in races of all standards from Meet and Train to National Championships. A token of the regard in which he is held was the special "This is Your Life" event organised in his honour by the club. He has a been honoured with an Athletics Ireland award for his contribution to athletics.

In his late 60s, Jim got a stroke. The consultant, a Dr Drea, recognised him and was eager to hasten his treatment. It turned out that she was the aunt of the rower Sean Drea who, like Jim, had competed at the Montreal Olympics. Before long Jim was back running and coaching, contrary to medical advice.

At the age of 75, Jim was still setting targets. He wanted to beat his age number in minutes for 10 miles each year and in 2014, he ran 74 minutes. While he might regret not running a sub-4 minute mile in his long career, that is but a small blip in a glittering career. He was very fortunate to be significantly influenced by family, place and friends. He still had to apply himself with hard training, discipline, self belief and a positive mindset. He was blessed with a physique that was suited to running and he never had joint problems. He was not interested in material things but inspired by the joy of running.

Major Achievements
Jim McNamara national masters T/F championships 2014

Senior: Best Time
Marathon: 2.14.57
Half Marathon: 65 min.

Master Road Times:
Half Marathon M/60 79.40m
15 miles M/40 79.28m

Top achievements: Senior
Olympic Games Marathon Montreal 1976
European Games Marathon Budapest 1966
European Cup Steeplechase Santry 1967
World Cross Country: 4 times on Irish team

EVELYN MCNELIS

Date of Birth: 30/1/1946

From the Mullet to Porto Allegre

By Willie McNelis

"You are never too old to set another goal or to dream a new dream."
– C.S Lewis

The distance from Belmullet to Porto Allegre, Brazil is some 10,000 km. This is the story of such a journey and some athletic achievements along the way.

Evelyn McNelis, or Ellie Ruddy as she is known locally, was born on 30 January 1946, in Belmullet, a picturesque coastal town in County Mayo. This parish, or the Mullet as it is more commonly known, is virtually an island off the northwest corner of County Mayo.

Evelyn, the youngest of 13 children, was raised on a farm and attended the local National School some 3 km distance, which was traversed each day on foot. Later she was a student at St. Mary's Secondary School 7 km from her home. The daily journey to school was done on a bicycle often in very inclement weather. These trips to school and helping out on the farm probably laid the foundations for a career in Master's long distance running that took some time to mature.

Evelyn moved to Dublin in 1964 and worked in Roinn na Gaeltachta until she married (yours truly) in1968. In 1972 she began her Teacher Training Diploma in St. Patrick's College, Drumcondra and graduated in June 1974. By then she had two small children. In September 1974 she took up a teaching post in the Holy Family National School, Rathcoole, Co, Dublin. She taught there for the next 35 years. Evelyn retired in 2009 having attained the position of Deputy Principal. Evelyn and I have four children and nine grandchildren.

Fast forward from the early 70s to the early 80s…

The present running boom probably started with arrival of the Dublin City Marathon in 1980. A small group of all male runners, some serious and some fun runners, used to meet at our house in Naas, County Kildare and start our training runs from there. This was the spring of 1981. One evening in March of 1982 Evelyn decided to join us. Two or three weeks later she was leaving some of us behind, yours truly included – the rest as they say is history.

*S*céal beag: One evening Evelyn and I for some reason were running on our own. We were about a mile into the run. We were doing the "Rathasker 8" an 8 mile run – all our routes had names. We were joined by Hugh Durnin of Clonliffe Harriers fame. The pace began to increase and increase – relentless stuff. I did get the trip, just about. I think it was after this gallop that Evelyn began to realise that she had some serious talent.

Evelyn McNelis

She joined Naas Athletic club and did group training with other club members. The late Des Connolly, who was coaching the ladies at that time, was a wonderful motivator and Evelyn was introduced to some speed sessions. Soon her times began to improve. Her first 10k was run in 42 minutes. Her next target was to break 40 minutes which she achieved a year later in the *Evening Press* mini-marathon.

Her pupils soon became aware of her achievements and Evelyn had very willing participants when she introduced athletics in her school. Her group of athletes were very impressed when one cocky twelve year old challenged her in a race over about 600 metres. She was preparing them at the time for the Dublin Schools Sports in Santry. The challenger was the best in the group and felt he could also take teacher on. Evelyn was reluctant to race him but the group persuaded her. On race day the challenger, lacking experience, started off at a very fast pace and soon began to fade. Evelyn was the winner. Lessons were learned that day and the same boy won a silver medal in the 600 metres in Santry a few weeks later. His pride was restored.

Although working full time and raising a family of three children by now, Evelyn continued to remain committed to her training. She took time out in 1985/86 when our fourth child was born. She couldn't wait to resume training and within a year was back racing again.

Our first foray abroad was in 1991 to Turku, in Finland for a WMA Championships. Evelyn was competing in the 10k on the track in the o/45 category. It being her first World Championship she was extremely nervous. However from the start she was up with the leaders and finished in the bronze position just two seconds behind second place. Four days later she won silver in the 10k cross country. It was a most memorable trip. The Irish team members on that trip, Pat Bonass, Nick Corish, Willie Dunne, Sean Cooney, Bobby King, John Buckley and the Champion twins were wonderful supporters. The parties we enjoyed afterwards to celebrate our success were the envy of the other countries.

There were many more trips to follow. In fact our annual holidays were usually planned around the European or World Masters Championships after that. Some great friendships were forged as we got to know competitors from the many other countries.

The European Championships in Poznam Poland was another very successful trip for Evelyn. Having finished finished 4th in the 10K on the track she was very disappointed as tactically she knew she got it wrong , going out too fast in the first half of the race. A few days later she redeemed herself by taking gold in the 5k.

Our most recent trip was to Porto Allegre in Brazil for the World Masters. It was very hot and humid but luckily on the day of her 10k track race

Evelyn and Willie McNelis

there was a deluge. Being well used to dealing with adverse weather conditions from an early age, Evelyn was able to cope with the conditions. She finished second, although the flooded track resulted in slow times.

Her favourite training ground is The Curragh. She considers herself so lucky to be able to train here. It offers such a variety of routes. You can run for miles in blissful freedom.

Evelyn's love of running has spanned three generations. All of our children have been involved in athletics. Our daughter Sandra was quite competitive and participated in many races with Evelyn. Unfortunately, due to an injury she no longer competes but still manages short runs to maintain health and fitness. Evelyn ran a leg of the Bonn marathon two years ago with our son Liam who lives in Bonn.

She continues to be very actively involved in coaching the younger members of Naas club and has enjoyed considerable success with her young charges. Two of our grandchildren are members of her group. She is still as committed as ever to her training and hopes to continue competing into the future.

PADRAIC MAY

Date of Birth: 1/5/1940

Analysis of a Sporting Life

"Nothing ventured, nothing gained"

Already it's the month of May. How time seems to fly especially when you have just celebrated your 74th birthday. At the moment I am sitting here on my patio soaking in the beautiful view of the Ox Mountains in the distance. Once I took this beautiful scenery for granted but now with age and maturity, nature is much more appreciated.

Just 100 metres away is my birthplace – the little village of Adare – which is tucked away beneath those same hills and as I reminisce and daydream, I hear in the distance the piercing sound of children at play. Indeed it is with a little nostalgia and envy that I pause to listen. Yes, once I was one of those happy little boys playing on the main street just immersed in my own small world, which was limited to the horizon in the distance. These echoes of the past take me back back back into a daydream.

Padraic May

It seems only yesterday that I was whisked away to boarding school St Nathy's in Ballaghaderreen. I felt my parents were mean and inconsiderate to disrupt my fun and games but then I discovered Gaelic football. For the first time ever, I became a member of a team – a team which went on in 1957 to win the only Hogan Cup in the schools 200 year history, a team also beaten in the final by St. Joseph's, Fairview in 1959.

With such credentials, that same year I entered University College Dublin. Needless to say, there was a little pressure on me to try out for the college team but after spending 5 years in boarding school, the training, discipline etc. was not appealing. My focus was more on social activities. However, before the end of my first academic year, somehow I ended up participating in the long jump at the UCD handicapped meeting which surprise, surprise, I won. Now I got the attention of Jack Sweeney, the college coach, and consequently became a member of the athletic team. Up to this, athletics was something I never took too seriously but I did win 2 Connacht Colleges medals during my football days at St. Nathy's. This began a succession of victories in the summer of 1960. My first success was winning the Leinster Long Jump and then proceeding to win both the All Ireland Junior and Senior NACA Long Jumps in Iveagh Grounds with leaps of 6.71 metres and 6.37 metres respectfully. The latter event was somewhat memorable as the first three competitors jumped the same distance but I won on count back.

After this, I went back home to county Sligo for the summer months where I lived a leisurely life. There was not much happening there athletically. Anyway trying to get to events proved impossible. We had no car. This was a time to get back to my roots. Indeed most activity revolved around the hayfield and bog. However, I did begin to practice the triple jump somewhat casually at first and soon realised that I could be a threat to more seasoned campaigners.

Returning to UCD in October 1960 was not as daunting as before as this time I felt much more confident. At the time, discussions were on-going to arrange an athletic meeting between Trinity College and UCD without contravening International Rules. You see those colleges belonged to different athletic associations. The idea got so much interest in the media that finally in 1961 the big occasion arrived – 4,000 spectators were said to be there but alas I could not compete. To add to the misery, we lost to Trinity by 87 points to 73.

Just a week earlier, I had broken my wrist and this created an insurance risk if I was allowed to compete. In no way was I going to miss the Leinster Championships in Gorey. My pride was at stake. I could not give up my title without a fight so despite being left off the UCD athletic team, I decided to pay my own way and compete independently even going so far as to camouflage my cast with a long sleeved tee shirt. The stubbornness paid off as I retained my Long Jump with a leap of 7.40m and to add to the occasion I got 3rd in the Triple Jump at 14.01m. Incidentally, that distance in the long gump was my own personal record. The next day in the national paper, Sean Diffley, a sports reporter, highlighted my victory with the heading, "Maye may get in World Class."

Still despite all the glory and attention, I decided after exams to pack my bag and go to London and work for the summer. I had been promised a job in the office of Kerry Murphy. At the time, I got £8. s1. D 4 take home pay for 5 and a half days work. My first wage packet ever and I felt so independent.

The year 1962 was a relatively quiet one. I did compete with Connaught against Ulster in the Gerard O'Duffy cup where I won both the long jump at 6.7m and triple jump at 14.12m. This was a competition begun in 1943 to promote friendship and understanding with our northern neighbour. Actually in 1993 to celebrate the 50th anniversary of this competition it was decided to choose an atheletic achievement that stood out over the 50 years and yours truly was chosen.

Seemingly at the time I was winding down my athletic participation. My final exam for BA degree was in 1962 and H Dip in 1963. I signed up to spend 2 years with SMA (Society of African Missions) in Nigeria. In all my college experience I won 7 UCD medals which are like coins and one intervarsity medal. While in Africa I did compete for Ondo province at West Nigerian

Championship but opted out of going to the finals in Ibadan. My presence was too conspicuous and this made me uncomfortable.

At that time, the facilities were extremely wanting. Open space was a precious commodity when you are at the equator; consequentially athletic tracks were part of the school compound. The natural vegetation was thick equatorial forest. Considering that basic electricity was wanting, as was great to have some semblance of a track. Light was provided by a generator when it worked and water was delivered by truck to a container in the ground, needless to say, had to be bolded and filtered before drinking. Without realising it at the time this began a long hiatus from sport – 37 years in all.

They say boredom gives pleasure to the most mundane activities and so it was with me. I spent 14 lackadaisical years in Chicago, USA leaving only faint footprints in the sands of time. However I did buy myself a pair of football boots and won six trophies with "McBride's team" over ten years. I played for Sligo in New York, receiving $80 expenses per game, until I got married in 1968. Years later I discovered that I was supposed to be at another function to receive player of the year award on my wedding day.

My fourteen years in America was a great eye opener. Coming directly after I taught Africa helped me compare situations. While in Africa I found the students had a great hunger for education while in America a much more casual approach was evident. On the other hand in Nigeria, you never had to cajole, push or force learning. Their appetite for education was immense. Mind you, we did have the cream of the crop students to our boarding school, St Thomas Aquinas, from all over Western Nigeria. In America, information was passed on in dribs and drabs and consequentially exams just tested a limited amount of knowledge before you passed on to a new set of facts. Students were much more vocal in class but not as adept as Nigerians in written work.

Having come home on a visit I was offered a job locally which I took up in 1980.

Eventually, I began to dabble in handball in the 1990s and ended up winning the 40 x 20 All Ireland Doubles in 1998 and both singles and doubles in the 60 x 30 court in 2000. In all, I won 8 All Irelands.

Again, misfortune struck as I damaged my right thumb putting an end to my handball prospects at that time. Somehow, I got led into Master Athletics in 2001. I had never heard of them till then. Rather sheepishly, I travelled to Tullamore and competed in the long jump only, winning it at 4.20 metres. This was just the encouragement I needed. As the years went by, I have added further disciplines to my repertoire. Actually, on my 70th birthday, I competed in six events winning all. Now at 74, I have grossed a collection of 111 All Irelands – this includes football plus handball – and 29 British medals and I can't wait to be 75. That sounds crazy wishing, my life away, but sure it's said that "age is only a word and not a sentence".

Sometimes I regret my laisser faire attitude to my sporting career. I was always a terrible role model – never really practicing what I preached. I depended on natural ability having ambivalence to dedication. Training and gym work were unpalatable. Today people raise an eyebrow when I tell them the bog is where I train. I find the softness of the surface and isolation conducive to my personality. Basically I am a shy person and even though I value attention, too much is overpowering. I suppose I am what I am and nothing will change at this junction. Indeed my run up for both long jump and triple jump is twenty-seven strides. And a shoe length, not very professional, I might add but this is how I do things.

Oops! Did I doze. It seems darker outside. No more can I hear those distant screams. What! Gee it's almost 10.00 o'clock! Is that the phone? Hi, is that you Michael? You know I just completed the project you wanted. No! I haven't it written. I'll explain later. Anyway, till then. Bye.

Top Senior Achievements
Long jump 23 ft. 51 inches

Master Achievements
Multiple master titles
Jumps and throws

ROBERT MILLER
Date of Birth: 13/9/194

Banking on Miller

"Wisdom is not a product of schooling but of the lifelong attempt to acquire it." – Albert Einstein

I suppose I began to be aware of running at an early age when the kids in our small road used to borrow my dad's watch (the only one that had a tiny second hand) to time themselves running around the block. At school, I was very small for my age until I was 16 and was in constant threat of being picked

Robert Miller

on by the bigger lads and so developed the art of running faster than they could.

My father was very athletic, enjoyed high jumping and he taught me to pole vault over the washing line using the line pole in our tiny back garden. When our school gym instructor asked for volunteers to learn to pole vault, I was the only volunteer but he tried to dismiss me as being too small and thin. However I accepted his challenge to demonstrate my skill and he put the high jump bar at its full height above the pole vault box and gave me a bamboo pole. I'm not sure who was the more surprised when I cleared it first time. I was in. Taking athletics seriously was also the best way to be excused from playing cricket.

At the school sports, I had to take second place in the 100 and 200 yards to a fine runner in my age group so I chose to try the hurdles which I could win. There was never a pole vaulting competition since I was the only vaulter. Apart from pole vault practise, I did little athletics training.

At Trinity College, I was persuaded by a class mate to turn up for the athletics team because they needed a pole vaulter. There I was able to get some coaching and lots of practice using the long jump run-up and pit. Yes, a long jump pit of firm sand at ground level. I soon learned how to vault and land on my feet every time. During these years I learned to vault reaching heights of 11 foot 6 inches, low by today's standards, but that was with a heavy aluminium pole that did not bend, and into the long jump pit. Fibre glass poles were available to those who could afford them. However we did have some fine competitions against Liam Gleeson (UCD) and Mike Bull (Queen's) and the fibre glass pole did not always win.

In the summer of my final year (my exams were in September) I took some time studying the 120 yards hurdles and worked out that it was possible to use just three big strides between hurdles and since this seemed faster I practised it. I entered the AAU Irish Championships that year of 1966 in both the 120 yards hurdles and pole vault. I won the hurdles easily as I was the only one using three strides but had a big problem as one flight of hurdles was incorrectly positioned. I was fortunate to get the silver medal in the pole vault in a very friendly competition with the two vaulters from Crusaders.

As jobs in Ireland were few and far between for mathematicians, I went to work in England that autumn and although I did have in mind living near a good athletics club, the job that offered the best salary was in Basildon, Essex. I joined the rugby club there who were delighted with my speed and the next summer I sought out the local athletics club. This was a club with a very small senior section, which did not have access to hurdles or vaulting facilities. So I concentrated on the 100 and 220 yards finishing mid-field in the local inter-club competitions.

In my first winter with Basildon, I decided to train hard during the winter using two booklets from the AAA on sprinting and hurdles training. I was by now working in London and two evenings a week, I would stop off at two cinder running tracks on the way home where repetition 100s or 200s were the basic sessions, sometimes joining a group of athletes from other clubs. On other evenings, I would jog and sprint alternately between lamp posts on the town ring road or do hops and bounds between 25s on the rugby pitch lit by the light from the same lamp posts. This was lonely and tough and the only fun was to take part in winter graded meetings at Crystal Palace where the shortest race was the 400m. Somehow I was always put in the slowest grade in the outside lane and each time won in the identical time of 50.0 seconds. I would just have loved it if, even once, this had been 49.9 seconds.

One of my best memories of my time in athletics was the joy of taking part in the club competitions the following summer where I was now the guy winning the races as my times went from 10.3 to 10.0 for the 100 yds and from 23.1 to 22.0 for the 220 yds. There was a particular thrill coming off the bend of the 220 knowing that if there was anyone close by, I would have the strength to run past them on the straight.

I moved jobs and home to live near Portsmouth and joined the athletics club there for a while. I did the occasional 120 hurdles but Alan Pascoe was their star hurdler at the time and they also had a very fine sprinter to whom I had to take second place in the county championships. I started to play more rugby that athletics while there.

I returned to Dublin when AIB opened their computer department and the next summer was encouraged to try out for a place on the bank's team for the inter bank competitions. I was pleased to find out that the speed was still there and I won that competition for a few years. As AIB's athletics captain, Bill Whiston, was also the captain of Crusaders, I was encouraged to sign up for them. I enjoyed sprinting with the club especially in relays and occasionally dabbled in the hurdles.

I more or less retired from athletics in 1977 but when Crusaders won the National Club Championships in 1978, Bill approached me again with the proposition that if I trained for the winter and got up to a good standard in

One of my biggest moments – racing against Pietro Mennea

the hurdles, there would be a place for me on the team for Lisbon and also on a bank team going to Paris.

Deja vu! Another winter of training, but this time at lunch time on the track at Belfield, this time based on repetition sprints and short runs over hurdles, culminating with aggressive sprint starts to the first hurdle. Again the first outing of the season – the Trinity Relays – proved the value of the training regime. Jimmy O'Neill joyfully told me he had timed my split at 15.3 secs, for me an excellent result. I only found out last year that my times that season were club records. I got the bronze medal in the national championships that year of 1979, a month short of my 36th birthday.

Selection for the Irish team followed, which really was what I was working for to overcome the disappointment thirteen years earlier when I failed to make the team after winning the 1966 national championships. However the race I remember best in 1979 was the 100m for Crusaders in the European Club Championships in Lisbon where I lined up on the start line with Pietro Mennea who was the current world record holder in the 200m. What fuss and palaver there was about that start!

The year 1980 was a magical one for me on the track when I won most of the inter-club events and the 110 hurdles national title in spite of being beaten in the semi-final. I'm normally a very relaxed athlete, but the morning of the 110 hurdles final, I was very focussed, visualising a very aggressive start across the first few hurdles. This came off brilliantly and the other competitors (about half my age) told me they were really put off with my fast start and although they did come back strongly, they just failed to catch me as I held on to my lead.

Three more international vests were awarded that year and I really enjoyed these trips and being part of the national squad. I even managed a 4 x 100 relay leg in Edinburgh.

I continued to enjoy club competitions over the next few years but with less success as some very fine young athletes emerged. However there was still a couple of good races in my Indian summer career. In the 110m hurdles at the National Championships of 1983, I was trailing Brendan Mullan when he hit one of the final hurdles. I went past to win my third national title one month short of my 40th birthday!

The following year, I was encouraged to enter the European veterans over 40 competition in Brighton. I was delighted to win the silver medal although a little disappointed as I was dead level with the winner at the last hurdle which I hit rather hard. He had been a very highly regarded international athlete in his time.

I retired soon after as I found training was causing headaches and, as Crusaders had slipped out of the first division, I would have no close competition during the season. So it seemed the right time. However I kept my lunch time habit of exercise but this time using fast walking around Sandymount instead. This has stood me in good stead as I joined a walking club in my 60s and now regularly walk the Wicklow mountains at a good pace. My hurdle training is very evident when I can step over barriers with a good trailing leg action and hop across streams to the envy of others.

Looking back over my career a few things are very clear to me. Training can have a dramatic short-term and longer-term effect. There is life after 35 on the athletics track. And most significantly for me, a little encouragement for an athlete can go a very long way. Many thanks to all those who dragged me out on the track and encouraged me to work hard when out there.

Major Achievements
National Champion
120 yards hurdles National 1966
110m Hurdles 1980
110m Hurdles 1983
Silver medal Europeans 110 hurdles masters
Irish senior international 5 times
Competing in 100m relay on Irish team

EDWARD MULCAHY

Date of Birth: 24/2/1933

A Giant of a Man

"The beautiful thing about learning is that nobody can take it away from you" – B.B. King

Born as I was in a small village in County Waterford, one of five children, three sisters, Anne, Mary, Eileen and a brother Michael, we all went to the same primary school. Times were hard; resources were scarce, with World War Two raging in Europe, and bombs dropping on our near neighbours England. Thankfully, we are all still alive and came together recently for a gathering at Clashmore, where we counted up our collective ages to be 413 years.

After primary school, I attended the Northern Monastery in Cork, a technical college run by Christian Brothers. While there, I stayed with my aunt Julie and uncle Paddy Ring in Foot Island, commuting each day to school by train. When I finished my schooling in 1949, I became apprenticed to Patrick Lucas, a master carpenter in Villierstown, for three years, something my parents paid a fee for, even though money was scarce. Villierstown was put on the map by John Treacy double world cross-country champion and Olympic marathon silver medal winner.

John's father Jack and his grandfather Redmond were great friends of mine and we often shared the task of turning dough in the bake house while waiting for the workshop to open. Jack encouraged me to work more adeptly and my skill in the art of bread-making improved with patience and practice. For three years, I cycled from home to the bake house and workshop. It was here that I learnt to play the bagpipes and read music from Paddy Parker, an outstanding piper and violinist, and also took up weight lifting. During my life, I have played the bagpipes, piano accordion the continental accordion and flute. I love Irish and Scottish music and my heroes were Dermot O'Brien and Jimmy Shand, both of whom I met. My favourite singer was Frank Fitzpatrick, who I met in Clonmel.

My first paid employment was building a technical school under the auspices of the VEC, an experience which gave me an insight into a broad spectrum of trades. Later I worked for Waterford County Council for four years; a time of great joy, since it was during this time that I met my wife Sheila Hussey from Sneem, in County Kerry. We moved to Sneem lock, stock and barrel in 1957, where I ambitiously set up an engineering business to support our four children. Shirley, Alan, Tony and Kenneth all came into this world as healthy as trouts.

All my life I was interested in individual sports such as boxing, tennis, sprinting and weight lifting. Team sports were less of a draw, as there are always dodgers on teams, unwilling to pull their weight. At the National Championships of 1963, I witnessed for the first time the 56 lbs weight for distance and saw a mighty man named Tadhg Twomey throwing this weight 15 feet (4.57m). After an introduction to Tadhg and a chance to try the weight for myself, I knew that I had a lot to learn and needed to strengthen up, if ever I was to live with the likes of him. After that, I regularly competed with Tadhg in open sports, at county level and at nationals; my best being 14'9" (4.5m) on a day in Listowel when I beat an outstanding thrower, Jack Dunlea from Killoglin.

Len Braham, a classy thrower who threw the discus internationally, then emerged. Tadhg and Len became known as "Giants of Irish Throwing". In 1973, Len recorded a might throw of 9.15m, an Irish record, at the Munster Championships in Castleisland where I finished second. Len taught me excellent training techniques, including light deadlifts, hack lifts, squats and 20 metre sprints for explosive power, always at 80% of maximum effort but high repetitions. Even after a hard day at work, I pushed myself in training. In 1975, Len and I travelled to the Highland Games in Durham, an experience never to be forgotten. Len, then the Irish champion in hammer, discus and 56lbs, won all around him, including the 56lbs for height. I lost a close friend and great rival when he passed away after a short illness in 17 February 2006.

About thirty years ago, a giant of a man named Gerry O'Connell from Ennis arrived on the scene and broke Tadhg Twomey's record 56lbs weight over the bar with a throw of 4.93m. As a super power lifter, I witnessed him pick up 740lbs (335.66kg) at a competition. Out of competition he threw 10m for distance, a feat he failed to achieve while competing.

While I have a great love for international athletics on television, I bemoan the lack of coverage for throwing and jumping. Although the field events could be enjoyed by many, they are tried by few.

In 1988, I went global, pairing up with Frank O'Connor, and with 7.72m, had the longest throw of the competition, becoming the first man in the world to win 56lbs indoors. Since then, I have competed many times in England, Scotland, America, Jersey and Northern Ireland.

My greatest throw ever was at the Irish Culture Festival Stone held at Hill College, Boston in 1995, when, aged 62, I threw the 56lbs a distance of 8.07m. Richard Jackson put it on his list of American records, claiming that it was the longest sling of a 56lbs weight by a man of my age on American soil.

My world came to an end in 1999 when my wife Sheila died of cancer at the early age of 63 years. She advised me to keep at the things I loved best and that was competing and music. So late in 2000 I just did that and I am glad I did and I sometimes feel that I get divine help. That year of 2000, I was invited to Rochester, Kent by Colm and Catherine Murphy to take part in the European 35lbs and 56lbs championships which I won.

Before the competition started ,I went to the toilet and when I came back, the throwers were standing around the throwing area and the weight was at the tip board. I picked it up, threw it over 9m and then saw it being measured. "Has the competition started?" I asked. Gordon Hickey one of England's finest shot putters spoke up: "It has son, but now it's over."

I went to Rochester for many years after that to compete in the championships. With the help of hammer thrower, James Nagle we started the Irish Throwers Club (ITC) and ran competitions for all the different events – Greek discus, stone throw, grenade and Goulding hammer, as well as the more familiar hammer, 56lbs over the bar and 56lbs distance. The venues were Castleisland, Dunboyne and later Templemore. At the start, the English would come for the 56lbs over the bar and distance since they were European and World Championships. Now these events are held in Stoke-on-Trent or Derby. At each meeting, we remembered some of the great throwers of the past like Len Braham, Ned Tobin, Dr Pat O'Callaghan and later Joe Nagle and a trophy was presented in their honour to the best thrower of the meeting. James Nagle was a great young organiser with deep respect for the men of the past as well being a great hammer and weight thrower himself and we all pray that he will take it up again.

Olympic shot putter Phil Conway was just one who attended these meets. The standard of competition was very high and in my age group, I had to watch myself very carefully with Mick McGarry from Dublin and Ian Miller from Scotland always ready to make an attack. It was hard to keep ahead of them.

I am over 80 years now and because of having arthritis in my left knee, can no longer spin in the circle with an implement. I can still get a fair distance with the discus, shot, javelin and hammer with a standing throw. The 56lbs suits me because it is thrown from a standing position anyway. My favourite throwers are Dr Pat O'Callaghan, Len Braham, Tadhg Twomey and Gerry O'Connell, while Patsy O'Connor from Brosna, County Kerry was by far the best all-round veteran athlete I ever met. In the 1970s, I was presented with one of my medals at the National Championships in Santry by by Dr Pat O'Callaghan, winner of hammer gold at the Olympics of 1928 and 1932.

In late 2003, I met my partner Maggie Guiney and after she took early retirement from her job managing six laboratories in London, we have sailed the seven seas on cruises around the globe. As well as knowing every weight thrower in Ireland and Scotland, Maggie loves the music and together we find peace and serenity and a lot of fun.

I credit my wellbeing, fitness and strength to never having smoked or imbibed the devil's brew, as well as the music and the love that

Edward Mulcahy

I have shared. I eat plain food – mostly milk, spuds, eggs and bacon, using salt and sugar sparingly. I like to say my prayers, and who knows, maybe the good Lord gives me that little push when I need it. Jim O'Shea, an international champion in his own right, and the secretary of Farrenfore Athletics Club, works with others, allowing the competition to happen. Maggie, my dearest, books the flights and hotels, and is there through thick and thin. I am a lucky man. I looki forward to competition at home and abroad, all the while enjoying every moment now. I am glad I was born in 1933 rather than 2003 because we had a wonderful time without the gadgets of today, which stifle conversation; a great loss.

One day, at Knocknagoshal Open Sports, two men near me were discussing the weight throwers. "This will be a good competition. You have Twomey, Braham, Justice and Mulcahy," one of them said. I moved near them. "Do you know Mulcahy?" I asked. And one of them replied, "Yeah boy, that swelled headed bastard from Sneem."

That day, I won the Kerry championship over the bar.

At the World Masters Highland Games at Inverness, September 2014, Eddie made two World records in the over 80+ with the 42lbs over the bar and the 42lbs distance earning the two gold medals. He also won 6 silvers with the 16lbs stone and hammer, 22lbs stone and hammer, the 28lbs sling and for good measure the caber toss.

Eddie is most thankful to his partner and manager Maggie Guiney who has been such a help to him over the last ten years.

The wonderful thing about competing in the Highland Games is the respect that is shown to the 200 athletes and the medal presentation ceremony is so well done, and so nice to see the tricolour flowing in the wind and above all the bagpipe music and the highland dancing.

Achievements

100 county medals between senior and masters
Munster Senior 11; Munster Master 92 (indoor included)
Irish All Ireland Senior 10
Irish Masters 104
English Masters 15
Northern Ireland Masters 7
European Masters 30
World Masters 29
World Masters Highland games 7
Kerry AAI Hall of Fame 2003.

MAURICE MULLINS
29/3/1941 – 26/12/2015

Eternity in the Present Moment

By Michael Gygax

"Every cripple carries his limp differently"

Maurice spent his life in education, as a teacher, head teacher in a reformatory school, and the last twenty-eight years of his career he taught maths and science in Balbriggan Community College.

A love of hurling saw him boarding in St Flannans school in Ennis, County Clare where he won a Munster Colleges hurling medal and a place on the Galway minor hurling team. He attended the latter half of secondary school in Rockwell College in Tipperary which instilled within him a love for sport which has been a lifelong passion. He was on the 1959 team that won the Colleges of Science Trophy for the best athletic colleges in Ireland. He went to UCG where he studied mathematics, physics and pure physics and played sports, but particularly liked hurling.

After graduation he went to England where he worked on a space program with Hawker Siddeley Dynamics as a professional mathematician. Despite enjoying the work he returned home to Ireland and worked in a number of teaching posts in the west.

Maurice moved to Dublin in 1973 and took up a post of principal at a reformatory school. It was during this time that he started to run, largely to give him freedom to think and unwind in the open air.

Maurice moved to pastures new where he taught science and maths to students in Balbriggan, just a short distance from his home. During the 1970s and 1980s he was involved with other like-minded people in community development projects within the town. They identified the need for sporting and recreational facilities and set about fund-raising and lobbying in the best interests of the community.

He also pioneered the staging of triathlons in Ireland, organized many ultra-distance races and was involved in IMRA races.

It is as an ultra-distance runner that Maurice made a name for himself in running, the longest distance run by him being from Cork to Dublin, an event where he ran for 140 of the 150 miles before the body gave up on him. In his own words, "he nearly made it". He has run many twenty-four hour races and has competed in races from Dublin to Belfast on a number of occasions. He has competed in the USA, a hundred mile race in the Rockies. In these races you do not stop, if you do the body gives up, so the mantra is to endure. He organized many trips away for team Ireland ultra-distance events.

He says he likes the mental side of things, the solitude; sometimes he cherishes company on these very long runs. It's time to dream, enter an altered state of consciousness, when movement becomes automatic. This trance like state brings you to a different place. It is an esoteric experience. Eternity is embodied in every single moment during the highs and the lows of an ultra-distance run.

Maurice was fascinated by human behaviour. He was a keen observer of the human condition, loved to test himself both physically and mentally and see others do the same. It was this impulse that brought him to Los Angeles in 2002, answered a request on an ultra-distance website for a feeder to a man who was running over fifty miles per day in high temperatures, from Los Angeles to New York, a distance of 3,000 miles. He drove a recreational vehicle

Maurice finishing a triathlon in his younger days

and accompanied the ultra runner on the long journey. The challenge was so great that his charge capitulated after fifty days.

Maurice studied hypnotherapy, qualified as a practitioner and loved to work with athletes to fulfil their potential. He believed that visualizing every possible situation, in a race or training can greatly enhance positive athletic performances. "To prepare well for an event, nothing is unforeseen." This technique he used himself when competing.

Maurice liked to sing and was a member of a barber shop group in Skerries for 30 years. He loved to travel and running was his passport to don the Irish singlet and compete abroad, explore far away hills and imbibe a spectrum of cultures. When he retired from teaching he headed to Australia where he back packed around for two months. He competed in most countries in Europe. He practiced yoga daily. Maurice was a storyteller and loved nothing better than being amongst friends and family.

Running in Moscow, by Maurice Mullins

Running is boring, or so the saying goes. In 1996, a six-man Irish team travelled to Moscow for the world 100km championships. The team consisted of the following runners:

- Eddie Harrison – holder of the non-stop record from Belfast to Dublin.
- Ray McConnell and Don McDonnell – whose duels for the 24 hour run kept the record at well over 130 miles.

- Michael Anglim – one of the best ultra-runners in the UK at the time. He has strong Limerick roots.
- Eugene Kavanagh – who was a founder member of the ultra-running movement in Ireland and a regular on distances over 100 miles.
- Maurice Mullins – one of Ireland's original triathletes and a veteran of over twenty 100km races.

The receptionist in the hotel said we had no booking made and kept us waiting for ninety minutes. I went to the back of her office and knocked at the door. Two minutes and US$5 later she dramatically found our booking. There was an office at the end of each corridor and guests were told to hand in their keys going down to breakfast. Royal requests are commands, and were sweetened by another crisp $5. No rubies or sterling were accepted.

The bribes were anticipated by us. It was 10.00 pm and we needed a meal. There was no food available in the hotel, or so we were informed. $5 later it suddenly materialised on the fifth floor, where hundreds of people were dining.

Returning the following night at about 10.30 I found a very depressed room-mate from the US team. He handed in his key on arrival but on principle would not part with a tip. He was left all day locked out of his room until the key dramatically appeared at 10.00 that night.

The necessity of a guide reared its head the first morning in Red Square. There appeared to be nobody who fitted the bill as successive trains came and left. I noticed an old man slumped by a wall and asked him if he could speak English.

His lips moved rapidly but no sound could be heard. By putting my ear near his mouth the replies to my questions were delivered in perfect English. A botched operation on his throat had left him without a voice box.

Vlad had been a translator on Russian delegations abroad where English was required during the Stalinist period. He had visited Ireland with a delegation and drank pints in the Guinness brewery among other places. Vlad was a welcome member of the Irish team. He enjoyed his new role as manager feeding us on the race day. We met him every day and he was full of surprises.

"The Kremlin is open today," said Vlad one morning. "When it's open again nobody knows." We took the opportunity and hot-footed it across the city.

On reaching the Kremlin, we were in the process of checking in our day bags when he told us to stop. "There is a fee per bag," he said, "so put all yours into mine." And he opened his expansive container. I looked down and there appeared to be an iron egg holder at the bottom, with one egg inside. With difficulty I took it out.

Maurice Mullins

"Vlad, why have you an iron egg holder at the bottom of your bag?" I asked.

His reply was dramatic: "If the only protein you got every month was one egg, you too would have an iron egg holder."

Having examined the inside of the Kremlin Wall the lads headed off to see the Russian White House, the government building that had been attacked with artillery three years earlier during the power struggle between Yeltsin and the Russian parliament.

Instead, I went into the Treasury, which was normally closed in those days. This is the museum that contains the gifts to the Romanovs from the crown heads of Europe during previous centuries. It was astonishing: lavishly decorated artefacts in gold, silver and diamonds.

What caught my eye among this magnificence was a huge carriage. When the Romanov family moved to St. Petersburg they still held formal family affairs like marriages and funerals in Moscow. When Peter the Great's daughter was to be married in Moscow, she was conveyed in this carriage. It was drawn in relays of 25 horses across the snow for 800km.

The carriage was so large it had three rooms. There was a kitchen with a stove that sent heat via pipes to a bedroom and sitting room. The whole carriage inside and outside was decorated with emeralds and diamonds.

Next day Lubyanka Square was on the agenda. Vlad brought us there reluctantly. When I asked him to bring us closer to the prison where the vans disappeared down to a basement, he flatly refused. In fact we could only see the square from a side road, rather like looking at Dublin's O'Connell Street from Henry Street. He wouldn't enter the square.

Early in the week we were approached by a young man of about 25 years selling tickets for the Bolshoi Theatre. They were costing US$16. I explained to him that we were just ordinary people who happened to run, not millionaires on a world trip. Our maximum spend was US$12. He told us to come back in 20 minutes. We did, and he had the tickets. There was a ballet that night and with 63 musicians, and it was a wonderful experience. We were seated directly under the royal box. We went a second night in the Bolshoi Theatre; not this time to a ballet, but a straightforward opera.

May Day saw a huge row in Red Square been Stalinists and the new regime, involving thousands of people. I asked Vlad to call an old lady over and we talked for a while. She said she lived 200 kilometres west of Moscow. I asked her about her life over half a century earlier: "What did you do when you heard the Germans were coming?" The reply was short: "We burned our houses and lived in the forest for two years."

Race day dawned. The course had the Moskva River on one side and a succession of apartment blocks on the other. I asked Vald who lived there and he said "ordinary people". I asked him about the size of the apartments. "Three metres by three," he replied. "But what if you include the bedroom and sitting room?" I asked, seeking clarification. "You heard me," he said, "three metres by three."

The Irish team was well past its best, but we still came a very creditable ninth in the race. I never found running boring. "But of for the touch of a vanished hand, and the sound of a voice that is still." – Tennyson.

To Vlad...

I called to Maurice in his home on 20 October 2014. We chatted for hours about life and his running career. Maurice is getting tired and needs to rest. Ten years ago he was diagnosed with prostate cancer, got a reprieve after treatment, when he ran three marathons but discovered then that he has secondary cancer which spread to his bones. He still does yoga and uses light weights every day. He looks pale but his voice is strong, a firm handshake and chuckles when amused. He can only walk for twenty minutes now and stand for five minutes. He misses the mountains terribly but his running buddies come and walk with him weekly in Ardgillan Park. Maurice continues to live a life where eternity is embodied in the present moment.

A documentary made by his daughter Deirdre Mullins is on YouTube, "Going the Distance".

Major Achievements
130 marathons races
Six or seven 24 hour race
Twenty 100 km races

FRANK MURPHY

Date of Birth: 21/5/1947

The George Best of Irish Athletics

By P.J. Browne

The greatest wealth is health. –Virgil

There is a misperception shadowing the athletic career of Frank Murphy. The received wisdom says that he was hugely talented but he did not realize his potential. He was one of the brightest stars who fizzled out. The reality is more prosaic but less romantic. The "George Best of Irish athletics"appellation hasn't done him any favors either, but we seem to revel in this kind of myth making. In truth, Murphy trained hard, perhaps too hard, and suffered injuries that went unattended or misdiagnosed. The recollections of his contemporaries dispel the ambiguities we cling to. What can be said with certainty is that Murphy was a considerable talent, a colorful, likeable character who got on well with nearly everybody, especially the ladies. He contributed substantially to the Irish tradition at Villanova

"I knew Frank when he was a student in O'Connell's and I was in Colaiste Mhuire. He was a year ahead of me and we competed against each other quite bit. We just hit it off very well together. Athletically he was clearly ahead of me, so there was never a rivalry or competition to speak of. We began to socialize even though we attended different schools. He got me to join him at Clonliffe Harriers, and that was the beginning of a great enduring friendship.

When we were at Villanova, Frank was at the top end of the scale, and I was at the bottom end. No question about that. Yet he always insisted that I would get the same as he got. He shared whatever he got with me. It was a natural trait in him, an amazing selflessness. It was through Frank that I went to Villanova. That indicates that he had the ear of Jumbo, but more important, that Jumbo respected and heeded his advice. Even as a freshman, Frank had impressed Jumbo. That was uncommon, and possibly unprecedented." Des McCormack, 1966-1970.

McCormack may not have been at the top end of the scale but he was no mediocre athlete. He was the dominant steeplechaser in Ireland and was national champion in 1969 (9:22.2) and 1970. He was a valuable member of the Villanova Cross country team when they won collegiate titles.

Frank Murphy became interested in athletics because of his love of football. "I was interested in Gaelic football and I wanted to get fit. We only trained one day a week with a match at the weekends. I joined Clonliffe Harriers at the suggestion of Bob Joyce whose father was a partner with Billy Morton. Billy had an Optician's shop and Bob's father worked with him. Bob was a high jumper.

I was only training a few months before I was entered in a race before Christmas, a handicapped 2 mile road race. I won the race off my handicap. Billy Morton came over to me and was amazed at the time that I ran. Now I hadn't a notion about times and so on. He urged me to keep training with the club and Brother Moore was trying to put together a school's team for the Christian Brothers Stretton Field summer games. He put me down for the 440, 880 and the 1 mile. I ran the three and won. I broke the school record on 2 occasions and came to prominence quite quickly.

I ran for Clonliffe in the All Ireland, the Northern Ireland AAA's and the Irish AAU. I won the 440 and the 880 in two school records on a cinder track. The school races were held in the Iveagh Grounds on grass. I was getting a lot of encouragement from people. Ron Delany spoke to my parents and told them he was representing Villanova and looking out for talent. I had two years left in secondary school and wanted to do my Leaving Cert. My father told Ron to come back in two years.

In the meantime, I continued to improve and I was on my way after finishing my Leaving Exams in 1966. I did my Leaving Exams twice. I passed the first time but was still eligible to run in the school championships. I was 17 and waiting the extra year was a very sensible decision. My father felt I wasn't mature enough to go earlier and he was right.

Billy Morton offered me his unique advice after I won the underage titles in Santry. Billy was his own man and he basically did whatever he wanted to do. He came up to me and he said: 'Murphy, you're going to be a great fucking runner and you'll have all these half-baked coaches coming to you and telling you what to do. Just tell them to fuck off.' That was vintage Billy, true to form.

"Leaving my parents for a new country, especially the United States, was a massive experience for me. The goodbyes at the airport were very tough and I was very homesick initially. So much so that I wanted to come home for

Christmas. My father told me that if I came home for Christmas, I wouldn't want to go back. He explained to me that I needed more time and I was only settling in after three months. I had a few aunts in the States and he suggested that I spend Christmas with them, and encouraged me to come home in the summer, and if I still felt like leaving we'd talk about it.

You can make your own decision then he said. Sure when I got home that summer I couldn't wait to get back, so it was the best decision I ever made. I got great support and encouragement from the likes of Ian Hamilton, who was already established at Villanova. That was the year Noel Carroll graduated. Because of taking time off for the 1964 Olympics, he had to come back in the fall of 1965 to finish his studies and graduate. He was a tremendous help to me as well so I put in my four years and graduated in 1969.

Jumbo

"I'd already had coaching with Brother Moore and also in Clonliffe Harriers, but nothing like Jumbo. You could see the professionalism coming through. He gave each athlete a lot of individual time and I got on very well with him. We had top class athletes there. Marty Liquori was a brilliant athlete, and also Dave Patrick. We had 4 sub four minute milers in my time there. Strictly speaking we really only had three. Chris Mace (England) ran a shade over four minutes. He was a killer in training but we always beat him in competition. It was tough.

We put two relay teams together one weekend in Modesto, California – the A team set a new record and the B team broke the old one We won the 2 mile relay and beat the best of the West Coast and we all ran sub 1.49. The second string won the two mile relay in sub 1.50. That depth of talent made it great because everyone had to work to hold onto his place. You would be dying to get on the team especially for the Penn Relays. Villanova and the Penn Relays were synonymous in those years. Jumbo would remind us – 'Your team is only as good as your fifth man.'

He didn't want us running with the older athletes although we trained with them so there was little or no competition for freshmen. One of my favorite memories is an indoor mile for freshmen when I finished second to Jim Ryun in 4.06, the best race of my freshman year. I could have made it on the senior team but that meant losing my last year of eligibility.

I never trained that hard when I was in Ireland, doing about 25 to 30 miles a week. Jumbo just put me on the program that they used and it was a normal progression. But it wasn't simply the severe training; it was the atmosphere, being around guys who were good and in some cases even better than me. Regardless of ability there was a kind of family atmosphere and the athletes trained together and socialized together.

I did all my best running during my years in Villanova. There are varying opinions about Jumbo. Noel Carroll, for example, completely disagreed with him on his outlook on training and togetherness. Jumbo insisted on the team concept, travelling together, neatness, ties, no long hair, none of which I had any problem with. If you were married you just wouldn't represent Villanova. That happened when Noel got married and he threw him off the team even though he was the best 880 runner that he had. Times change of course. When I was there you had to check out and check in if you

Frank Murphy

wanted to go anywhere on weekends. We were closely monitored.

Jumbo was a great motivator; he could build an athlete up to the point where he overachieved. He was superb at getting individuals to perform beyond their talent on a given day for a particular race. Many times they never again came close. Even so he was very mindful of your academic progress. 'Athletics may have got you here,' he'd remind us, 'but you're here to graduate.' He would tell you to stay away from training if you were doing poorly in class. He'd see to it that you got tutoring if you were weak in subjects. He was supportive in other ways as well; you felt like you could go to him and talk to him about anything. He was a father figure."

"Of all the Irish athletes there and certainly my contemporaries," Des McCormack explains, "Jumbo would have singled out Frank as the best overall person that he had. He had an enormous affection for Frank and a huge respect for the effort that he put in. With regard to student life, Frank was very intelligent. He was very diligent and a great note taker. He was fastidious in this way with lectures dated and so on. But it left him better prepared when the push came for the exams. He took his studies just as seriously as he took his running. Frank never had to attend summer school and he graduated with a good marketing degree. This meant I had a few lonely summers there without him when I had to remain on. Three times I had to go it alone when he left for Ireland. That was quite difficult for me." McCormack went on to have an outstanding business career after he returned to Ireland.

Murphy was a champion with few illusions about himself. He reacted to success with quiet humility. There was never a thought of vanquishing any athlete during competition. "My greatest achievement was winning the 1,000 meters at the IC4A and setting a European record. I beat Byron Dyce, a Jamaican Olympian. I raced really well at the Penn Relays."

"Villanova won 5 Championships one year and I won three watches and was voted best athlete of the meet. I ran a three quarter mile in 2.50 and I knew then that I could break 4 minutes which I did when I ran the mile two weeks later. I was only 3rd that time and Liquori was the winner. For the size of the school we didn't have a huge track and field team so that success was noteworthy. We won championships with just a handful of athletes who doubled up – you had Donnie Walsh, Ian Hamilton and Des McCormack all running cross country.

The 1968 Penn Relay Championships that Murphy scarcely mentions was widely acclaimed in the press:

"They said it couldn't be done, that no college track team could win five relay championships in the Penn Relays," the *New York Times* reported. "But no one bothered to ask Villanova, or Larry James, its speediest sophomore quarter miler, or indeed Frank Murphy. They waited until the one mile relay to complete their sweep.

James delivered the clincher with an unbelievable 43.9 second quarter mile that wiped out Rice University's 10 yard lead entering the last leg. It was the finest moment in the history of the Penn Relays, and was believed to be the fastest 440 leg ever ran.

Earlier in the afternoon, helped by the first of Murphy's two strong distance performances, they set a record in the four mile relay. James, Murphy, Dave Patrick and Charlie Messenger, each ran on two victorious teams today.

Yet each had enough time to rest between races. More important, Villanova concentrated on winning each relay rather than setting records and tiring its talented athletes. Murphy started the assault in the four mile relay with a 4.04 anchor leg in which he passed Byron Dice of NYU and Jim Baker of Harvard in a thrilling final lap."

Reflections

I loved my time at Villanova, athletically, academically and socially. I would recommend it to anyone who has the ability to get a scholarship, and not just to Villanova. It's a great experience for a young man and you can always come home. I had some great years especially 1969. I won everything in the indoor season, I won the British AAAs and broke Delany's Irish Olympic record. If I'd had the same level of fitness and was injury free in 1968 I might have performed better. I got a hairline fracture before the Games and it was diagnosed as shin splints. Dr. Pat O' Callaghan was the medic in charge of the team and I suggested he take some x rays. His response was, 'Who is the doctor, you or me?' He wouldn't listen to me. It was terrible. I got permission then to go back to the states because there was no medical support in Ireland.

My doctor at Villanova ran his fingers down my shins and felt three big lumps there, calcium deposits; the injuries were repairing themselves. A copy of the medical report was forwarded to the Irish medics who replied that the injury was one more commonly associated with a ballerina and quite unusual. An effing ballerina! He was trying to cover himself of course but I shouldn't have been running at all. I was the third fastest miler going into those Games and though they were held at altitude, I had reasonable expectations of getting a medal. In truth I wasn't fifty percent. I shouldn't have been there at all.

I encountered another problem in 1969 shortly after winning the AAAs. I asked the International Secretary if he could get me into races in Europe; there was three months between the AAAs and the European Championships in Athens. I needed the races. His answer to me was, 'what would they want you for?' Those were his exact words. Billy Morton got me into one race but I needed more so I went back to the States for the summer to work out and prepare. I flew directly from Philadelphia to Athens for the Championships.

I had a really hard race in the preliminary heat and |I needed a good blow-out. The problem was I hadn't raced in two months. Fair enough I finished 2nd to John Whetton and I had to settle for a silver medal. I set an Irish record in doing so but I didn't choke as people said. I was beaten By Whetton on the day and that was that.

Noel Carroll

It was really Noel who paved the way for me to go to Villanova. Ron Delany never came to track meets and it was only in the latter stages that he got involved. Ron was a great man to delegate and ask others to do things for him. Essentially he had no interest in giving back coaching wise and that was grand. He had a family to raise and other interests. Mind you it didn't do an athlete any harm to have Ron Delany in his corner but equally he made sure he got some recognition out of it. This is not a criticism of Ron, not at all. At times he tended to take more credit than he actually deserved.

I trained with Noel every day in College Park when I came home during the summer. He was graduating the year I was entering. We had great times.

Hall of fame 2014

In Mexico he pulled me away and told me my training wasn't right. Jumbo was down there; the team manager wouldn't listen and it looked like I was going to be sent home. I was doing a crash course all wrong. The team manager was trying to get in my head to tell me what to do. Noel was a very effective coach. When we were training, we'd run up to the line and from a standing start he used to time us. He believed in doing short distances flat out which suited me after a year in the States and enabled me to reach a second peak. We did these workouts on most days and people would come out to watch us.

Des McCormack provides a unique glimpse into college life with his best friend Murphy. "Frank got on with everybody and he was hugely popular with an array of Villanova athletes – basketball players, swimmers, footballers. They gravitated toward him. A lot of them wouldn't have known about his commitment to training because he tried to project himself as the Georgie Best of athletics. Best was becoming the international superstar.

I'm convinced Frank felt he could do the same in athletics and he cultivated this perception of himself as the talented athlete with a fondness for the booze and the bright lights even though he never had a problem with alcohol. Frank worked his arse off even as he was telling people, 'ah sure I don't care it doesn't matter.' He trained twice and sometimes three times a day. It was natural for him to nurture this image and it was no effort to maintain it. There was no deviousness or cuteness about it. People wanted to retain the playboy image of him; we all have a soft spot for the George Bests of this world. It's no surprise that Frank and Best would later become great friends.

For years I've been hearing that Frank didn't train hard enough, he didn't put it in, and he was a choker and couldn't cope with the big meet pressures. That's a load of nonsense. They got it all wrong about Frank. I'd say every athlete asks himself the question, did he get the most out of his talent, especially when his career has finished. I'll answer that for Frank. I think he got 99.9% out of it and that's a wonderful thing for any athlete. Given his circumstances he couldn't have done much more. After living with Frank for four years, I can safely say he left no stone unturned. Let me put it this way. If Coach Elliott was talking to you about Frank, he would tell you exactly the same, because if you weren't putting the work in, by Christ, Jumbo would be onto you."

Tom Donnelly, a teammate of Murphy's, remembers a very dedicated athlete. "He was very talented, but he was a hard worker. He may have given off this air of indifference but it was obvious to those who saw him train that he was willing to put the time and effort in. He was such a competitive athlete that he may well have over trained. It's a very fine line and injuries are hard to avoid. The regret is that injuries did come at key points of his career but even so he was a team guy for Villanova and his collegiate record speaks for itself."

It wasn't all plain sailing for Villanova's Irish athletes. Like many foreign athletes they got caught up in the feud between the AAU and the NCAA. In hindsight, the intensity between these two feuding bodies is scarcely credible, but the fear among athletes was very real. In February 1967, Ian Hamilton and Murphy were among the athletes barred from competing by the AAU after they appeared in the USTAFF meet in Madison Square Garden. The two Irishmen told the Associated Press: 'We were told by Mr. Elliott two hours before the meet that if we didn't run our scholarships would expire this summer.'

Murphy was unhappy about this threat and the fear of losing his scholarship. Jumbo was bluffing, of course, but the young athletes may not have fully understood the broader perspective. The federation did not seek an AAU sanction for its meet. International rules required that an athlete competing out of his country take part only in meets sanctioned or approved by the governing body of the nation he was in. Murphy and Hamilton appeared as guests at the next meet and watched their teammates compete. Murphy's unease was inevitable. In his experience with athletic bodies in Ireland he found that the needs of the athlete were scarcely considered. The power struggle for control of amateur sport in the USA mirrored the infamous split that existed in Irish athletics for far too long.

Murphy's athletic career came to an end just before 1976. It was the culmination of what he calls "a slow drift away from the sport. There was no structure in place in Ireland after I left college. You're trying to find a job with no one looking after you. I had gotten married and I had no money to show for all the running. I was trying to get a business career off the ground. I'd like to have extended my career at the 5000m distance. I had the strength and speed and the attributes necessary to make a right go of it but I had to accept the inevitable. I had a great career in spite of the injuries and setbacks. It was only in later years that I began to understand that I was part of the tapestry of the Irish tradition at Villanova, and I am very proud of that association and it is very satisfying to know that I might have inspired a few of those who followed on after my time there."

Murphy eventually settled into a varied but ultimately successful business career in Ireland. Murphy's charisma never faded; he retains his endless good humor, and he can still light up a room by his mere presence. He takes a good deal of slagging about his fashion sense, the silk shirts and the ties picked up in Milan. Invariably he is impeccably turned out, a class act in every sense of the word.

Editor's note: Frank never competed as a master but I have included this piece since Frank is such a significant part of the history of Villanova and Irish athletics. It adds a link to Noel Carroll, Eamonn Coghlan, Sonia O'Sullivan and Marcus O'Sullivan who are included in this or the next volume.

PADDY MURPHY
Date of Birth: 20/11/1944

You Are in the Army Now

By Michael Gygax

"Discipline is the soul of an army. It makes small numbers formidable; procures success to the weak, and esteem to all."
– George Washington

Paddy Murphy by his own admission had the perfect job for thirty-one years, a member of the army based in the Curragh close up to his home in Kildare town. He married young and shirred six children. Each morning he arrive for work at 9.00 am and were on the grass by 9.30 doing his morning run with the lads or more politically correct term, his colleagues. Commandant Hegarty was a key person behind the development of athletics in the army. He wanted to build up the army athletic team for national and international competition which became a viable alternative to the USA system and a complimentary outlet for the club system for young men who wanted to pursue an athletic career. Historically Ronnie Delany and Noel Carroll spent some time in the army.

After their morning training session the lads went to the gym and tidied up, before lunch and rested for a while before their afternoon run. They would usually run twenty miles per day; a routine he admits meant he was constantly tired. The lads were self-coached; one might imagine depended on a wing and a prayer, but there was some sense to their methods as lads adapted gradually to training and were not forced to do workloads their bodies were not ready for. All that said although they had access to hospital facilities, but physiotherapy and rehabilitation were practically non-existent. The lads did no stretching or weights, training consisted of running miles, sessions and hills.

This was in contrast to the American system which gobbled up vast numbers of Irish young athletes who were never heard of again, breaking down under the college regime which acted more like a murder machine than a carefully crafted theatre of development in an ideal world one would imagine it would be.

Paddy Murphy

Paddy's own son Niall Murphy held the Irish record for junior 3km and went to Providence College but fared poorly in the aforementioned environment. In paddy's words, "they ran the steam out of him" and he found it hard to adapt from a rural setting to a big metropolis. He now resides in the USA and runs a retail outlet and the family visits him regularly.

Paddy s father died at 37 years of age, when he was 14 years old and in order to help his mother left school and worked on a chicken farm for 3 or 4 years, starting at 8.00 am and finishing at 6.00 pm. He progressed from there to working in a factory making wallpaper, a job that entailed working a machine. When he got an opportunity to do the overtime he jumped at the it as money was scarce. He got married at twenty two years of age and it was his neighbours the Morrissey's were constantly at him to go running, so he joined Kildare athletic club and started, usually at night after a day's work. At first he did not show any great promise but enjoyed the buzz.

He joined the army in 1974 at 28 years of age, not to improve his running but because it was a better job than he was in. He landed on his feet, so to speak, as his running career took off. He was now being paid to something that was essentially his hobby. He did not have to do overseas duty but did race overseas for the army in inter army games, an annual event he greatly enjoyed. He cites the North Africans as being particularly strong in these competitions. To qualify for the team it was a simple enough process, finish in the top six in the army cross country, a race Paddy won many times.

Paddy Murphy

The army traditionally have three a number of avenues to compete, army games, national championships, business houses athletic association, open races and of course masters nationally and internationally. Paddy won the national 10km on the track and was runner up on a couple of occasions in the 5km. He enjoyed competing with the army team in the business houses athletic association and with Jim McGlynn, Herbie McElland and Brendan Downey were a formable crew, very difficult to beat. In 1984 when Paddy hit his fortieth birthday the army decided to support him, sending him to the world masters championships in California. He was in superb form and won the v 40, marathon in a time of 2.21.

Masters competition in 1984 was in its infancy, weighing nine stone, Paddy was in the shape of his life. The *Irish Runner*, like masters athletics, was in its infancy, Paddy Murphy's photo winning the marathon appeared on the first cover of the magazine, a news read which has endured. There are a number of strategies to becoming a good miler, one being off a strong distance base, another mixing strength and endurance weights and circuits with speed sessions and lower mileage. Pat Murphy was a high mileage man and one of his comrades and stable mates were Brendan Downey was a proficient miler. He ran four minutes flat for a mile, and in the late seventies finished third behind Eamonn Coghlan and John Treacy in the national 1,500. He made the world cross country on a number of occasions and won television sets and other prizes in races in the seventies the length and breadth of the country. Jim McGlynn, another athlete with a good pedigree, won the Glasgow marathon, ran 47 minutes for ten mile and just fell short of making the marathon team (European trials) in the trials in Limerick 1982, he stormed into the lead with only a few miles to go, but the wily Dick Hooper caught him and the wheels came off Jim's bus. In all the proceeding races Jim had beaten Dick with consummate ease. Jim McGlynn raced well in his forties; an event to remember was him winning the national masters cross country. Jim suffered a severe stroke in his late fifties and spent over half a year in hospital. He lost a lot of his memory. He is now recovering and when Pat Murphy heard this news he set about to contact him. Before he made got in touch Jim himself drove down to meet Pat, who was delighted to see that he was on the mend and appeared in better shape than he imagined.

The general consensus is the army served many of the soldiers well in terms of athletic development, but it lacked a structure and long term vision. The lads were generally left to their own device and they made the most of limited resources. Most soldiers who were interested in athletics had to do it in their own time. Historically, The Curragh had one of the first rudimentary indoor tracks in the country but it was burnt down in the late seventies and was replaced by a gymnasium Pat and his comrades trained out of there for three decades.

Many a Derby winner ran around the Curragh and Paddy thought he might qualify for the Olympics or win a national marathon but his ambitions were thwarted by Paddy and Dick Hooper in the trials in 1979 and he felt that third place in the trials for Los Angeles behind Jerry Kiernan and Dick Hooper but the selectors picked an unknown quantity over the distance, John Treacy. His silver medal in those games silenced his critics and left Paddy Murphy with no complaints.

Achievements

5km 14.00.3

10km 29.17

1500 3.54

1/2 marathon 63.54

Marathon 2.16.48

3km 8.15 cork

National masters title

Clonliffe 20 1.37 approx. Following wind

Silver 5km

National 10 km champion

1984....2.21.48 California. Sandino

1985 5km 10km silver. Rome

TONY MURPHY

Date of Birth: 8/7/1942

You Will Be Okay Son

"Running has been good to me and if I had it all to do again I wouldn't change anything. I made so many friends and enjoyed myself so much."

My participation in athletics started in an almost flukey sort of way and was most fortuitous in many ways. In 1958 while I was still a member of the Boy Scouts my troop had their annual camp on the McCalmont estate in County Kilkenny, near Thomastown, now better known as the famous Mount Juliet Golf Course. One of our daily activities was a swim in the local river, however, on one day the river was rather swollen and for safety reasons we were not allowed to swim. Having made the journey to the swimming location, what do we do now? Someone made the decision to run back to the campsite and the brave Tony managed to make it back first although it was not a race as such. The next day we had a paper chase and I was sent off as the hare because of my exploits the previous day.

Not too long after the annual camp the annual scout sports were held in Santry Stadium and the leaders of my troop entered me for a mile race, again because of my exploits at annual camp, and I managed to finish 2nd with no training. Later that year through the winter there were a few cross-country races organised by Ignatius O'Brien, The scoutmaster with the Synge Street Troop and again I was entered by the leaders of my troop, mind you I had fancied being another Ronnie Delany and I had listened on the radio to the commentary by Liam Brown on the famous mile race at Santry Stadium in 1958 where the first five finishers broke 4 minutes and Herb Elliot had set a new world record but I had done nothing about it.

I now had a little incentive and got another pal in the scouts to start doing an occasional training run with me, I put in reasonable performances in the races mentioned and Ignatius O'Brien must have spotted some degree of talent because he got me to join Donore Harriers during the summer of 1959, when they used Irishtown stadium for summer training, the track at Irishtown was the same as the track at Santry but was rarely used. This was a fairly handy location for me because I lived in Donnybrook at the time. I could have been joining any club, I knew nothing about Donore or where they were located or what sort of club they were. However, I became an active member and started attending training sessions at the clubhouse at Island Bridge and progressed fairly rapidly through the ranks.

The following year, 1960, as part of the Donore team we won the AAU novice cross-country championship, then in early 1961 the AAU junior (grade) CC Championship, we should also have won the all-Ireland junior but some of the team ran without shoes on a very difficult course at Dundonald, outside Belfast, and we were beaten. However, we made up for it in 1962, winning on the Phoenix Park racecourse. That same year Brendan Dunne and myself were selected on the first ever Irish team to compete in the under 20 International cross-country championship in Sheffield in England, it was only the 2nd year of the under 20 championship. I also finished 2nd in the under 20, 3 miles track champion ship that same year. On that day I had spent a long time before the race on "guard of honour" duty in O'Connell St. because it was the Patrician year and the Papal delegate was arriving in the city for the celebrations.

I have attached a chart outlining all my championship performances over the years, unfortunately I did not keep records of times etc., or paper cuttings, something I very much regret at this stage of my life. My best ever time was probably a 6 mile race I ran on the old cinder track in Santry in 28.46, probably worth at least a minute faster on today's tracks.

I had great success in open road races on an individual and team basis over the years all over the country, the most important and favourite of which was probably the Crusaders road race around Ballsbridge, Donnybrook, Clon-skeagh and Still organ road, because this was my first big open win and it was local to where I lived, it was also my most successful having won it in 1964, 1974 and 1979, and I also had a few 2nd's in it. I suppose championship victo-ries should top the list but I have to say I got great satisfaction from many other races depending on who you beat e.g., I know he won't like me saying this but I remember beating Paddy Smee of DCH in a track league over 400m hurdles, I think he had been the national champion and of course I was known as a middle and distance runner but I could hurdle because I was a steeple chaser. I think he probably underestimated what I might have been capable of but the last few yards were excruciating hanging on for victory.

Tony Murphy

The biggest achievement for me and Donore Harriers was our 2nd place in the European Club Cross-country Championship in Arlon, Belgium in 1966, the first time any Irish club had taken part. Our team of Tom O'Riordan (5th), Jim McNamara (11th) and me (12th) were beaten by the top class English team Portsmouth Harriers made up of Tim Johnston, Martin Hyman and Bruce Tulloch. This was a European Championship but we never got a championship medal, which would have been silver, and that is obviously missing from my medal collection, another thing I regret.

Athletic activity, training, racing etc., took over a large part of my life and indeed a lot of my social activity was also tied up with the club and athletics in general. When I got married in 1969 and started our family I was very lucky I was able to continue my running career and over the years my wife and family travelled all over the country to races with me, something I think they all enjoyed and they got to places they might not otherwise have visited. It was probably hard on my wife because I was, thankfully, in full time employment with PMPA, and training every day after work, either at official club training sessions or on my own on other days when children needed putting to bed and bedtime stories etc., but my marriage was strong and survived and we are still together 45 years later.

Training was hard with a tough group of the best runners in the country all driving each other forward; it was almost as hard to win a Donore Harriers Cross-country championship as it was to win a national title. Training sessions ranged from long easy runs to interval sessions over all sorts of distances e.g., 12 interval miles, 40 interval 400's, and everything else in between, hill repetitions up and down Knockmaroon, something you couldn't do now because of traffic. Indeed I recall the very first twenty mile run I did with all the top guys in the club at the time, Bertie Messitt, Willie Dunne etc., while I was still very much a rookie. Needless to say I was dropped off the pace about half way, out around Leixlip, having started at the clubhouse at Island Bridge. I had to make my own way back via the Strawberry Beds and Phoenix Park and thought I'd never make it. When I got back everyone had gone home and Eddie Hogan was waiting for me in the lane and put his arm around me and said "you've made it son", and I did.

Over the years I have done many things in Donore Harriers. I took over from the renowned Eddie Hogan as club captain and coach, was active as a committee member and club official for many years culminating in becoming club President in 1983 following on another great club servant, Tommie Hayward. I am now a vice president, an honorary position conferred of people who have given outstanding service to the club.

I spent a few years in England where I also had reasonable success running with Ealing and Southall A/C. I lived for a short while in London where I worked with the AA and then moved to Basingstoke in Hampshire where the AA had moved their headquarters, I continued running with Ealing & Southall and also ran with Basingstoke A/C as a 2nd claim member. Indeed 2 of my children were born in England.

My international career did not result in anything worth reporting except for victory in one road race in 1972 in Alencon, France, although I remember beating Jim Hogan in the Rue De Pravo in Czechoslovakia in 1966 I think. First international appearance was as a junior in 1962 and last in a track international in Bielefeld in Germany against Germany and Romania in 1974.

Unfortunately, a pelvic injury just after I had won the national vets cross-country championship at Kilmacow in 1983 curtailed my career and I eventually gave up in 1988 having struggled to keep racing the way I used to with much reduced training in the intervening years.

Athletics was good to me, I would not change anything, and I made and have some great friends and as I said at the start, it was all down to a chance in joining Donore Harriers back in 1959.

PAT NAUGHTON
Date of Birth: 18/9/1932

Not a Care in the World

By Peter Gleeson

"I do not have a care in the world"

Patrick Naughton may by 82 next birthday, but he carries himself like a man half his age. He bounds up the steep stairs to our agreed meeting place, the newsroom of his local newspaper, *The Nenagh Guardian*.

Age has not lowered his centre of gravity. He is still tall and erect, un-bowed by his mature years; still looking every bit the 6 foot 1 inch lean, athletic frame he has always been.

But what else to expect from a man who has spent most of his life running, throwing and jumping; whose amazing athletics career did not reach its zenith until he was into his seventies, a decade when he bagged all his five European Masters Track and Field Championship medals. Like a good wine, Patrick has got better with age.

In fact, he considers his fifth Euro medal win, a bronze at the Outdoors Championships in Hungary in 2011 – his third Euro bronze for the event – as his sweetest, considering he was competing against "young fellas" in the Over 75 category. At the time he was just a month shy of his 79th birthday.

On top of all that, Patrick has previously won a silver medal in the outdoor championship in the pentathlon, and a bronze for the same event in an indoor championship. And that's only the international stuff.

On the home front, he has competed in every National Masters Track and Field Championships since he was 40. That's 42 years of consistent competing from which he has bagged a total of 272 national medals – "three quarters of them gold," he says.

For a man with fast twitch fiber muscles (running 11 seconds for the 100 metres in his prime), he travelled way outside his comfort zone during the first marathon craze in the 1980s, finishing a Dublin City Marathon in "a little over three hours", at the age of 45.

And then there were his days as a senior athlete when he won a total of ten national medals. He was also a member of the Nenagh Olympic Athletic Club men's 4 x 100 metre relay squad that broke the national record in the mid-1950s and a founder member of that club during that era.

Patrick, a multi-events specialist, won the National Decathlon titles in 1957, 1959 and 1960. "I was second in 1958. I was beaten by the Cork foot-baller Pat Moore who was a top-class sprinter," Patrick recalls.

His medal haul at national senior level also includes four for the 400 me-tres hurdles, a silver in 1959, and three bronze.

Patrick has been an athletics fanatic for most of his life, the flame sparked by the glittering athletics era into which he was born. He came into the world on September 18th 1932, just weeks after a fellow Nenagh man, Bob Tisdall, won gold in the Olympic 400 metres hurdles in Los Angeles. An Irish team member with Tisdall was Pat O'Callaghan, a Tipperary-based doctor who retained the hammer title he won in Amsterdam in 1928.

Twenty years earlier Johnny Hayes, whose parents were Nenagh emigrants, won the marathon while competing for the US at the London games (1908).

Pat Naughton

And then there was the big burly New York policeman Matt McGrath, born just outside Nenagh, who won the hammer event at the Stockholm games in 1912, and silver at the games in 1908 and 1924.

"We had a school teacher, Jim Madden, who used to fill us with stories about these great athletes that came from Nenagh and Tipperary. It really motivated me to start competing at running and jumping and throwing," says Patrick.

He recalls hithhiking as a teenager in 1950 with his friend Donal Murphy to nearby open sports events in places like Roscrea and Moneygall, winning medals at novice level. Sixty-three years later, he is still competing, and enjoying it now more than ever before.

"The only complaint I have is a bit of rheumatism in my neck, but my wife Joan says I have been complaining about that for the past 40 years. My approach to my ahtletics career from now on is a little bit like that of the recovering alcoholic – take each day as it comes.

I thought that when I got to 70 that the best of my career was over. But now, looking back on the past decade, I see that it was the greatest chapter of my sporting life when I won all my European medals."

By today's standards, Patrick's training methods may seem rudimentary, but they have certainly worked for him. "I love growing vegetables and I have always viewed the digging and lifting in the garden as my part of my weights and conditioning regime.

Sean and Pat Naugton kept indoor athletics on the map in Ireland – Nenagh Indoor running track

I never liked the cold, so over the winter months I do a lot of my training in the house. Every day I stand in the kitchen and go through the movements of throwing the shot or the javelin. I still do exercises in the house every night and morning, mostly for flexibility.

I have devised a running circuit around the kitchen, sitting room and the hall, which, done ten times, equates to 400 metres. You can do so much training without going out your front door, and still win medals at the highest level."

Patrick says that a well-balanced diet that he sticks to has paid dividends. And, he is also a great believer in the power of meditation – even though that's not the word he uses to describe his daily "Cut-out", which he has been practicing now for almost half a century. "I think we could take a leaf out of the book of some of our European partners and take a siesta," he says. "I was suffering from burnout in my early thirties. My father died suddenly in 1960, and being the eldest in the family, I took it very hard. I was also after doing many years of hard training and competing, much of it in the many open sports competitions that used to be held all over the country back then.

"I remember being on a lot of medication for lethargy and going to a woman doctor in Nenagh who said to me, 'Pat, all those tablets will kill you; you have to come off them'."

"She sat me down and got me to look out the window of her surgery into the distance. She told me to relax and to repeat to myself, 'I don't have a care in the world'. After a while doing this I could feel energy flowing into my system. So, every day at some stage, when I feel like it, I just cut out for a few minutes.

"For me, this has been a great practice prior to competition as it helps me to focus and to conserve energy for the task ahead. It really worked for me, too, when I was in hospital and awake getting two cataracts removed from my eyes and a hernia repaired. It took the fear away.

I often think that when I'm going to die I will be lying there relaxing saying to myself, ,I don't have a care in the world – being positive."

Life for Patrick has not just been all about athletics. A father of four and grandfather of six, he spent 20 years working with O'Dwyers Wholesalers in

Washington Street, Cork ("they sold everything from a needle to an anchor"), before returing to his native Nenagh at the age of 40 to work in the clothing and household retail store which his father co-founded in Pearse Street in 1930 – Gough O'Keeffe & Naughton's.

Along with his brother Sean (a superb sprinter in his day, and former national hurdles coach), and business partner David O'Keeffe, Patrick spear-headed the running of the store for four decades. He and Sean (80) only re-tired in November 2013 after deciding to close the business, which had long been an institution in Nenagh and North Tipperary.

In retirement now, he has plenty of time to prepare for the competitions ahead. Much of his days are spent training and tending to his small herd of cattle which graze on a farm he inherited from an uncle on the outskirts of the town ("The farming is more weight training").

And though he has lived more than his three score years and ten, Patrick has no plans to hang up his spikes. However, after badly injuring his collar-bone while doing bend sprints on the Nenagh Indoor track, he was gutted to miss the World Masters Indoor Championships in Budapest in March 2014.

"The first time I had any prolonged injury was last year [at 80] when I took a fall racing over hurdles and pulled my hamstring," says Patrick. "But a friend of mine Jack Powell [a vet in Nenagh who still practices even though he is now 100] told me I should stay competing until I win 300 national masters medals."

If Patrick is going to take this target seriously, then he still has some run-ning, jumping and throwing to do – and 28 more medals to win.

As he grows older, he enjoys the way life cycles along. He is full of pride that his own offpring pursued athletics. His son Joseph competed at interna-tional level at the decathlon and his grandson, also Joseph, is a national long jump champion and a Munster multi-events champion.

Masters athletics has been kind to Patrick, not least for the sport and ac-complishment. He first travelled abroad to compete at 45 and has since com-peted and toured in ten countries. He is hoping to see a few more before finally calling it a day.

Major Achievements
272 National Master Medals
National senior decathlete champion 3 times 1957/59/60
Second and third senior national 410 yard hurdles
10 senior national medals; 5 European championship medals
National Master Athlete of the year 2014
O/50 7 national titles same day [100m, 200m, high jump, long jump, shot, discus, javelin]
O/75 Silver medal pentathlon European Championships Slovenia

O /75 Bronze High Jump
O/80 Bronze Medal pentathlon San Sebastian
5th in world Games Pentathlon O/45 Gothenburg
Part of a 4 x100 meter Irish senior record team with Nenagh AC
Marathon O/ 45 3 hours 10 minutes

LIAM O'BRIEN
Date of Birth: 11/10/1954

The Flying Corkman

By David O Dwyer

*"That is what learning is. You suddenly understand some-
thing you've understood all your life, but in a new way."*
– Doris Lessing

Liam O'Brien as a man is in many ways defined by his athletics career. It is quite possible that he has never been flustered or stressed in his life. That is certainly the case when it comes to his athletics career. "Do enough to win" has been the guiding principle and with an envious list of titles and impressive times it is hard to argue with such an approach.

Liam has won a national medal of some description over a 30 year period from 1967 to 1997. His 11 national titles in the 3000m steeplechase is certainly one of the most under-rated achievements in Irish athletics. Most people would consider this to be a slight on their achievements, not getting the recognition they deserve. For Liam this is something he laughs off with a pithy comment about not wanting to be the centre of attention.

A lengthy career has meant that those 11 titles were won over 3 decades from the first in 1978 to the last in 1994. One of the standout features of that period was in the depth of talent in the steeplechase event in the country at the time. In fact Liam held the national record (8:27:27) for a period before one of his closest rivals, Brendan Quinn, bettered it with a time of 8:24.09 that still stands today.

Liam set that national record at the AAA championships on 24 June in Crystal Palace when qualifying for the Olympic Games in Los Angeles in 1984. The obvious next step for most athletes would be to map out a detailed training plan that would lead up to the heats of the 3000m steeplechase in Los Angeles. Running road races would not be part of most track athletes plans. However for Liam it wasn't quite like that. A mere 4 days later, after returning from London he was competing in the Ballycotton 5mile road race near his hometown of Midleton. He was after all the defending champion and was keen to win the 4 race series. This wasn't just a case of his commitment to the local run-

Liam O'Brien

ning scene. It was also a case of "this is what got me where I am so why change it?" The same can be said for the type of training that Liam undertook. Two sessions a week, 400s on a Tuesday, 1,000s on a Thursday plus hills on a Saturday with a long run on a Sunday was the staple diet. Not forgetting of course the Wednesday night club run that was meant to be a recovery but more often than not ended up as a time trial. His commitment to the local road running scene was not diluted by his Olympic experience. His first race back was the final race of the Ballycotton series in Shangarry, which he won by the way.

The Olympic experience didn't daunt Liam. He was literally able to treat the race just like any other he had toed the line in the past. He was scheduled to run in heat 3 of the steeplechase. Far from being overawed or intimidated by the experience he was able to stay focussed on the job in hand, which was trying to qualify from his heat. The call room may have been in the belly of the stadium but by keeping an ear cocked for the starting pistol of heat 2 he was able to determine what time he needed to run in order to qualify as a fastest loser. He ran 8:31 and duly qualified for the semi-final. The final was a step too far however and he bowed out with 8:34 in the semi-final.

Liam was in a minority in that Irish team in Los Angeles with regard to not having taken up the US scholarship route which had been well trodden by almost all of the top Irish middle distance runners of previous generations. Instead Liam attended to NCPE/Thomond College (Now UL) to train as a

Liam O'Brien

teacher. It was while in Limerick that Liam was exposed to a more regimented training regime and this helped him to made significant progress.

On completing his studies in 1977 Liam returned to Midleton, having first spent a 12 month stint in Bantry in West Cork his where he took up a teaching post in Midleton CBS until his retirement in 2010.

Los Angeles was not the only major championships that Liam competed in. He also competed in Rome in 1987 at the World Athletics Champion-ships. In total Liam won 33 official international caps, between 1977 and 1995 which puts him joint third on the all-time list of international caps. There is no doubt that Liam could and perhaps should have qualified for additional championships including the Olympic Games in Moscow in 1980 and Seoul in 1988. The absence of any real structures to help "home"-based athletes into top class international races in order to gain a qualifying time probably meant that Liam did miss out on these occasions.

Liam displayed a huge versatility as an athlete and this is shown by the number of races and titles that he has won from 400m hurdles up to the half marathon as well as numerous honours in cross country.

The lure of masters competitive athletics did not burn long with Liam but he did manage a significant victory in the US when he won the Crescent City Classic (CCC) 10k road race – masters section in a time of 30:51 in 1995. In very warm and humid conditions Liam led from start to finish with a 4:38 first mile. This is one of the longest running road races in the US and at the time this was a significant victory. Competitive masters athletics was not going to keep Liam for long and he retired from competitive racing in 1999.

Regrets?

For such a successful career there aren't too many regrets but one is definitely not having run a sub 4 minute mile. It was certainly within his ability but it just didn't happen.

Liam has continued his long association with the sport throughout his teaching career and beyond. While teaching at Midleton CBS Liam was instrumental in getting individuals and teams involved in the sport of athletics, particularly in cross country. Any past pupil will recall the 1000m time trials that they had to partake in as a fitness test in an attempt to unearth the next gem.

He is still actively involved in the administration of East Cork AC and has his long association with The Cork City Sports has come full circle and he has been the Meet Technical Director for a number of years.

Fifth in ten-part series highlighting the best Irish masters performances. In July 1995, 1984 Olympian Liam O'Brien ran an impressive 8.48.65 for 3000m steeplechase (M40-44) at the World Masters in Tailinn, Finland. This Irish masters record has stood for more than twenty years with no sign of being touched.

Liam O'Brien ran 8.48 for the steeplechase when he was over forty. This was the second best time in the world at the time and short of the world record held by Gaston Rolands from Belgium. 8.41

BERNIE O'CALLAGHAN
Date of Birth: 6/11/1945

Footsteps in the Sands of Time

By Patsy McGonagle and Michael Gygax

The word legend is often bandied around but it is the term which best describes Bernie O'Callaghan. He has been involved in athletics since the early 1950s, as an athlete, administrator, coach, author and statistician, and held the position of National Race Walking Coach from 1978 until 2007, and is credited with developing the event to the position that it now holds. A founder member of Donegal County Board he is a life Vice President of the County Board and President of the Ulster Athletics Council.

Leader of the Pack – Bernie leads the pack in a one mile race in Gormanston College in 1964

As a senior athlete he won seven National Senior individual titles and six team titles with Donegal, and held six national senior records. He won his first National senior medal in 1975 and his last in 2007. He was an Irish Senior International from 1978 until 1987, and was the first Irish walker to win at international level away from home when he won the 10,000m walk in Edinburgh International in 1981. He was the first Irishman appointed an IAAF International Race Walking Judge in 1994. He was selected on the County Donegal Athletics team of The Millennium in 2000 and inducted into the Ulster Athletics Hall of Fame in 2008.

His enthusiasm for athletics is still infectious and he has passed on his love of the sport to his family, He and his son Pierce are one of only eight father and sons in Irish athletics history to have both won Irish senior athletics titles. Pierce is the youngest person ever to have been elected to the BLE Management Committee and has worked as Director of Competition with Scottish Athletics and Director of Communications with the European Athletics Association and is currently an elected member of the EAA Competition Committee. He is an also an IAAF International Race Walking Judge and has been a judge at the Olympics in Beijing and London as has been appointed to judge in Rio in 2016. Roisin, who died in 1997, was National Junior Indoor 1,5000m walking champion. Bee is currently the Anti-Doping Coordinator with the International Paralympic Association based in Germany and Bee was also a consistent medallist in All Ireland Juvenile walking events daughter Siobhan won the novice title at the Dublin International Grand Prix of Race Walking and was Kildare Senior race Walking Champion on several occasions. Fionnuala represented Meath at the National Community Games finals and also walked for her School in both Leinster and All Ireland schools Championships. Pierce is currently based in Baku Azerbaijan and employed as a consultant by the Azerbaijan Government to help them host the first European Olympic Games which take place in June 2015.

Bernie has also been prominent in the administration of Irish Athletics at National level over the years, having been elected to the Board of Athletics Ireland in 2002 and also served for many years on the BLE/AAI Juvenile Committee, Coaching Committee and Competition Committees, elected to the BLE Senior Activities Committee in 1977 and held the position of International Secretary of the Irish Masters Athletics Association for six years.

He has managed and coached many Irish teams at European and World Race Walking Cup and was Irish Endurance Coach at two World Track and Field Championships in Edmonton in 2001 and in Paris in 2003 and at CISM (World Military Sports Council) cross-country championships in Pensacola, Florida in 1982, Fermoy in 1979 and the Curragh in 1994 and track and field championships in Warrendorf, Germany in 1987. He was elected to the CISM Technical Committee in 1982 at the Cross-Country Championships in Pensacola, and awarded the CISM Medal of Honour in 1994.

Bernie won the Javelin in the first Donegal Senior track and Field Championships in 1970 and while he was based in the Army won Meath and Kildare senior titles and since his return to Donegal in 1997 has continued to compete at senior level and is the County Senior Champion in the Javelin and 1,500m walk in 2013. In recent years he has also excelled in Masters athletics and has won medals at European level in the 3,000m walk, and 5km walk, and World medals in the 10Km walk and 20Km walk and UK medals in Indoor 3,000m, and outdoor 10,000m

He is the author of two books, *A Chronicle of the Ordnance Corps During The Emergency* and *Footsteps in the Sands of Time*, a very detailed twelve hundred page history of Donegal and Ulster athletics during the period from 1969 to 2009.

In 1992 Bernie founded the Dublin international Grand Prix of Race Walking, which attracted athletes from all five continents and regularly had walkers from as many as forty countries taking part each year and was ranked at number two Grand Prix in Europe by the European Athletics Association in 2001. Pierce and Bernie organised the event together after 2000 and many athletes achieved their Olympic qualifying standards in the Phoenix Park, and Nathan Deakes of Australian set a World Record for 50km there in 2004.

As well as athletics Bernie has also excelled in other sports and has represented Ireland in Sea Angling and was a member of the Irish European Shore Angling Championship winning team in 1963 and played hurling for Donegal from 1975 to 1987, he won a Donegal Senior Hurling Championship in 1964 with Erne Valley, an amalgamation of Killybegs and Ballyshan-

Bernie and Pierce in Santry after Pierce's victory in the BLE senior 10,000m walk

non Hurling Clubs and also won Hurling Championships with Donaghmore in Meath in 1974 and 1976.

Bernie and his family have also experienced great sadness in their lives with the death of their beloved daughter Roisin at age eighteen in 1997. Some people in such circumstances are overcome by sadness while others manage to rise above their grief and become agents of change and self-fulfilment, strive to make a difference because of or in spite of their own personal struggles. Bernie O'Callaghan coach, athlete, manager, administrator and writer is such a man.

When he retired from the army in 1997 he was appointed as the first Sports Development Officer for Donegal in a Joint Peace initiative with Northern Ireland called Youth Sport Foyle and he moved back home where he could recharge old batteries with family and lifelong friends, people who understand him best. The project became an instant success powered by Bernie's knowledge and enthusiasm so much so that it won the Laureus Sport for Good Award from the World Academy of Sport and received funding of over €500,000 over the next three years. It is interesting to read the citation that accompanied the award. "Youth Sport Foyle has proved very successful at bringing young people from diverse religious and political backgrounds together. It should be used as a template in other war torn regions of the world."

As a result of this success Bernie and Aileen McGlynn, his opposite number in Derry, were invited to Aras An Uachtrán to meet President Mary McAleese and they were subsequently invited, as the keynote speakers, at a major Conference entitled Peace Through Sport in Ein Gedi in Israel. As a result of this conference which had delegates from all over the World. Bernie proposed that a group of athletes from Israel and Palestine be invited to Ireland to live and work together and be trained as soccer coaches. In all twenty coaches came, ten from each side spent almost a month in Donegal and received their coaching badges at the farewell dinner in Jackson's Hotel, Ballybofey. On their last day in Donegal they played a soccer match against a Youth Sport Foyle team the game billed as The Middle East v Ireland and was played in Finn Park, Ballybofey. To see both Palestinians and Israelis playing together in a team was an inspirational sight for all who were privileged to witness it. The final score was Middle East 2, Ireland 1. In a few short years Bernie had gone from being a UN Peacekeeper in the Middle East to become a catalyst to bring the two sides together rather than keeping them apart in the Lebanon.

While he was with Youth Sport Foyle the project was visited by committee members of the World Academy of Sport including its Chairman Olympic Legend Ed Moses and Olympic Champion Sebastian Coe, World Cup Winner and former European Footballer of the Year Bobby Charlton, English cricket legend Ian Botham, Indian cricket 1983 World Cup winning Captain Kapil Dev and former wheelchair Olympic champion Tanni Grey Thompson.

Patsy McGonagle has known the real Bernie O'Callaghan, the highs and heartbreak, as they have shared a lifetime in athletics together. They first met on September 1969 when they were both on their first day teaching in Glenties Comprehensive School they formed an instant rappor through their mutual interest in athletics Patsy newly married had just returned to Donegal after studying in St Marys College Strawberry Hill while Bernie was returning after three years teaching in Dublin they struck up an instant friendship that has endured through the intervening years.

When I speak to Bernie about Patsy, the tone softens to that of a blood brother; a deep affection resonates in his voice. Bernie, a passionate man, is driven by love of his children, sport, friends, family and Donegal the earth mother. These inspire him to excel in many spheres of life, despite of or maybe because of his life experiences, which has morphed into a mutual understanding, and an appreciation of life that only deep friendships can generate.

The name of Olive Loughnane is familiar to everyone, a silver medallist, (now upgraded to Gold following the disqualification of the Russian winner for a doping offence) at the world senior championships in Berlin 2009, For Bernie her career has certain poignancy. His daughter Roisin had beaten Olive in the BLE Junior Indoor 3,000m walk in 1995 when she was just 16. Roisin seemed to be on a cusp of a wave of athletic excellence also winning silver medals in the AAA track championships in Birmingham and in the Road Championships in Sutton Coldfield, and silver in the Tailteann Games a position which in later years would have earned her selection for the Schools International, some highlights in an all too short life.

Today, Bernie is Station Manager of South West Donegal Community Radio which is based in Killybegs. He anchors a three hour Breakfast Show three times per week. He also makes the seventy mile round journey to Ballybofey, where he is the Finn Valley AC Javelin and Walks coach, three times every week, as does his wife Mary who coaches sprints, hurdles and relays. He is getting back to training again, as he approaches his seventhieth birthday, so he will compete in major championships once again in the future. But a day does not go by when Roisin and his other children are not in the forefront of his mind.

National Senior Championships

3000m walk winner 1979, 1980, 1981 bronze 1982, 1983, 1987, 1988, 1989
10000m walk winner 1980, 1981, bronze 1987
20km walk winners 1980, 1981 bronze 1977
20km walk team winners with Donegal 1999, 2000, 2001

Five National Senior Records

3000m walk 12.54.20 Army Championships Curragh June 1980
3,000m walk 12.41.7 Belfield June 1981
10000m walk 46.24.20 Army Championships Belfield May 1981
10000m walk 46.23.00 National Senior Championships Santry May 1981
10,000m walk 45.29.4 Belfield May 1982

National Senior Relays

2 x Javelin silver with St Andrew's AC in 1975
3 x 1600m inter-county walk winner with Donegal 1999, 2000, bronze 2001, 2002, and 2004
3 x1000m indoor inter-county relay winner with Donegal 2000, 2001 silver 2002, 2003, 2004,

BLE/AAI Masters Championships

5000m walk winner 1985, 1986, 1987, 1988, 1989, 1990,
3,000m walk winner 1987, 1988, 1989, 1990,
Javelin winner 1986, 1987, 1988, 1989, 1990, 1991, 1992, 1994, 1995
10km run team winners with Donegal 2003

UK Masters Championships

3000m walk winner O/45 in 1994, O/50 1995, silver 1996, 1997
5000m walk silver O/55 2001
10000m walk winner O/55 2001

European Masters Championships

3000m indoor walk bronze in Birmingham 1997
5000m team walk silver O/65 with Ireland in Ghent 2012

World Masters Championships

20km team walk bronze O/50 with Ireland in Gateshead 1999
20km team walk bronze O/55 with Ireland in Brisbane 2001
10km team walk bronze O/55 with Ireland in Riccione 2002

FLOR O'LEARY
Date of Birth: 15/1/1934

St Finbarr's A.C., My Spiritual Home
By John Walshe and Fergus O Donovan

"Keep it going as long as you can"

Flor O'Leary was just twenty years old in 1954, the year that Roger Bannister broke the four-minute-mile barrier. Sixty years on, the man from the Mayfield area of Cork City is still setting records and is himself somewhat of a barrier breaker as well.

In the year of 1994, on a windy March Sunday in Ballycotton, Flor ran 10 miles inside sixty minutes at sixty years of age.

"It was the previous April, on the way home from a race in Dungarvan, that I first mentioned my hopes of achieving the feat the following year," he recalls.

"I trained away and raced as usual during the summer of 1993 and around Christmas time I started to think about Ballycotton, although I didn't tell anyone about it.

"I used to train on the track at UCC on Tuesday nights with Pat O'Neill and Liam O'Leary where we did sessions like 10 x 600m and then we would do hills on a Thursday night. When we were doing the hillwork, I always thought of the hill at eight-and-a-half miles at Ballycotton."

Flor ran a couple of cross-country races and one four-miler before the big day. Conditions at Ballycotton that year weren't the best, as he describes: "There was a gale there that day; it was against us for the first five miles. My first mile was 5:35, which was a bit too fast and I was well under 18 minutes at the three miles.

"I reached the five-mile mark in 30 minutes even – wind-blown but relaxed – and still confident I could break 60 minutes. Shortly after, Willie O'Riordan joined me and we ran together until nine miles. Head down at the hill, short strides to keep up the painful effort. Thank God the hill is over and only one mile to go.

"I could see the 400 metres to go sign and I thought of 400m repetitions at UCC. I just wanted to finish at that stage, someone passed me a few yards out but I couldn't do a bit about it. I saw 59 on the clock and I knew I had broken the hour."

Flor's time that day was 59:15 and he finished 117th overall out of the 1,020 finishers. Later in the same year of 1994 he ran 2:48:48 in the Dublin Marathon for another Irish age best.

Remarkably, twenty years on, he is still rewriting the record books. Having turned 80 in the middle of January 2014, over a period of seven days Flor lowered three Irish indoor records by more than 25% in each case.

He set new marks of 40.65 for 200m and 3:43.23 for 800m at the Munster Championships in Nenagh and then the following week establish a new M80 record of 7:25.04 for the 1500m at Athlone, a massive two-and-a-half minutes faster than the previous best.

Like most Cork youngsters, the first sport Flor dabbled in was hurling. "I started athletics around 1956, at that time it would be mainly track and I ran everything from the sprints up as there were very few road races."

Despite the lack of races on the tarmac, it didn't stop him from having a distinguished record over the marathon distance. Along with that 2:48 at 60, he also had a first, a second, a third and a fourth in the Munster Marathons of the 1960s and 70s.

"I don't have much idea of the times I did," he modestly states before producing a certificate from a file which reads: 'Flor O'Leary of St Finbarr's finished second in a time of 2:25:27 at the Munster Marathon, 1971.'

"I was mixing all the distances; I even made the St Finbarr's relay team a couple of times in the 4 x 200m and 4 x 400m. I suppose I never really trained for the marathon – although I would do a few 20 milers at the weekends – and I always felt the shorter stuff helped me. Speed work will never hinder you."

A proud 'Barrs man all his life, Flor has served the club well, both as a competitor and as an administration where he has held the posts of treasurer and president. He is also a true athletics fan, one of the many events attended being the Commonwealth Games when they took place in Edinburgh in 1970.

There he witnessed some famous victories from the likes of Ron Hill, Ian Stewart and Lachie Stewart – the latter defeating Flor's hero, multi-record holder Ron Clarke. "They were something else, those games. Myself and Jack [O'Leary – no relation] and our wives went over, as did Fergus O'Donovan from the club."

Flor O'Leary

"I also saw Peter Snell running at Santry, but I missed the night that Herb Elliot broke the world mile record as we were on holiday in Butlin's at the time and had no way of getting into Dublin."

And now, having reached another milestone, Flor O'Leary is still looking forward. "I know I can improve on my M80 1500m record outdoors, I felt I should have ran faster indoors but I didn't have the confidence as I was after having a disastrous 12 months with injury."

And his advice to anyone contemplating retiring from the sport at 50 or 60? "Keep it going if you can at all, for your own health's sake and everybody else's health's sake!"

Fergus O'Donovan on the History of St. Finbarr's

St Finbarr's Athletic Club, founded in 1951, was only a pup when Flor O'Leary joined it in his early twenties. The competitive year consisted of the summer track and field season(end May to end August), with novice and open sports almost every Sunday, and the winter cross-country season i with county novice, junior (now called intermediate) and senior championship races. The faster runners might go on to provincial and Irish championships level. The only road races were the Irish Marathon Championships and an occasional four-mile race before a sports such as at Ballyhooley.

Novice sports days were intended for beginners and once an athlete had won six events, they were promoted to the open ranks. Typically, there were at least two sprints, two middle distance, two jumps and and throw with first and second prizes at each meeting. The programme would also include or four grass track cycle races and a single column report would appear in the *Cork Examiner* the day after. Novice County Championship (measured in yards) meeting and "farmed out" championships at metric distances were also held. The sports, held on grass tracks of varying standards, were very popular and attracted large entries.

Among the venues for Novice Sports were Minane Bridge, Rising Sun, Caharagh, Aughadown, Leap, Aghina, Nadd, Ballyclough, Glenville, and Montenotte. Non- championship events were run off with some ad hoc handicapping. Local sports committees organised the meetings with Cork County Board approval. A novice athlete started at the handicap limit (100yds for the one-mile, 50yds for the 880yds, 40yds the 440yds, 20yds the 220yds and 6yds for the 100yds) with similar limits in the field events. When you won a race, your handicap was reduced (15yds in mile,7.5 tds in 880yds etc) and half of that for a second place. If you had won an Irish Championship race, you started off scratch. Although handicaps gave the beginner a gradual introduction to higher standard competition, it was difficult to catch even newcomers at the limit and finishing times were never for the full distance. Because winning off scratch was almost impossible, sports committees who wanted the prestige of an Irish champion competing would put on "Short limit" events, where the limit was halved.

The 'Barrs committee of the 50s organised and motivated their athletes effectively. Because few club members had cars, lifts in hackney cars from the Woodford Bournes corner were arranged so that athletes could get to their competitions. The August bank holiday weekend was a particularly busy one with novice meetings at Nadd, Leap and Glenville and the 'Barrs "mentors" doing their best to a car load to each.

Coaching was athlete-to-athlete irrespective of club – training schedules and experiences were shared. In the mid-1950s, Roger Banister's sub-four minute mile had us reading Franz Stampfl 's book *On Running* and adding interval training to our schedules. Herb Elliott's 1500m victory at the 1960 Rome Olympics where he bettered his own world record with a time of 3:35.6, led us to sand hill running a la Percy Cerutty, while the successes of Peter Snell over 800m and Murray Halberg at 5000m meant that Arthur Lydiard's 100-miles a week programme of training becoming the aspiration. The earliest formal coaching courses were at the summer school of athletics in Loughborough, England and were attended by Larry O'Donnell and Pat Naughton of St Finbarr's and Fr Nessan of Hilltown (later Leevale).

In the mid-1950s, track suits, spikes or road training shoes were not available, even in Elverys, then Cork's only sports shop. Tennis shoes (rubber dollies) were worn for warming up and road training, which itself was not that widespread. The logic of keeping the legs warm was immediately obvious to me and the first "track suit" was usually an old pair of grey flannel pants with a piece of cord threaded through the turn-ups.

The first St. Finbarr's member to win an Irish title was Charlie Vaughan who, after a silver in the 60yds in 1954 and bronze in the 220yds a year later, won the 440yds in 1957 and again in 1958. That was the beginning of a "dynasty" of 'Barrs men (sometimes in UCC singlets) who won Irish 440yds medals: Jim McKenna (UCC), gold, 1959; Cashel Riordan (UCC), gold, 1961 and 1962; Martin Lynch, bronze, 1963; Gerry Murphy, bronze, 1965; and Mick Dooley, bronze, 1966.

Although Charlie Vaughan was the first 'Barr's Irish champion, Sean Dobbyn was the first Irish champion to become a Barr's man which he did in 1953. Before joining the club, he has won five gold (440yds, 1948, 880yds and 1 mile, 1951, 880yds, 1952 and 1500m) and at least two silver (880yds, 1949 and 1950) medals while running for Ballincollig.

In the early days of the club, three associations governed athletics in Ireland. The National Athletics and Cycling Association of Ireland looked after the sport in all the 32 counties of the island but was excluded from international competition after 1934 for political reasons. Although it had only about six affiliated clubs, all of them in Dublin, the Amateur Athletic Union was recognised internationally. Athletics in the Six Counties was administered by the Northern Ireland Amateur Athletic Union, which was affiliated to the Amateur Athletics Association in Great Britain.

Because St Finbarr's was an NACAI club, any athlete aspiring to international competition was forced to join an AAU club in Dublin, so foregoing local competition. Not until 1967 and the foundation of Bord Luthchleas na hEireann as the ruling body for the sport did this situation change.

In Cork in the early 1960, road relays were added to the winter season programme, with one and two miles legs at races held in in Blarney, the Lough (organised by St Finbarr's) and Farrenlea Road, where UCC were the organisers. St Finbarrs did very well in these relay races, with teams of mostly middle distance runners. This lead to longer four mile to seven mile races which saw runners such as Barry O'Gorman, Liam and Finny Long, and John Buckley coming to the fore, both on the track and on the roads. Other fixtures intorduced at the time included the Cork to Cobh 15-mile and indoors athletics at the Curragh.

At the Irish Marathon Championships of 1966, which finished during the Irish Track and Field Championships in Banteer Stadium, Jack O'Leary was second on 2 hrs 26 mins and Fergus O'Donovan 17th in 3hrs 2mins. A year later, O'Leary finished third in the first BLE-organised National Marathon, held in Dublin. In 1969, Denis Quinlan was second behind Oughterard's

Mick Molloy in the BLE Marathon from Thurles-to Cashel. Although he was not allowed to score, the St Finbarr's trio of Jack and Flor O'Leary and Fergus O'Donovan finished first team.

Len Braham was one of the most enduring and talented St Finbarr's athlete winning discus, hammer, and 56lbs for distance titles in 1973 as well as a second place in the 56lbs for height. He would win five national discus titles between 1872 and 1977, and other titles in the 56lbs events for distance and height, as well as the hammer, with his last outing coming in 1985.

With the athletic landscape continuously evolving and changing, St Finbarr's is experience an influx of members who love to run and socialise thanks to the recreational running boom. St Finbarr's, one of the oldest clubs in the country, has seen many changes and has endured because it provides competition, friendship and spiritual nourishment to members and friends regardless of ability.

JEAN O'NEILL

Date of Birth: 18/2/46

My Running Life: Orienteering, Veteran Athletics, Mountain Running

"Experience is not what happens to you; it's what you do with what happes to you" – Aldous Huxley

Jean Dowling-O'Neill has had the best of times and the worst of times. Born February 1946, she lived in a patriarchal world, where young "ladies" were expected to be seen and not heard.

She kept her head down – studying, learning music and dancing, and keeping active through the Girl Guide and sport. She got on with her life, never conventional, and paying little attention to what people might think or say about her.

Jean's sporting career had started at school, where she played netball and hockey. As a winger in hockey, she was so fast that, later on, when playing club matches, she was often pulled up for off-side.

At the age of twelve, she had joined the Irish Girl Guides following her older sisters Claire and Anne. She was keen Guide, earning lots of badges. She loved the regular hikes which included lighting fires and cooking a meal outdoors and the annual camps, usually in Ireland, though on one occasion they travelled by ferry to Wales. In 1962, Jean was part of a group of thirteen guides and two leaders joining around 13,000 others from all over the world at an International Jamboree in Denmark. There were other trips – all overland – to Belgium and to Our Chalet, an international Guide house in Switzerland. Jean went to become a Girl Guide Captain and would continue guiding until well into her adult life.

At school, Jean couldn't wait for 4.00 pm when there was an hour of sport every day, plus a match on Saturdays. Add to that orchestra practice twice a week and piano lessons as well as her Girl Guides and it was a busy life.

Jean recalls those hectic early days: "In April 1964, my older sister Claire Dowling – now Walsh – asked me to come with her to 'the stadium' on a Saturday morning. I didn't know what I was going to-the only stadium that I knew of was Harold's Cross Greyhound Stadium, visible from the bus on trips into Dublin's city centre.

"As it turned out, she was taking me me to a women's athletic match at Santry, where she was competing. Claire and about fifteen other women had been training at Santry since the previous October when Billy Morton held a meeting at Moran's Hotel to discuss setting up Ireland's first women's athletics club. I was enthralled by the girls I saw running, jumping and throwing and joined Clonliffe Harriers the following day.

"So started my running life. I was aged 18, and had left school the previous summer. There was no athletics for girls then; our school sports (if there were any) consisted of dribbling a hockey ball slalom-style, or throwing a netball around a circle of girls, piggy-in-the-middle. We played both hockey and netball and I loved both. Our games uniform was a school shirt-style blouse and a divided skirt which had to be no more than two inches above the knee.

"I began going to Santry for training with the late Harry Cooney and Noel O'Rourke two or three times a week. We did everything – running, throwing, hurdles. It was impossible to find running clothes, so we made our own shorts from a pattern, with a zip on the side. Baggy tracksuits could be tracked down though, for a long time, I wore a long jumper and pulled it over my knees when I sat down. Spiked shoes in our sizes were also a problem. Later, we bought 'knicker shorts' by mail from England after we saw them advertised in *Athletics Weekly*; I still have those shorts. In those days, women did not wear trousers; skirts or dresses were the norm. The Catholic Archbishop of Dublin at the time was John Charles McQuaid, an austere man who disapproved of men and women mixing at sporting events and whose dictats ruled our lives.

"During the next few years, I progressed from 100 to 220 yards, then to 440 yards. I ran in Irish Championships, graded meetings and lots of open sports, including trips to Northern Ireland where I competed against Maeve Kyle and Noeleen McGarvey. My times were mediocre: under 13 seconds for 100 yards, later under 14 for 100m; about 26/27 seconds for 200m, and 60 or 61 seconds for 400m. In the few 800m I competed in my times were in the 2 minute 20 second range. In 1968, I got married and had my daughter, and got back running quite quickly.

"In the summer of 1970, my times came down every time I competed; I put this down to the hormonal benefit of giving birth. My personal bests dropped to 12.3 secs for 100m, 25.5 secs for 200m, 57.1 secs for 400m and 2 mins 9.9 secs for 800m. That time for 800m came in Belgium where I was running as part of an Aer Lingus team. The 800m was run on a cinder track and I came second to the Belgian record holder, Francine Peskyens, who had to break her own record to win, after overtaking the Dutch record holder, Elly Ernst, on the finishing straight. My performance meant that over the next few years, I was invited to compete at several meets in Belgium and made the Irish team.

"In 1970, Clonliffe Ladies decided to enter a 4×400m team in the WAAA Championships, which were held in Crystal Palace. On the team were my sister Claire, Padraigin O'Dwyer, Ann O'Brien and me. For Paid and me, it would be the first time to run on a tartan track. We felt we could do well, but never believed that we would come second in an Irish record time of 3:45.8 which lasted for several years. We were very excited!

"In 1971, the WAAA Championships were in Birmingham and, this time, we won the 4×400m in 3:49.1. We also won the 4×800m in 8:48.8 on a different weekend, with Jean Appleby running instead of Padraigin. In 1972, the team of Paid, Jean, Claire and me came second in the 4 x400m and third in the medley relay – 2×200m, 1 x400m, 1x 800m. My late husband, Brian, had arranged sponsorship for the team and travelled as our team manager. Unfortunately, he was detained by immigration at Birmingham Airport and we had to travel on alone. We found him after the race lying exhausted beside the track under a tree!

"These were golden years for me. After my second baby in 1973, I was troubled by injury when I attempted to compete. Finally in 1978, I equalled my best time of 57.1 seconds for 400m, and was again selected for an Irish team.

"In winter, I still played hockey, so did not do much cross-country running. I didn't really enjoy it, though I loved the freedom of running in the grass and muck. The races were usually held in the fields behind Santry stadium. Afterwards, we would fetch basins of water from the boiler room in the nissen hut where the men had their changing rooms (ours was a sort of lean-to under the concrete stand; no running water) and washed ourselves followed by our shoes!"

Jean O'Neill

She remembers the great Billy Morton, who founded Santry Stadium. "Billy Morton gave us great encouragement. During big track meetings in the summer, he armed us with collection buckets to help defray the stadium's debts."

Jean worked in various jobs before forming her own company in 1980 when the family returned to Dublin after spending time in Lesotho where her husband Brian was working for Aer Lingus. While in Lesotho, she ran an international company with two other women and continued her involvement in guiding; her daughter Deirdre enrolled there.

When her involvement in guiding petered out, she became increasingly involved in orienteering and discovered that she was in her element. "My involvement in the Irish girls guides introduced me to the sport of orienteering and in 1989, I joined Fingal Orienteers, which is based in Swords. Navigation skills as well as fitness are key attributes for the sport, which is held mostly in forests, open country and mountainside. Events may be as short as 1.5km or as long as 10km, with shorter sprint events usually taking place in parks and around suburban streets. Competitors pick up a map and set off individually, visiting a number of set "control" points on a course marked out on the map. At each control point, the orienteer "punches in" uses a timing device worn on the finger. Choosing the best and fastest route around a course is the object of the exercise.

"There are orienteering festivals all over the world. I often plan my holidays around these events and compete regularly in masters events; orienteering has become an important form of eco-tourism. To date, my highest placing was a fourth in the 2011 World Masters Sprint Championships held in Hungary and I am proud to have won multiple Irish titles as I move through the age groups."

Like many orienteers, including her daughter Deirdre, Jean took to mountain running through the annual IMRA summer evening league. "I went to look initially and then joined in and really enjoyed it. There is great variety of terrain, and while the uphills are a struggle, the downhills make up for all the effort, and I find it very thrilling."

Jean was lucky to be employed by Aer Lingus, with the perk of cheap staff airline fares. This has allowed her to travel to sporting events all over the globe. When she travels, she stays in hostels or camps, or with running friends and is always good for a stint at the piano, leading a late night sing-song. Her love of sport is equalled by her love of music – in her mid-40s, after six years of study, she gained performance and teaching diplomas in piano playing from the Royal Irish Academy, the Leinster of Music and the London College of Music.

In 1991, Jean was introduced to the world of masters' athletics by her Clonliffe club mate Pat Bonass who encouraged her to enter that year's European Championships in Turku, Finland. Since, she hadn't competed on the track in over ten years, she took a lot of encouraging but, once persuaded, started training for speed again and entered a 400m race at a Dublin Graded Meet about five weeks before travelling. The plan was to break 70 seconds for the distance, but unfortunately, she pulled her achilles tendon in the final 50m of the race. She didn't travel.

It would take another four years before she made her international debut at the World Masters in Buffalo, New York in 1995. By now she was just six months shy of her 50th birthday and at the top of her age class. Not at all deterred, she ran in both the 200m and 400m, making with 200m semi-finals in 31.01 secs and timed at 67.21 secs in the 400m. She also ran in the 4×400m as part of an Irish team.

A highlight of the trip was meeting Robert (Bobby) Charlton from Australia, a chiropractor who treated both Jean and Evelyn McNelis on their first day in Buffalo. Until his death in December 2012, the couple got together every year for months at a time, mostly in Australia. In 1997, they went to the World Masters Championships in Durban, South Africa, where Bobby got to know all the Irish, with his accent caused great hilarity. "One day when we were all on the beach, he remarked in his Australian accent: 'there are a lot of wives on the beach!' It took a few repetitions before we realised he was saying 'waves'."

Again she had signed up for the 200m and 400m this time in the W50 age group. In the 200m, her time of 30.38 secs was an Irish record. In the 400m, she was in medal contention but ran out of steam and came 4th in 67.99 secs. At the 1996 European Championships in Malmo, Sweden,

Jean had also came fourth in the 800m in an Irish W50 record of 2.43.05.

In 2001, the World Masters Championships were held in Brisbane; although she wasn't competing, Jean flew out from Ireland and Bobby drove up from Melbourne – it took him three days. They stayed with the Irish team and Bobby proved a valuable asset, with a stream of athletes coming to him for massages, among them Donore's Jim McNamara and Ann Woodlock. After that, a visit to the Donore Harriers clubhouse by the "real" Bobby Charlton to give massages was a regular feature of his trips to Ireland.

Her final international outing came in 2004 when Jean travelled to the 2004 European Championships in Aarhus, Denmark. At home, Jean continued to competes most years at the Irish Masters Championships in Tullamore, where several age classes are run together, giving her competition from younger athletes. At the time of writing, she still has two Irish records to her credit. In April 2010, she set a W60 record for 200m of 36.53 secs in Santry. In August 2012, she ran 1:22.53 for 400m at the National Masters in Tullamore, which was a new W65 record.

Mostly, she sticks to orienteering which, with its varied terrain, isn't so hard on the legs. She's far from the only family member involved in the sport. Her sister Claire is still competing regularly, while Claire's son-in-law Aongus O Cleirigh was many times Irish senior champion and continues to pick up titles in the masters age groups. Claire's daughter Patricia – a former Irish 400m international – also competes regularly, as do their children Cathal, Dara and Emmett. Jean's daughter Deirdre is also following in the family tradition of combining running and orienteering, along with her husband Pat Ryan and their two children.

Athletics, orienteering, music and travel have combined to give Jean O'Neill a life full of fun, friendship and adventure. Who could ask for anything more?

JIMMY O'NEILL

Date of Birth: 11/9/1941

Jimmy – Tough of the Track

By Brian Timmons

"Live as if you were to die tomorrow. Learn as if you were to live forever." – Mahatma Gandhi

Back in the day when I was a kid of 8 or 9, Jimmy O'Neill was at his peak as an athlete. I was an avid reader of comics at that time, in particular the Hotspur and the Hornet. I am talking about the 1960s.

At the time Jimmy would have been keeping company in 800 metre races with the likes of Noel Carroll, Basil Clifford and Derek McLeane. It was a golden era of 800 metre racing in Ireland. Jimmy's talent was such that he was selected to represent Ireland in 800 metre relay races with some of those illustrious names.

But because Jimmy's early racing career coincided with those names, he did not win many races when in that company. And the fact that Noel Carroll continued to race at the highest level for many years meant that Jimmy rarely succeeded in winning the big 800 metre races. That was never a deterrent to Jimmy. Jimmy loved competing and as he describes it "the fun of racing". That love of racing was to foreshadow a long career and some remarkable developments in his later athletic career.

There were two comic book heroes from the 1960s era who had captured my imagination. Both in their own way inspired me to take up running years later. One was Alf Tupper, "the Tough of the Track". The Tough would only win the race if he had eaten a single of chips (wrapped in the previous day's newspaper) an hour or two before the race. I tried it once or twice but I'm afraid that diet never worked for me personally.

The other comic book character was called Wilson. His Christian name didn't seem to matter and was never mentioned as far as I recollect. Wilson was a mythical figure, more at home on the cross-country circuit than the racing track beloved of Alf Tupper.

The amazing thing about Wilson was not just that he continued to participate in elite races as he got older. He continued to perform at his peak into his 60s, 70s and 80s. As far as I recollect, he was still winning races at the age of 150.

Inspired by Wilson and Tupper, I took up running myself with Crusaders. Louis Vandendries was my first point of contact as Chief Coach. He was ever present and Jimmy was also a constant presence at training sessions and club runs. Though Jimmy had a certain reserve, he would always welcome newcomers like myself, inviting us to join him for interval runs on the Crusaders green beside their old club house in Serpentine Avenue and

Jimmy O'Neill

on club runs around the leafy precincts of Ballsbridge and Donnybrook.

Jimmy had a love of the 200 metre interval sessions. This involved running several groups of 200s with a 1 minute interval or sometimes a longer interval if it was near to a race. When it came to racing Jimmy believed in doing very little running in the days beforehand and usually no running on the day immediately before the race. That is something that requires a degree of restraint and discipline.

Jimmy reminded me of both Alf Tupper and Wilson. Jimmy is a very different character to Alf and as far as I know he never preceded his races by wolfing down a single of chips. But his economic, streamlined running style always reminded me of Alf.

Jimmy's racing posture (and Alf's!) was perfect – arms and legs moving in unison like pistons. For both, that classic style and economy of movement applied especially when they were racing.

But it was Wilson in particular I used to think of when I'd see Jimmy racing. Wilson was ageless. Jimmy seemed to have accessed that same mysterious quality especially as he got older. In addition Jimmy retained the ability to go into the zone mentally. His expression always assumed a look of studied focus before the race.

I recall once seeing Jimmy lining up to compete in a graded 400m race meeting at Belfield. All of the other participants looked at least two decades younger and I found myself admiring Jimmy's courage. Jimmy won that race in some style, his competitive instinct kicking in over the last twenty metres as he moved from third to first. It was a competitive edge at the close of the race I had also seen in the late great Noel Carroll who Jimmy would have raced against many times.

I remember offering my congratulations to Jimmy after that graded meeting race. He was breathless, leaning forward with his hands on his knees, completely spent with the effort. He could not respond and I was a little concerned for him. He eventually managed five words: 'I love beating the young fellas'.

Jimmy has been involved with Crusaders continuously as an athlete since 1957, joining at the age of 16 while Ireland was still basking in Olympic glory achieved the previous year by another Crusader, Ronnie Delany.

He has remained an active Crusader ever since, not just on the track but as a coach and in the Committee room too.

Most of the unsung heroes of Athletics Club committees take up the role when in the twilight of their athletic career or after they have retired. Jimmy began working at Committee level at the age of 22 when at his peak and he has had almost unbroken service in the interim. He has seen the club make the very successful transition from Ballsbridge to Ringsend with a significant increase in membership.

Those who have served on voluntary Committees will know it can often be a thankless time consuming task. Jimmy has had over 50 years service at Committee level which for ranks me that is up there with all of Jimmy's athletic achievements.

Jimmy's spirit of dedicated voluntary commitment also extended to officiating at many races and track meetings over the years. He was a dual player at many graded meetings. As well as competing, he would often be seen officiating at the same meeting. Though not in the races he was competing in!

Jimmy worked for over 40 years as a manager in Kelso a commercial laundry. During that time he and his beautiful wife Helen raised three lovely daughters: Sarah and Tessa who became athletes with Crusaders themselves and Nicole who didn't take up athletics. But her children have recently joined Crusaders!

I had assumed that Jimmy didn't have time for any other recreational outlet but I recently discovered that he was a scout leader for over 45 years with the Scouting Association of Ireland which was since absorbed into Scouting Ireland. Jimmy was involved there at many levels including adult leader training.

When I drifted away from running in the mid-90s Jimmy was still going strong. He seemed immune to the injuries which were enforcing retirement on athletes far younger than him. He was again reminding me of the afore-

Jimmy O'Neill

mentioned mythical Wilson. In fact, in the spirit of Wilson, Jimmy's best days were still to come.

In 1997 Jimmy set a new national 400m record for the over 55 years Veterans category of 55.70 seconds and a new 800m record of 2 minutes 6.9 seconds. In the same year he won the gold medal in the world veterans 800m championship and bronze in the 400m. In the European indoors Vets championships he won gold in both the 800 and 400. In the process he had to run four races in three days which is an indication of both his stamina and his competitive instinct.

Jimmy went on to set an Over 60s 800m record of 2 minutes 16.04 seconds and 57.08 for 400m. For the uninitiated, the latter time is 3 seconds a lap under four minute mile pace by a man of over 60.

Jimmy's interest in scouting and athletics converged on one occasion in his very early athletic career.

It was when the Irish athletics selectors decided that Jimmy should be selected for his first call up to international duty. But when the call went out Jimmy was not to be found. It was established eventually that he was on a Scouting Jamboree, camping in a remote area of County Wicklow. It was far away from any phone contact of any sort – long before the days of mobile phones. His location was uncertain. A search party was duly dispatched. Jimmy was eventually located and retrieved in time to fulfil the call.

And Jimmy is still running. *Go mairfidh sé an dá chéad!*

Major Achievements as senior

Pacing Kip Keino in mile
Three bronze medals National championships
Selected to run internationally over 800m

European Masters Championships

1997 Birmingham European Indoors 800m Gold
First ever 400m Gold /With world invitation O/55
2001 Bordeaux France European Master [I]Gold O/55
2002 Potsdam European Master[o] Gold O/60
1999 Malmo European Indoor Bronze O /55

World Championships

1997 South Africa 800m Gold 400m Bronze
1999 Gateshead World 800 Silver O /55

BRENDAN O'SHEA

Date of Birth: 6/1/1943

Where Have All Our Good Marathon Runners Gone?

"An rud is anhamh, is iontach"

In my young days handball was my game. In fact I was quite a good hand-baller, playing Interversity handball with UCG, now known as NUIG. But in my late teens/early twenties I needed to wear glasses. It may be hard for those younger than 40 to believe that in the 60s contact lenses or even plastic lenses were not available in Ireland. Glass lenses were made of glass. So I reckoned it was only a matter of time before I would get a ball in the eye which could cause serious damage to my eyes. I did not fancy that happening so decided to quit handball and take up some sport where glasses would not be a major problem. I decided that distance running would be the sport.

In 1965 I joined the UCGAC. I had no expectations of being a top class athlete as I had never done any athletics prior to this. Running internationally for Ireland never crossed my mind. In the first year of my athletics career cross-country and some 6 mile road races (we had no fancy 10ks in those days in Galway/Connacht) were my events. I usually made the scoring team but rarely won. One member of our team stood out above the rest for respect. His name was Colm Roddy. What set him apart was that he had run a marathon. Quite a good one also, something around 3 hours. So in my second year of athletics in 1966 I decided to have a go at the Marathon.

In those days there were very few marathons held in Ireland. The only thing that I knew about the Marathon was that it was very long and probably very tough. I entered the National NACA Marathon held in Banteer, County Cork. A typical field for a marathon in those days would be 20. If 30 athletes turned up one would wonder where they all came from. To move on I lined up at the start, ran 26 miles 385 yards, most of it on my own and to my complete surprise finished 5th in 2-34. I was shocked and amazed. That set me on the road to be a "marathoner". It effectively orchestrated much of my future life, as an athlete, as a distance running coach, as an observer of marathon runners and standards.

It is worth dwelling a moment on that first marathon as it is still clear in my mind 48 years later. Like one's first kiss one never forgets. We got ready for the start in a corrugated shed which was acting as the changing room. As I was then only 23 the other runners looked quite old to me. They were probably in their thirties. I reckoned they knew more than me and were better marathoners. The guy next to me took from his kit bag a jar of wintergreen and proceeded to rub it into the whole of both legs. He then proceeded to massage it into the rest of his body wherever he could reach. The smell was powerful. Almost intoxicating. When he was finished with the wintergreen he rummaged in the bag and took out a jar of honey. After some furtive looks around he turned his back to the rest of us and poured all the honey into his mouth. In my innocence I thought " wow this guy must be good". In the race I never saw him. Did he finish? I doubt it, he probably spent a good bit of time clambering over fences to get into fields.

The course was from Banteer to Mallow and back. There were no thousands of spectators lining the course cheering us on. The only spectators were the cows in the fields bordering the road who probably got great fun watching the daft humans running on the road. Periodically like children they would break into a gallop and run along with us for a while. There was little in the line of water and certainly no isotonic drinks or energy gels.

Having finished I was making my way through the crowd at the end to the changing room when I met a friend of mine from UCGAC, Liam Kavanagh. I can remember vividly what he said to me as if it were just yesterday He said "where did you fall out?" I answered, "I did not fall out, I finished in 2-34."I was amazed. He was amazed. The plan had been to try for 3 hours!

I left Ireland in September 1966 and spent the next 5 years in England and USA. I continued my marathoning, winning some, not winning others but generally finishing in the top 5. It showed me that while I was not particularly good over shorter distances such as 6 miles or even 10 miles I was relatively much better over the marathon distance.

Those were very exciting years in USA. They were the days of the Vietnam War Protests, Flower Power, Peace and Love. They were also the days of LSD.

LSD came in two shapes. One was the drug LSD which was all over the place. One could trip over it if one were not careful. The second form of LSD was a type of marathon training, Long Slow Distance. This may not surprise people now but at that time it was revolutionary. It said there was no need to do speed work when training for the marathon. Just go out and run long distances slowly for a high weekly mileage of well over 100miles. One needed plenty of time for this and good weather as one was out for a few hours every day. Not surprising it was popular in California. While not a complete LSD fan it made sense to me as a training philosophy for the marathon and is the bedrock of my training programs.

When I returned to Ireland I found myself in the golden era of marathon running and marathon runners here. It is hard to appreciate how fantastic that era was. I remember thinking some years later that, if a Marathon Team Championship existed at the time for teams of 5 or 6, Ireland would probably be in the top 3 along with UK and Japan. We had colossal quality and depth. During the 1970-1979 decade Irish marathoners and Pb times included Danny McDaid (2-13), Neil Cusack (2-13), Pat McMahon (2-14), Jim McNamara (2-14), Sean Healy (2-15), Donie Walsh (2-15), Des McGann (2-16), Brendan O'Shea (2-16), Tony Brien (2-17), Willie Dunne (2-17), John Sheridan (2-18), Mick Molloy (2-18), Eddie leddy (2-18) etc etc. This does not tell the full story as many of these ran multiple sub 2-20s. And we were all homebred Irish men. I am pleased to also point out that 5 of that list were from my club, Donore Harriers.

The 1980-1989 decade was even more golden. We had John Treacy (2-09), John Woods (2-11), Dick Hooper (2-12), Jerry Kiernan (2-12), Louis Kenny (2-12), Kingston Mills (2-13),Eamonn Tierney (2-16), Paul Craig (2-16), Brian Keeney (2-16), Gerry Staunton (2-16), Paddy Murphy (2-16), Ray Treacy (2-16), Robert Costelloe (2-17), Jimmy Fallon (2-17), Michael Byrne (2-18), Gerry Deegan (2-18), Jim McGlynn (2-18). Again many of these ran multiple very fast times, in particular John Treacy, Dick Hooper and Jerry Kiernan.

The 1990-2000 years also produced many good times with some of the previous list continuing to produce fast times. We had new entrants into the list with Andy Ronan (2-11), Roy Dooney (2-13), Tommy Hughes (2-13), Jerry Curtis (2-14), Jamie Lewis (2-14) producing sub 2-15 marathons. A further 8 produced times that were sub 2-18.

And then the well dried up. Since 2000 only 3 Irish men ran sub 2-15. They were Mark Carroll (2-10), Mark Kenneally (2-13) and Martin Fagan (2-14).

Brendan O'Shea

The picture is less dramatic with our female marathon runners as it was only in the 1980s that female marathoning became generally accepted and women were allowed compete in major marathons. Carey May (2-28) was the first to make her mark internationally winning the Osaka Marathon in 1983 and 1985, Caitriona McKiernan (2-22) set the marathon world alight with a series of great times during 1990s. Sonia (2-29) was the third athlete to run sub 2-30 in 2005. Since then we have had no female athlete come close to sub 2-30. However it is good to now see a cluster of women around 2-35.

Why has this famine of fast marathon times happened at a time when there has been an explosion in the numbers running? There has also been an explosion in the prizes for winners, often in the thousands of euro? There have been a number of theories brought forth. I cannot say what the reason is but perhaps it is some combination of the following;

- Athletes are racing too often. I am a firm believer that top class marathoners need to be fresh for the race. They should be 99% fit and not 100%. Races should be planned in advance to fit into a specific marathon program.

- The races should be competitive where the top athletes race against each other. Currently athletes can pick and choose so that they don't compete with the other top runners. In the 70s and 80s we did not have so many races so that the top runners had to compete against each other on an on going basis.

- Perhaps they are overtraining. I think the LSD concept has been lost.

As most of us work full-time we have limited time to train. So here is my idea of a good training program for a sub 2-20 marathon:

1. A long run of 22-26 miles at a pace 1min/mile slower than marathon pace on road which has some easy hills.
2. A fartlek session of 2.5 hours on grass
3. A tempo session of 6-8 miles at a pace 15 sec/ mile faster than marathon pace
4. A 15 mile run at a little slower than marathon pace to be done on road.
5. Two days of 10 mile run at relaxed pace on grass.
6. A day off or if you feel the urge to run 5 days relaxed on grass.

Each session has a specific purpose, they are not simply combined so that you get the mileage up. The 6 day program totals approximately 85 miles/week. The 7 day program 90 miles. These sessions are not written in stone but provide the basis of a good program in itself or slightly modified. This worked for me as it enabled me to run 2-16 when winning the Berchem International Marathon in Antwerp 1972. But then each athlete has his/her own opinion.

Top Achievement as senior
National Marathon Champion 1973
Berchem Marathon Antwerp 2 hours 16 minutes

Senior best times
Marathon 2.16.50
Half Marathon: 63 minutes approx.

World Master championships
1983, Puerto Rico, Marathon, Bronze

Master Best times
Half Marathon: 67 min approx.
Marathon: 2.24 Belfast

PAT O'SHEA

Date of Birth: 17/4/1950

Kerry's Toughest Men

By Michael Gygax

"Everybody has a talent, it is important to recognise it and develop it"

How an environment shapes a man? On a recent visit to Annascaul, I followed the footprints of Tom Crean, one of Ireland's greatest explorers. I learnt of a man who fled home as a fifteen year old boy and joined the British navy in 1901. One of ten, from a poor rural farming background, he was a tough, good humoured, gregarious individual. He participated in 3 Antarctic exhibitions between 1901 and 1920, known as Heroic Age of Antarctic expedition. His comrades included Robert Scott, Ernest Shakelton, Worsely. During these expeditions, gales, freezing temperatures and enormous swells hampered their progress over unchartered territory. Crean's exploits were initially poorly documented because he did not keep diaries and his heroics only later became recognised. When he returned home in 1920 he opened up a pub called the South Pole and" kept mum" regarding his 3 epic expeditions. He received the Albert medal for bravery after putting his own life in imminent danger, succeeding in saving the lives of his comrades by having them rescued against all the odds. His brother Cornelius, a member of the R.I.C. was shot and killed by the IRA during the war of independence. Some of Ireland's republicans may not have taken kindly to any Irish person joining her majesty's forces, so he never spoke of his exploits. Even his children were unaware of the extraordinary feats of their father.

On the Tom Crean festival weekend, I went searching for another tough man, Pat O'Shea, still alive and running from a neighbouring district on the Ring of Kerry. Like Crean, he comes from a family of ten children.

Pat resides in Cahirsiveen capital of Iveragh Peninsula, a small town nestled between the Beenetee Mountains and the River Fertha. On any day, summer, winter, spring and autumn the mountain ranges on the Ring of Kerry

Pat O'Shea in competitive mode

are likely to bring down precipitation in the form of mist, rain or hail stones. It is a damp unforgiving terrain. Locally, sits Carrauntoohil the highest point of the Macgillycuddy's Reeks range, boasts of being Ireland's highest peak, and overshadows Cahirsiveen.

Knowing the reputation, but not the location, of his residence, I made local enquiries of the whereabouts of the runner Pat O'Shea. He runs that bed and breakfast over there, a local man points out. On this day, the wind raged putting a stop to boat trips to the nearby Skelligs. Waves crashed ten metres tall against the nearby cliffs off Bray Head, Valentia Island.

Pat had just returned from a local sports day where his grandchildren were competing. He talks enthusiastically about their athletic prowess. Pat, now a retired fireman, runs a bed and breakfast and looks after his wife who has developed a severe form of Parkinson's, is wheelchair bound. She is in need of full time care and attention, which Pat provides daily.

Pat has won many NACA national titles, the triple crown of marathons in 1985, 86, 87, his best time 2 hours 26 minutes. He ran most of his marathons under two and a half hours, normally finishing somewhere on the podium. Training twice a day, running over 100 miles per week, Pat Bonass, a master stalwart, came down to look for the elixir which shaped Pat O'Shea. Pat explained that he did most of his training on White Strand, which lies close to his home. Pat expected to see miles of windswept strands. Instead he found that White strand was a small inlet and Pat had forged his training route over a 400 metre circuit. "If you do enough of them, sure the miles add up," he quips.

The Atlantic Ocean is freezing cold even at the height of summer. At the end of each run, he baths his body in the Atlantic swell. He rubs seaweed deep into his muscles which he feels has kept him reasonably injury free.

Pat was a relative latecomer to the sport, starting at the age of twenty-seven. He initially served his time locally as a fitter before taking the boat to England. Five years later he returned in 1973 and took up employment as mechanic. He was encouraged by his younger brother Michael to take up running. Michael ran rings around him. Still at school, he was the golden boy, winning medals at national schoolboy level. At first Pat was huffing and puffing and hardly able to run across the road. He gave up bad habits like smoking and drinking late into the night and started running miles and miles. He overtook Michael who still competes at a very high level. The O'Shea brothers are local celebrities, featuring regularly in *The Kerryman*.

He avoids the road and keeps to the beach in order to avoid injury. He has only been up to the peak of Carrauntoohil once. He does not travel to go to

Pat O'Shea

the long beaches of Inch or Glenbeigh, the distance being too far. He keeps it local. Pat keeps his training simple. He runs between fifty and seventy miles per week. His brother Michael still calls him, to join him training. Running is part of the rhythm of every day.

Pat has become a regular participant on the master's circuit, competing in the nationals, Europeans and world championships on the road, cross country and track championships. He enjoys travel and dons the Irish singlet with pride and distinction. Despite his relatively small stature, he resonate athleticism and focus. He boasts fitness that many twenty year olds would envy.

In 2005 Pat became a world champion, winning the 8km cross country in San Sebastian. His dining room is a shrine to a man who has reached the top of his sport. Medals of every hue adorn the mantelpiece national, European and world. A photograph of Pat O'Shea in all his glory crossing the finishing line depicts the rest of the world sprinting to get the lesser spoils, behind him. Pat smiles in satisfaction. Tom Crean, if he was still alive, would be proud of his near neighbour.

Major Achievements as a Senior

National NACA Marathon Senior 1985 2.26 Gold
National NACA Marathon Senior 1986 2.30 Gold
National NACA Marathon Senior 1987 2.29 Gold
National NACA Marathon Senior 1988 2.29 Silver

Masters Major Achievements

National Marathon [Dublin City Marathon] 1992 2.35 Gold
National Marathon [Dublin City Marathon] 1993 2.31 Silver
National Marathon [Dublin City Marathon] 1996 2.36 Gold

CARMEL PARNELL

Date of Birth: 8/7/1955

Better Late than Never

By Hugh Parnell

"The more difficult the victory, the greater the happiness in winning."– Pele

My earliest memories of my mother's athletic career take place in muddy fields somewhere in rural Ireland, as I trudged through mud in an over-sized raincoat that nearly tipped off the top of my boots, thinking about how I was missing my Sunday cartoons. With my younger brother, Colm, at my side, we would strategically move around the course to instructions of military precision from our dad, Hugh, to cheer on Carmel, as she would cruise through the course spraying sprinkles of mud behind her. I was six, maybe seven years old at that time, but it was years before this that it all started.

It was during the one of those feverish crazes that captures the public imagination every so often that hooked Carmel on a sport that has played such a key part of her and our family's lives. Like line dancing to Achy Breaky Heart in the 90s, people in the 80s were swept up in marathon running, and in the midst of this came Carmel. Without adequate training, she set off to complete the Cork marathon with the simple motto of "just don't stop". She finished the race, and despite not being able walk for about a month afterwards, the euphoria of it all had caught her and she set her eyes on the Dublin marathon soon after. These experiences sold my mother on athletics, and putting marathons aside, she began training with Leevale Athletics Club in 1983 at the age of twenty-eight.

It was at Leevale where she met my father, who was a coach in the club at the time. With my dad coaching her the following year she got her first cap for the Irish Cross Country team. It was considered old in the 80s to be starting out in athletics at that age, leading a journalist on the radio to comment that it was "better late than never". My mother got a second cap for Ireland that year, the highlight of which was running against Zola Budd and getting her autograph at a presentation afterwards. When she began her training, she never could have imagined where this would take her, because soon she found herself dragging her family, willingly of course, to cheer her on around Ireland and even Europe.

Many Sundays were spent in the back seat of a car, staring at roaming fields as I tried to stave off motion sickness and boredom. This boredom was resigned solely to the commute to the race; once we arrived, we entered a world that vibrated differently from the normal pace of the day. These fields, that during the week were the home of grazing animals, all of a sudden transformed into a buzzing hive of anticipation and activity. Athletes togged off and lined up. Spectators readied their cameras and found the optimal viewing location. Everybody had their role and hurried about to fulfil it. My brother and I rarely stayed in one spot during Carmel's races. My father would plan an elaborate route around the course for us to take so that we would pop up at key spots to cheer her on. I have always felt there was more to this than met the eye, some ulterior motive at play; get the pair of them running, I suspect. These trips to cross

Carmel Parnell

country events took us all over the country, from rugged fields of Connemara to the sprawling Phoenix Park, where the sound of galloping deer in the distance matched that of the athletes as they ran by.

My mother ran in many 3000m races for Leevale on the track, where she was often competing against younger women, some of whom were half her age. When she rounded the track to cheers of 'come on mom' from my brother and I, she would often remark of a fleeting sense of embarrassment at this haunting reminder of her age, as she coursed along, pace for pace, with these younger women. Despite that, there must have been a creeping notion niggling in the minds of those other women that "I can't let this old timer beat me". In a way, this exemplifies the exquisite nature of the sport in that it transcends all. Age, fitness, and all other trappings can be tossed aside with relative simplicity; slide on a pair of runners and hit the road.

It was in my early teenage years that Carmel decided to venture to the World and European Championships. We decided to make this a family holiday, where time at the athletics track was interwoven with trips to the beach and tourist destinations, such as the Berlin Wall; a sombre reminder of division and oppression. These trips took us to San Sebastián, Spain, for the World Championships where she received silver in the 5,000 and gold in 10,000; Poznan, Poland, for the European Championships where she won gold in the 10,000; and Potsdam, Germany, for the Europeans again, this time winning gold in the 5,000. Cycles along the lakeside or lounging at beach were often followed by the day's events in the arena, a fantastic mesh of activities.

In Poland, on the day of the ten thousand meter race that Carmel was participating in, the sweltering heat of the day managed to penetrate even the most shaded areas. With perspiration pouring down my face I stared out across the arena, intermittently cheering on my mother, as she rounded a track that seemingly contorted in the shimmering haze of the heat. Through this mirage the athletes would burst and powerfully stride forward while I stood motionlessly, melting piece by piece. Armed with a large bottle of water for protection, I was bewildered how anyone could maintain any semblance of composure in such scorching conditions. I remember hearing that the temperature was in the region of forty degrees, but I cannot be certain due to the time that has passed, and the youthful desire at the time to exaggerate a story. That being said, the heat that swept across the arena is something I will never forget, and it was in these conditions that saw my mother towering in the

Carmel Parnell

centre of the podium later that day, not with only a gold medal, but with the championship best time of 38.29 that still hold to this day.

While I have managed to make it to many of my mother's successes, I have never made it to some. One in particular is the British and Irish Cross Country Championships. None of the family has ever made it to this event. It takes place annually on a Saturday, a workday for my father, preventing us from travelling. Even though we were not there, my father would plan meticulously ahead so that Carmel would be in peak condition for the championships. This has led to us missing her winning eight gold medal and two silver medals in eleven starts. At times, this leaves me wondering how much help our vocal support actually lent to her performance. These were disappointing to miss, but no doubt, there will be a few more successes to come.

Carmel would often speak about the high one would get when they are locked into the zone, the runners high. A high that despite your movement you are never chasing, it lies right there in the moment. While I never followed in my mother's footsteps as an athlete, I do at times strap on a pair of runners and follow her trail down country roads and through suburban estates, my feet springing from the asphalt into the machine motion of a runner locked into its momentum, as I cruise along with the wind caressing my cheeks. It is in these instances that I realise the beauty and joy of this sport that my mother has loved most of her life. It is in these climatic moments of freedom, where all is lost except motion, that you find yourself floating on the crest of a majestic wave. It seems it is my mother's love of the sport, more so than her great accomplishments that will keep her running through the hills of Douglas and around her beloved UCC farm for years to come.

Top Achievements: Senior
2 Irish Caps Cross Country 1984/85

Top Achievements: Masters
British & Irish Masters: 8 Gold & 2 Silver
European Championships: 2 Gold & 1 Silver
World Championships: 1 Gold & 1 Silver
World Champion 10km 2005

FRANK REILLY
Date of Birth: 18/11/1945

An Anglo Irish Tale

*"Let go of certainty. The opposite isn't uncertainty. It's openness,
curiosity and a willingness to embrace paradox, rather than
choose up sides. The ultimate challenge is to accept ourselves exactly as we are, but never stop trying to learn and grow."*
– Tony Schwartz

Born Francis Reilly in the townland of Tierlahood, parish of Laragh,
County Cavan, the third child of a family of nine, four boys and five girls,
he was educated at Tierlahood NS.

In those days all male children were expected to serve as altar boys from
around the age of nine after having learned the Latin required. There was a
rota and apart from serving on Sundays we were required to serve during the
week before going to school and also during school holidays. In my case this
involved a walk of about four miles.

In those days Cavan had a decent football team and every schoolboy hoped
to grow up to emulate their heroes. I remember one evening in Breffni Park
when Laragh schoolboys were playing a game against Kinawley a club from
across the border in Fermanagh when some of their supporters seemed to be
playing a funny game behind one of the goals. Instead of catching the ball
they seemed to be trying to hit it with their head. On enquiring from my team
manager what they were doing I was informed not to get involved as it was
illegal and you could be banned from "proper" football for life. As I couldn't
contemplate that fate and couldn't see a policeman to arrest them I decided to
move to the other end of the field.

Also in those days TV hadn't arrived so we listened to the radio to hear the
exploits of Ronnie Delany and when the races were over we would go out into
the field by the grocery store "not everyone had a radio" and run around hoping
that one day we might be the one on the radio. We were over the moon when

he won gold at the 1956 Olympic Games in Melbourne, "the only male Irish athlete to win a track Olympic gold".

Having reached the ripe old age of 13.5 and as I had passed the leaving cert the previous year I was allowed to leave school to commence work in a grocery store in the summer of 1959. This was a bicycle ride of about six miles, "my first and only bicycle". I stuck at it for about fifteen months and on hearing that lads were being recruited for the catering trade in England, I enquired from a friend who was already working in the business and he invited me over to Wantage, near Oxford, so I left home aged 15 in 1961 to make my fortune. My friend was as good as his word and got me a job as a commis chef in a hotel in Banbury from where I attended catering college one day a week in Oxford.

On my day off I sometimes went to the local park, where I came into contact with that funny football again. As I was fairly sure nobody was going to report me to the Irish GAA I decided to join in but was swiftly put in as goalkeeper as I was told I had a "bad habit" of catching the ball. All my friends were amazed that I was working as they had to stay at school until their sixteenth birthday.

Around this time I had a nasty experience with cigarettes which led to a life as a non smoker. I invested heavily in a swanky cigarette case and a packet of Benson and Hedges and set out to impress my friends, but never got that far as when I took my first few pulls I got a coughing fit, my eyes were watering and my mouth tasted as though I had been poisoned so I threw the cigarettes and case into the open fire of the hotel TV lounge and called it a day.

I worked in Banbury until Spring 1963 and then went down to a hotel in Ilfracombe in north Devon for the summer season and when I left in October I said goodbye to catering. My next port of call was my present domicile, Manchester.

I was invited to Manchester by my cousin who was a keen Gaelic footballer and also a Man U supporter. On arrival in Manchester I was informed that we were going to Old Trafford the following day "Sat" to watch Man U play Fulham. This held great expectation for me as I remembered from my schooldays the teacher having kept me in class at lunchtime for misbehaviour, she then took pity on me and gave me a newspaper to read. The main headline was about the Munich air disaster in which most of the Man U team were killed. The survivors were still playing so it was a great thrill to see Charlton, Foulkes, etc; also the legendary Johnny Haynes of Fulham. I have been a Man U fan ever since.

My cousin also introduced me to the local GAA scene and over the years I played for both St Brendan's and Oisins with varying degrees of success. I also got involved with the local soccer club St Marks so was playing games most Sats and Suns. During one of our Gaelic practice sessions at Brooklands in

Frank Reilly

1965 we were surprised to see the then Man U goalkeeper Pat Dunne with a pair of boots slung over his shoulder and asking if he could join in. He practiced with us on a few occasions and invited a few of us to an informal session at one of Man U's training grounds. However I didn't make it as I went down with appendicitis and ended up in hospital. If only?

In 1973 I married my wife "Dot" a Manchester lass and the following year our son Michael was born. This settling down came as a great shock to my bachelor style of life as I had been my own boss since leaving home in 1961. Having accepted my inevitable fate I decided to accept more responsibility at work and moved up to the position of site foreman with a construction company. In the next couple of years more promotions followed and I became site manager. By 1980 I was looking for a new challenge and joined what was to be my final employer, Redrow Construction, as an engineer, a job that would last for 29 years until my retirement in 2009.

During the period 1973-1986 I continued to play football "both codes" on and off as time allowed. I travelled with my work all around England and Wales and sometimes didn't see my family for weeks at a time. Around 1986 Redrow entered a team in a corporate running series and anyone with a sporting history was invited to take part. So started the slippery road to what was to become "a life on the run". Training intensified and over a period of two years our team became good enough to win the series cup. Who needs Ronnie Delany?

On my travels I had the pleasure of training/racing with numerous athletic clubs, Prestatyn, Hereford, Bicester, etc; and found them most helpful with regards to not only running but as a source of local knowledge about procurement of labour, etc; which was my responsibility as new contracts were won.

Another of my stops was within reach of Mt Snowdon in North Wales where I joined the Eryri club on their weekly training runs out of LLanberis. These were basically a group of mountain goats who had a dislike to road and track running, so after suffering an initiation of running up and down Snowdon things got worse as I was taken on a tour of all the mountains surrounding LLanberris. Having survived this I was accepted as "one of the boys" and the did me the honour of speaking in English when I was present. At local races they used to joke that I was the cause of late starts as they had to repeat the pre race instructions in English just for me, for safety reasons.

By this time I was a member of my present club Stockport Harriers and was called upon to represent the team at road, track, xc and fell races as work would allow.

In 1996 I was selected to represent my native country for the first time at the Home Countries XC International in Irvine, Scotland and was lucky enough to be part of the winning O/50 team. We were then told that we were the first non English men's team ever to win gold medals at the event.

This was a great boost to confidence and encouraged me to set my sights even higher, so I went to The Hague, Holland in 1997 for the European Road Champs to run in the 10K event where I finished 3rd O50. In July 1997 we were in Durban, South Africa for the World XC Champs, "another bronze medal".

1998 and we went to Kobe, Japan for the World Road Champs to run the 10k event, which went over and back across the newly rebuilt Akashi bridge, the original having been destroyed in an earthquake that killed several thousand people a few years earlier. The start was a shambles as there were about 20,000 participants starting in age order groups at short intervals and as the faster runners from the older groups caught the slower ones of the younger groups the road was blocked and chaos "among other things" ensued. Having suffered looking at hiking boots, fancy costumes and people carrying enough water for a short holiday I finally found enough running space to finish 3rd O/50, another bronze medal. However along with Monaghan's Brendan Sherlock and Wexford's John Sheridan we won the O/50 team gold medal.

Further International races at home and abroad followed "with varying degrees of success" but that all elusive individual gold, or even a silver, medal was still not achieved. However this was to change in May 2001 when we went to St Paul's Bay, Malta for the EVAA Road Champs.

Having lost out on winning the gold medal by some 5 secs in the 10k, at least I got a silver, my hour arrived the following day in the half marathon when I finally got onto the top step of the podium as O/55 champion. Hearing the National Anthem being played was very emotional and brought back memories of the great Irish athletes who had inspired me down the years: Ronnie Delany, world xc champ and 1984 Olympic marathon silver medalist John Treacy and "the king of the boards" Eamonn Coghlan, to name just three.

July 2001 and we were in Brisbane, Australia for the World Champs. Hostilities kicked off with the 10k XC event and guess where I finished? Yes 3rd again. There was quite a bit of drama over the awarding of the team medals as was so eloquently told in an article written by one of my teammates Pat Bonass. Three days later and I lined up for the marathon event which was run out and back along the Brisbane river over a two lap course which had 180 degree

Irish Team – Adam Jones, Frank Reilly, Pat Bonass

bends at the bridge ends which were crossed numerous times. It was a very warm day but despite the heat and blistered feet I managed to win the o/55 gold medal. Another trip to the top of the podium, it doesn't get much better than that.

Having said that 2002 was to bring a real surprise. After helping my club to the O/50 road relay champs gold medal in Sutton Park, Birmingham I went out to the World Road Champs in Riccione, Italy with the intention of having a holiday and using the races as training which went according to plan. With the races out of the way we all went for a meal and a few beers and then came the surprise. Martin Kelly the then President of the IVAA, who was supposed to be in South Africa suddenly appeared and commenced to make an announcement. I nearly went into shock when he said I had been voted IVAA "Athlete of the Year" for 2001. I was given a framed certificate so I had to believe it was true. I was nearly lost for words but eventually I managed to thank all for the honour bestowed on me. I was also advised that there was a trophy, "The Tadhg Lynch Award", that would be given to me on arrival back in the UK and when my good friend and teammate Pat Bonass presented it to me at my home in Stockport I felt truly humbled, when I looked at the names already on the trophy amongst them was Eamonn Coghlan. It definitely doesn't get better than that.

The year 2004 saw us in Cape Town, South Africa for the 35m Two Oceans road race which runs from the University campus at Newlands across the city from the Atlantic to the Indian Ocean and back.

Survival was the name of the game and eventually the finish line was reached. In 2005 we journeyed to Monte Gordo, Portugal for the EVAA road champs where the highlight was winning the O/55 XC relay team gold medal.

In 2006 we were in Linz, Austria for the World Indoor Champs. The snow was so bad they used a bulldozer to clear the XC course just before the races began. I was delighted to win gold in the 3000m track and the 8K XC plus a bronze in the half marathon. Along with Pat Bonass and Pat Healey we won team silver in the XC event missing gold by 1 secomd. In 2007 I was in Regensburg, Germany for the EVAA Road Champs where it was yet another bronze medal in the 10k.

Having suffered with a knee injury in 2008 which worsened and kept me out of action for all of 2009 and half of 2010 I finally got back training in July and by December was back running competitively. January 2011 and it was back to Cape Town, South Africa with my present training partner Derek Walton of Altrincham RC where we competed in races ranging in length from 5k to 30k, with wins in the O/60 category keeping us fed with seafood vouchers. March 2011 and we went to Ghent, Belgium for the EVAA Indoor Champs where I won O/65 gold in the 3000m track and 5000m XC events, Another couple of emotional trips to the podium.

The last couple of years have been testing as I have suffered a series of running-related injuries, but these seem to be starting to improve and I am back in light training and looking forward to the future. As some of my training mates are in their middle eighties I hope to continue running for some time yet and meet up again with my many good friends around the world, God willing.

PAM REYNOLDS RIELLY
Date of Birth: 29 May 1945

Sport Adding Sweetness to Life
By Michael Gygax

Lucy: "You learn more when you lose."

Charlie Brown: "Well then I must be the smartest person in world!!!" – Charles M. Schulz, Peanuts Treasury

Pam always considered her life as a bit of a disaster, early years at school she was considered a low achiever, colloquially known as a dunce. She found it hard to write well, often spelt backwards, had difficulty with numbers and the whole of the experience was overwhelmingly frustrating. Today she would be diagnosed as having dyslexia. One of five children, her father was a farmer in North County Dublin in the District of Garristown, where he bred horses on a small scale. When she was not walking horses gently for an hour or so, she was falling off them, so she never became a horse whisperer. Her twin brother Peter, who is manger of Ballymcall stud farm in Dunboyne is the only other family member to take up running. He ran 12 to 14 city marathons, a few more than Pam.

She went to boarding school, one might believe it was a privilege, but her schooling life was by and large a negative experience. Her first jobs were menial and unfulfilling. At about the age of twenty five she gave up work altogether to look after her mother who suffered a stroke.

Pam was always interested in arts and crafts, developed good skills in sewing, needling crafts and dress making, but there was never a career in it. One of her abiding passions is philately, or stamp collecting, and she has a full range of Irish stamps going back to 1929 when the first Irish stamp was issued.

She was lucky to inherit a house form her aunt when she passed on. Her brother took over the family farm.

In 1973 she decided that she needed a holiday, so she was drawn to Castlebar International walking festival, a recreational event which entailed walking twenty five miles per day, for four consecutive days. The first day or two was lovely and very enjoyable but the third was a disaster, as her body began to cry that she was not fit and it appeared that she had bitten off more than she could chew. She tagged along with some lads from the FCA which kept her going but if an ass, nag or goat had offered her a ride home, she would gladly have taken it. These hundred miles took her thirty hours and sixteen minutes to complete, which left her feet blistered and sore and she sank beside her mother in her chair for a month afterwards unable to move, her exertions had taken such a toll on her, but a seed had been planted.

That was when racing bug took over and for the next 4 years (with better training) she got her time down in 1976 to 21 hours. Looking after her parents were a full time job, so she found it hard to get away at weekends but she did start regular training.

She saw a picture in the paper of an English girl, after winning the English AAA's 3000m race walk. Thinking this would easy after the 100 miles. She was soon to discover that race walking when done at speed takes endurance, strength and speed and it is a lot different than a casual walk in the park. She could find no girls race walking in Ireland but identified a man, John O'Leary who race walked for Ireland and was a member of Clonliffe Harriers. So she joined the north county club and was kindly coached by Richard Davis. Race walking was in its infancy in Ireland, so there was little competition for men but practically non for women, and there was no female races in the early days at all, so she ended up racing against men. The men treated her well; she never finished last and was considered one of the lads. Needless to say, she broke record after record at every distance, easy to know why, since she was the only female competitor.

Her first all-female race was in the English WAAA in London 1976. She had never seen a tartan track, let alone walked on one but she was happy to finish fifth in a time of 28.31.2 for 5km. She remembers it was won by the top English girl setting a new world record, beating the Swedish record holder. In the race, she was the first Irish woman to contest a walking event abroad. Between 1976 and 1991 she went over to London, for many 5k and 10k races and always finished in the top half of the field. She also competed in some races around Europe.

In the women's 10k in London in 1978 it was the first time they were awarded a certified to women who got under 1 hour for 10k. She qualified by doing 59 min. 12sec. finishing twelfth place. Her 5km race in London in 1977 with the time of 27.54.-4 put her twenty-fifth fastest time in the women's world list in 1977. In this year she decided to have another try at longer distances, as she seemed to be a tortoise rather than a hare. She went over to the Isle of Man, for their 50k race where she won it in 6 hours 44 min. 40s. It was a course record that lasted for about 10 years.

In 1989 she left Clonliffe Harriers and joined St. Andrews A.C. in Ashbourne, County Meath, a club that was nearer her home. One of the top race walkers at the time Bernie O'Callaghan was a member, and the top Irish race walker so she could train with him. The club was founded in 1955 recently celebrated the 50 years of women's athletics. In 1964 they were the third club in the 26 countries, and the first in NACA club to take in women and girls as full members. In 1967 they joined BLE.

Nineteen eighty was to be a world race walking championships for women to be held in New York, but the USA had boycotted the Moscow Olympics and all international competitions were up in the air. The race was on and then off all summer, but she had bought a ticket and ended up competing on the fifteenth of August with only six teams competing. Her strongest race was 10km where she finished fifth in a time of 55 minutes and five seconds. She stayed with some long lost cousins in New York.

Pam Reynolds Rielly

This was the same year as the first Dublin city marathon. So she had about 6 weeks to get in a lot of extra training miles in. She completed the distance in 4 hours, 48 min 02 race walking. It turned out to be the best time of all the nine Dublin marathons she did, competing each year for nine years. The only year that she did not finish was 1981 as she had been sick the weeks before it. By 20 miles she felt was going backwards, so that was enough

The year 1981 was the first where there was an official 3000km race walk for women included in the national championships. Twelve walkers turned up and it was won by Mary Hennessy in 15.48.02. Pam was second in 15.55.06, but she was now thirty-six years of age, the rest of the girls were younger and fresher than her. Her time that day, 33 years later, is still the Irish Masters record for the over thirty-five year age group. In 1986 the first National 10km road championships National Championships were held and she won it in 58.56.

For the next twenty years or so, she had had good fun taking part in the World and European masters, but the competition was very fast and furious, as usual, and she was on her own, with plenty of competition around the world, but none in Ireland.

A new era was dawning in race walking as women's race walking became an Olympic sport. Times got quicker, athletics became more professional and she found herself out of her depth. The times got so much faster and also the style, more active which makes a bigger difference between running and walking. But since she has aged and grew stiffer, she cannot master the new style. She has been given many a red card for lifting, leaving her frustrated when not allowed to finish some races. Her last international race was in LAHTI Finland in 2009.

Paddy Rielly, a near neighbour of a half a mile and stalwart competitor and official of St Andrews Athletic Club Ashbourne, became companions and friends after she joined that club over twenty years ago. He worked for Unidare as a metal worker making water pumps. He took up running in 1957 when athletics had got very popular with younger people after the 1956 Olympics when Ronnie Delany won a gold medal. He first joined St. Mary's A.C. in Garristown later joining St. Andrew's in 1965 running short distances and high jump. Due to domestic reasons his training and competition were limited. When his father died as a relatively young man, he was left to look after his mother on their small north county seventeen acre holding.

Cars, petrol, sandwiches, tea and conversation have been shared with him over two decades of going to and from race meetings and athletic competitions. Paddy later took up field events, and marathon running, and decided do the Dublin City marathon. His greatest athletic moment was in the hammer event. He beams with pride as he remembers his biggest claim to fame, when he was 3rd in the hammer which helped his club win the team event, in the National Senior track and field league championships when he was over fifty. He says it is the training more than competition that gives him the greatest pleasure but he still competes with a pacemaker, some arthritis and other mechanicale foibles thrown in.

Some people started to comment that Paddy and Pam were an item, so frequently they were together, but they were really only good friends but the idea started to take on a life of its own. The winter of 2009 was particularly cold and although there is more meat on an Ethiopian chicken than Pam, it seems like a good idea to preserve heat, they decided it would be nice to keep each other warm at night, away from the chilly chimes, so they decided to get married, a notion that they kept secret even from their own family. They are of a generation where taking a pre-nuptial dip or a test drive went against their holiest beliefs, so they quietly got married in a small county church in the presence of six witnesses. They are quiet people and dislike pomp and ceremony. They then went to the world masters championships in Finland where they competed and enjoyed their new life as a couple. They later had a party for their two families, on their return from Finland.

Major Achievements as a senior

1977 IAAF World Race-walk world Cup 5k. 14 the 27.58
1977 50km 6 hours 44.04 Isle of Man
1978 Frediskstad Norway World race-walk women 10km 20th 58.24
1979 First European Communities women's race-walk champ France road
10km 11th 57.35 5km 27.51

Masters Major Achievements

National champion track and road
M 50 2005 Silver European Masters 20km 2 hours Portugal
Personal Best times: All Master national records at the time
In 1999 best time of 27min.45sec. for 5k. was still 16th in the Irish Women's Race
walk best 50.
Best Marathon Walking 1980: 4 hours 48.02
at a much slower pace for about one hour.

BRENDAN SHERLOCK

Date of Birth: 7/4/1946

"Keep On Running, Keep On Rocking"

"Sports is human life in microcosm." – Howard Cosell

I was born the 13th child of 14 in a small village called Tydavnet, a few miles north of Monaghan Town. I didn't take up formal athletics until I was 35 years old. As a child we had to walk 2 miles to school but I would rarely walk, preferring to race my siblings. With hindsight, it was not unlike the upbringing of Kenyan children who also run everywhere and this may have sown the seed for my love of athletics.

As a teenager I played Gaelic football with my local underage football team, Scotstown GFC, but I didn't pursue this much further as the roaring 60's hit and the lure of the band halls and dances were too strong. I fell in love with the buzz of live music and followed that path by joining The Ventures Showband in my late teens. This brought me all over Ireland, the UK, Canada and America

While on tour abroad I would sometimes go for a run to relieve the boredom of the day time and to get some fresh air into my lungs to counteract the smoky atmosphere of the dance halls and night clubs, but again I didn't take it seriously. Having moved to Canada in 1974 with my young family to continue my music career, the odd run and playing football with Chinese lads in Vancouver's Chinatown on a Saturday morning was about the height of my physical exercise.

On my return to Ireland in 1977 and set up my own business, owning a chip shop. This combined with raising children took up most of my time but when we were established back in Monaghan I started to run with some locals to keep fit one day a week. In 1981 I suggested to the group of casual runners that we aim to run in that year's Dublin City Marathon. They laughed at me and thought I was crazy. I proved them wrong and in October I lined up at the start line with 3 month's jogging under my belt. Much to my (and everyone else's) surprise I clocked a respectable time of 2 hours 52 minutes. About 2 weeks later, my local running club, Monaghan Phoenix, approached me to see if I would run with them in the County Cross Country Championships. I was both thrilled at being asked and terrified, having no experience of cross country running and not knowing what a pair of spikes were!

Much to the surprise of my fellow athletes, I won my first competitive race. Due to my inexperience, my team mates had suggested that I sit back in the pack and try to hang on to win a team prize. Halfway through the race my renowned impatience got the better of me and I said to the guy beside me that I was going to take the race up a notch to try bring everyone on. No one followed and the gold was mine.

From here I went on to run in the Ulster Novice Championships in Derry. I fell in a puddle of water at the start of the race and as no one could avoid it, they all trampled over me leaving me resembling a colander with the

Brendan Sherlock

holes of spikes in my back. I pulled myself up and with sheer doggedness I pushed myself to the front of the pack to steer clear of any further collisions. With 200 meters to go I was winning but Derry's Peter Mitchell had other ideas and eased past me, leaving silver as my prize. I moved up to the Intermediate class and won that 2 years in a row.

A lot of my senior year's success was due to the strong athletes around me and the competition to try to make the team. Runners such as Dermot Clarke, Francie Boylan, Donal O'Mahony, Noel Kennedy, Pauric Gollogley and Tommy and P.J. Coyle, among others, made it a challenge to get to pull on the green, white and black stripes of our club. With my 40th birthday closing in, it was time to make a move into the Masters world.

My first experience of National Competition came in 1986 in Navan for the National Cross Country Championships. I took home an individual bronze medal with the late P.J. Fagan and John Buckley taking gold and silver respectively. This medal inspired me and marked my arrival in the elite Veteran athletics world where I continued to accumulate National Medals. I was then invited to join the Irish team on their trip to the European Championships in Malmo, Sweden in July 1986.

Sweden marked not only the start of my international career but also the start of some of the best days of my life. On the day of the opening ceremony in Malmo, there was a heatwave. I was advised not to go to the ceremony as I was running in the 10k that evening and the heat would leave me dehydrated. Home alone at our hotel base, boredom struck. I was on the sixth floor and decided to open the window facing onto a main street, grab myself a glass of water, and sit on the windowsill to get some sun on my legs and watch the world go by. After approximately 5 minutes, I could see 2 rescue trucks coming down the street followed by a police car. I was curious as to what was going on and looked around me to see what was happening. I looked down and saw a small group of people standing on the street below looking up. The trucks pulled in under my window and one of them started to raise the rescue basket up towards my window. It dawned on me that, due to a high suicide rate at that time in Sweden, they had assumed I was going to jump.

I immediately climbed back in the window, banged it shut and ran up a few more flights of stairs to the roof. It was like the hotel was built upside down as the lawn was on the roof. I took a peep over the wall and could see that the commotion below was continuing and they were scanning the windows with the rescue basket looking for the "jumper". I saw there was a young lady sunbathing (topless!) on the roof so I casually walked over, took off my t-shirt and lay down beside her. The police, having searched the hotel, arrived on the roof but thanks to my quick thinking, they assumed I was with the young lady and didn't ask any questions.

One of my Ireland teammates, Sean Callan, made friends with some of the locals the next day and was told about the "suicide" attempt at his hotel the evening before and that it had made the city's newspapers. I had told Sean about the event and this became a running joke for the rest of the trip.

This was not the only event of the Swedish trip though. One of our team mates who will remain nameless almost came a cropper on a sunbed. An athlete's wife was going to use a sunbed and myself and my running mate, having never seen one before, decided to go with her and try it out. When we got there I went in first and the salon attendant explained how to use it. When my time was up, I came out and told my team mate to go in. The attendant was not around so I told him that he had to strip totally naked and lie on the bed. When the attendant came back I told her that he had gone in but didn't know how to use it. She went in to explain and he got such a fright he sat upright and banged his head off the lights above him and had to fall back helpless while she laughed at him.

My next international sojourn was to Australia in November 1987. I ran the 5k track on the Wednesday night and 10k cross country on the Friday,

T.J. O'Loughlin (Tipperary), Brendan Sherlock (Monaghan) and John Buckley (Cork) after winning the European Road Championship 10k in Venice in 1991

finishing 6th and won a team silver medal. On the Sunday morning I ran the Marathon and with a mile to go, I was joint 2nd with a Greek athlete when suddenly I got violently sick. We had been on target to run 2 hours 25 minutes but due to unclean water I had drank along the route, my race was ruined and I finished 7th in a time of 2 hours 30. My personal best for a Marathon had been achieved in London in a time of 2 hours 28 previous to this, so I felt very disappointed despite having won my first world medal.

Two years later I travelled to the USA to run in the World Masters Games in Eugene, Oregon. In order to acclimatise I spent the previous 2 months in Edmonton, Canada where I had lived in the 70s. While there I ran a 10k race and then was asked by The Chasquis Carucas to run on their team in a Rockies relay. It was a 150 mile relay between Jasper and Banff and I had the 2nd leg running a distance of 12 miles at 7000 feet above sea level. I was handed the baton in 33rd place and handed it over in 2nd place for our team to go on and win the masters event. This was a once in a lifetime experience that I will never forget. A few weeks later I ran with this team again in another relay in the mountains and once again we were victorious.

I think the mountains beauty stole my cross country abilities as my race in Oregon was disappointing in comparison and I finished in 9th position.

Next stop on my travels was Turku in Finland once again for World Masters Games. Team Ireland won the Cross Country race with John Buckley winning the race outright, with John Sheridan, myself and T.J. O'Loughlin making up the team to take home the gold.

A few weeks later we travelled to Venice to take part in the European Masters 10k Road Race with John Buckley again taking the gold and I was third. Our team consisting of Buckley, O'Loughlin and Sherlock took home the gold.

The world games returned to the USA with Buffalo the venue in 1995. The cross country event saw Denis Noonan, John Sheridan and myself take the silver to a strong but dubious Russian team. My individual placing was 6th but I improved my rankings by taking 4th in the Marathon behind the Russian winner of the Cross Country race. This was despite having to stop twice in the pouring rain to tie my shoe laces and not having had time to warm due to registration issues!

In March 1987 while working, I fell off a roof and broke my ankle in 2 places and cracked the 6th and 7th vertebrae. It took the hospital a few days to realise that my back had been broken and when the consultant discovered it, he said that I was very lucky, because if I had moved in the wrong way I would have severed my spinal cord and would never have walked again. I spent the next few months in a wheelchair and body cast but decided to travel to Durban, South Africa to support the Irish team anyway.

As soon as my ankle was healed, I used an exercise bike to try build up my legs while still wearing the body cast. When it was ok to do so, I started running in my local swimming pool and as soon as I was able, I was back training fully. Almost exactly a year to the day of my accident I took part in the World Road Race Championships in Kobe, Japan and I helped the team to win the gold.

My last international race was in Spain in 2000. In the preparations I had severe pains in my knee but I didn't let that deter me and travelled with the team. We won the gold in the 10k on the Saturday and as we had no fresh legs for the half marathon the following day we competed again and picked up the bronze.

A few weeks later I had an appointment in Blackrock Clinic to remove cartilage but when they examined it they discovered that there was no cartilage left and the bones were rubbing against each other. They advised that I should stop running. I did so for a few months and then started again but not at the same highly competitive level as before.

I have made lifelong friends in my team mates and had a lot of fun and laughter in many different places all over the world thanks to athletics and my ever patient and loving wife Maura.

Senior: Best Time
Marathon: 2.28; Half Marathon: 70mins

Master Road Times:
Half Marathon 69.33 Age 40; Marathon 2.30 Age 40

PAT TIMMONS

Date of Birth: 25/11/ 1949

Health Matters

By Sean McGolderick

"Proper nutrition and recovery is as much a part of my training as hard sessions or long runs."

Pat Timmons did not run his first track race until he was 53! But he has been making up for lost time ever since. A multiple winner of National Masters' titles in middle distance events, he's also medalled at the British indoor and outdoor championships, won bronze at the European championships and set a few new age category records along the way.

As befits a true blue Cavan native – he hails from Crosskeys – his first love was Gaelic football, though he did run on the St Patrick's College cross country teams in Cavan while a student there. He moved to Dublin in 1971, played Gaelic football with Erin's Isle and later coached juvenile teams in the club – two of his protégés, Charlie Redmond and Mick Deegan, later went on to win All-Ireland medals.

By the time his 30th birthday was looming he was no longer doing any exercise. He had changed jobs; he was doing a lot of driving, eating too much sugar laden food, smoking 20 cigarettes a day and feeling unwell.

So unwell, in fact, that he went to see his doctor. "He told me straight away that I wasn't exercising enough," recalls Pat, who did a routine blood test during the visit. The test revealed that Pat had dangerously high levels of triglycerides in his blood.

"It is a 'first cousin' of high cholesterol. The cure was quite simple; I had to exercise rigorously for half an hour three times a week in order to get up my heart rate up. When I asked the doctor what would happen if I didn't do the exercise he remarked 'I won't make you any promises past 40. And by the way, I also want you to give up the cigarettes.'"

So for the next couple of months Pat went running three times a week – mostly during his lunch break. His triglycerides level began to fall. "A friend

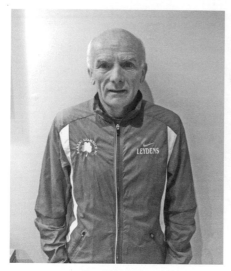

Pat Timmons

of mine was going running a marathon so I asked the doctor whether I could run one. He said there was no need; but there was nothing stopping me. However, I would have to stop smoking."

By now Pat had progressed to running five days a week; his weekly mileage hovered around the 30 mark and he continued to make valiant efforts to give up the fags. Then one night while running on the Howth Road on Dublin's northside it all came together.

'I'll never forget it, it was a Thursday night. I was living in Donaghmede at the time and I had a circuit I used to do, through Baldoyle, the Howth Road and Raheny village. I was going lovely, but then along the Howth Road I found I couldn't breathe though my legs were flying. I had to cut short the run and head up the Kilbarrack Road." Pat never smoked again. "The need to run was greater than the need to smoke."

He subsequently ran three marathons in Dublin, Cork and Galway and one 10km race in the space of seven months; achieving his goal of breaking 3.30 in the latter event in 1984 when he clocked 3:29.34. He never ran a marathon again.

Instead he concentrated on shorter events – particularly 10km road races – he posted a decent personal best of 35.48. By then he was a member of Raheny Shamrock AC and was also coaching juveniles in Kilmore AC, then a feeder club for Raheny, where his young daughter Nicola was a member.

During his late 30s his personal circumstances changed; he moved house, changed job and gradually stopped competing regularly. He celebrated his 40th birthday by virtually quitting running and playing a lot more golf. "I think the golf became all consuming."

A decade passed before Pat caught the running bug again. In the meanwhile he had piled on well over a stone in weight. "My 50th birthday was on November 25th, 1999 and I went for my first run that day. I set myself a target of running the Raheny 5 the following January.

"I re-joined Raheny Shamrock's; my aim was to break 40 minutes in the race. On two months' training I did 37.30 and I thought I was fantastic. I enjoyed it so much that I kept running and my times kept coming down in every race."

The chances are that Pat would have seen out his athletic career as a road runner were it not for the promptings of two of his training partners at the time, Martin Treacy and Paul Brady. "I used to meet up with the two lads in Malahide Castle for training, though I wasn't able to stay up with them for too long.

"One evening we were doing strides after a run and Martin said to me, 'you have great leg speed. Would you not consider doing some track races.'"

Pat was unconvinced; even less so when he went along one evening to see a Dublin County Board graded meeting. "There was no way I was going out on the track and getting laughed at."

But eventually curiosity got the better of him and at the ripe young age of 53 he entered the 800m and 1500m at National Masters Track and Field championships in Tullamore. He still had never tested himself on a track so one evening he decided to go along to the ALSAA Complex near Dublin Airport to do a 600m trial ahead of the championships.

Olympian Dick Hooper was timing an interval session with one of his young protégés, Richie Yeates the same evening. "I jumped in on one of Richie's efforts hoping to stick with him for as long as I could. He was doing 800s and I planned to stop at 600m but I felt so good I kept going. He eventually pulled away from me but I did 2.22 or 2.23 for the 800m."

The following week Pat went to Tullamore and won a bronze medal in the 0 50 800m before securing gold in the 1500m in the same category – but he didn't realise he had won the race when he crossed the line.

"I didn't know anything about how the races were run and didn't understand how many runners were from other categories in the same race. I crossed the line in about tenth or eleventh place. It was somebody from my own category who finished behind me who told me that I had won.

"Walking off the track that evening I knew that track racing was for me. I just loved it."

Over the next few years Pat enjoyed a stellar career in masters' track competitions. Self-coached, he took a more scientific approach to training, using a heart rate monitor and sounding out every coach he met for advice, hints and tit-bits of useful information.

"I was like a sponge; I liked to pick the brains of anybody I felt knew what they were talking about. I just loved the track. I probably fell much out of love of road racing at the time; I should have been doing more road races just for the fun of them."

Then his life hit another speed bump – a blood test taken during a routine check-up in March 2008 revealed that he was suffering from hemochromatosis, which in layman's terms means an excess of iron in the blood. Ironically, most runners seek ways of increasing their iron levels as it boosts the production of haemoglobin, the agent that transports oxygen rich red blood to the muscles. The notorious banned substance EPO does the same thing!

But as Pat describes it the extra iron he was producing was "rusty". Not alone was it no use to his athletic career, if left untreated it would unquestionably shorten his life. The standard treatment for hemochromatosis is the removal of the excess iron by phlebotomy – in other words blood donations.

Initially Pat had to give nearly a pint of blood once a week for seven weeks. He didn't realise the devastating impact it would have on his running at that time. "It literally drains you for racing; I remember I went to do a 800m in a Graded meeting and I had to stop and step off the track after 500m."

The scientific literature suggests that it takes the body two months to restore its oxygen capacity to the levels they were at prior to a single donation of blood.

His condition quickly improved and has now stabilised. At the moment there is an eight month gap between donations. After those early weeks, Dr Noel McCaffrey provided him with invaluable advice on training and racing. It helped too that he was able to persuade his medical team that he could give donations at certain times of the year. "I couldn't give a donation in June/July ahead of the National Masters' championship but I would do in August when they were over."

Career wise his best year was in 2010 when he competed in the O 60 category for the first time. "All Master athletes have a honeymoon period when they move into a new age category before it slides away in a non-linear manner over the 5 years."

Pat had a dreamlike 2010 season starting with the National indoor O 60 titles at 800m and 1500m in Nenagh, followed by the British indoor titles at 1500m and 3000m in London. The outdoor season brought double gold in the 800m and 1500m at both the National championships in Tullamore and the British championships in Cardiff. In July he won bronze in the 1500m at the European championships in Hungary and also that year set a new Irish O60 record in the 1500m (4.51.41).

This sequence of successes at home and abroad led to Pat receiving the Athletics Ireland award of National Master Athlete of the year for 2010.

A life-long teetotaller, he still has the "sweet tooth" which caused him so much angst when he was in his twenties. The difference now is that he controls it.

"At the end of the outdoor track season in August I take three weeks off. I don't do anything apart from the odd jog. I feast on scones, buns, cakes and biscuits and I stick on the guts of five to seven pounds."

Then he gradually reduces his sugar intake before cutting it out completely, save for a taste of dark chocolate after a meal, two months before competition starts. "Once the speed work starts the sweets go. It's as simple as that. There can't be any half measures."

Ruefully he recalls that he simply wanted to lose weight when he took up running again at 50. "I wanted running to enhance my life but not dominate it. I think that got a little compromised. I would still hate to think it dominates my life but it is a very large part of it. Having said that, running has enhanced my life and health."

"I have never lost my enthusiasm for it possibly because I have very little mileage on the clock. I love it, and I love the comradeship around running. There is nowhere to hide once the gun goes. Sometimes it is the performance and not the result that counts. I've won races when I've known I ran tactically poorly; on other occasions I got beaten but ran a Pb and felt great."

On the night before his final marathon in Galway in 1984 Pat fell into conversation with a couple of runners, one of whom went on to win the race the next day. "I didn't know this at the time but I was asking them for advice. I told them I wanted to break 3.30 and that was about as fast as I could run. They gave me good advice and encouragement and one guy turned to his friend and said 'We will be running about 2.20 pace tomorrow which is our best. This guy is going to be running at his best for nearly 50% longer. Fair play to you.' That remark gave me such a boost that I have never forgotten it."

Masters' running is the only sport where competitors look forward to getting old! In November Pat will celebrate his 65th birthday – his passport into a new category. Robert Frost's words spring to mind:

> The woods are lovely,
> Dark, and deep,
> But I have promises to keep,
> And miles to go before I sleep
> And miles to go before I sleep.

Top Achievements Master
27 National titles over middle distance, indoor and outdoor.
7 British Masters titles over middle distance, indoor and outdoor.
Bronze medal individual at European T&F championships in Hungary 2010.
2 European Gold team medals.
One European Silver team medal.
One World Silver team medal.
Masters Athlete of the Year Award 2010

Ann Woodlock
Date of Birth: 4/11/1938

Treasure- races, Faces and Places

By Frances Macken

"It's not what you look at that matters, it's what you see"
– Henry David Thoreau

There are three types of treasure in the life of Ann Woodlock, namely faces, places and races. Ann has jogged behind prams, run through the Phoenix Park on innumerable occasions with her friends, known as the "Miss Marples", and crossed hundreds of finish lines. At the time of writing, Ann is 76 years old and living in Drimnagh. She meets regularly with her running coach Jim McNamara who she says is an inspiration to her.

Ann was born on 4 November 1938 and is the second eldest of eight. She attended the Goldenbridge Sisters of Mercy (also known as Sisters of Cruelty) School. "Some of the nuns were cruel, but not all. It didn't matter if you had a mother and father at home.

"I did the exam for secondary school and came top of the class, but as my family could not afford books etc. I did not receive the gold bound bible, which was the prize. I never got that bible as I left and went to a technical college. When I was there I won a scholarship in Irish but I was offered a job as a shorthand typist at the same time. I took that due to the shortage of money."

Ann married at twenty-three. Within eight years, she had five children – all under the age of seven. "Life was busy," she recalls, "but I had to have some time and interests for myself." She joined a local badminton club, despite great opposition from her husband who was of the firm opinion that a woman's place was in the home. Nevertheless, Ann made it work and balanced sport and taking care of her young family.

"I wasn't bad at the badminton but after a few years of it, I developed tennis elbow. So I moved on to something else!" She took up swimming next, then life-saving classes, and then she became a swimming teacher. All the while, running was a motif in Ann's life. "I even ran with the pram."

She started running races in her forties and with a glint in her eye she states, "I was hooked. After a race we would have a bag of chips and a bottle of lemonade. We really had to cop on!

"Life was a challenge but I battled on. We had a holiday every year – thanks to the children's allowance! I remember counting them (the children) all on to the bus, and again when getting off, when we went to the beach."

She sought solace in running. When Ann is in motion, her mind quietens.

"What a wonderful way to lose yourself. Running … and talking! I am told I am good at that. You could confess that you had murdered someone during a run and nobody would remember by the end of it."

Ann went on to join the Irish Masters Association, a defining moment. She travelled all over the world, "in the company of wonderful people", to Durban, South Africa in 1997; to Moscow in 1998; Malmo, Sweden in 1999, and Brisbane in 2001, for example.

"I have medals from Sweden, Moscow, Finland, and France. My last trip was to the Budapest World Indoors where I won silver in the 3000m and bronze in the 1500m race. I have met some amazing athletes, like a little Indian woman, full of wrinkles. She was the post woman in her village in the mountains and in her nineties."

Ann's sporting prowess is something of a family trait. Her grandfather was a professional cricketer and travelled throughout Ireland, teaching British officers how to perfect their technique. "When the British left Ireland, he lost his job. My father played soccer with St. Patrick's Athletics in the 1920s. He and his brother Bobby, an All-Ireland Handball Champion, were the first to have a four seater tandem bicycle in Ireland. They used to have girls on the back, until they crashed it coming down Knockmaroon Hill."

Ann's sister Aileen is very involved in motorbike racing and has completed circuits of Ireland. Aileen never broke a bone, that is, until she was marshalling. Another one with a daredevil streak, she was also a member of the WAF's.

It is evident that Ann's grá for running has been a catalyst for a great deal of positive and interesting events.

"I have the most wonderful friends through running. From John Kavanagh (RIP) at Guinness's to Lindie Naughton. Donore Harriers has been great. Meeting my Coach Jim McNamara and before him, Willie Smith. I look at the young women in Donore Harriers, how different it is with the support from their husbands and partners and children, all cheering them on.

The conversation turns to drugs in sport. Ann has another great anecdote. When Ann's cat Pixie was getting sluggish as she aged, she took her to the vet

Ann Woodlock

and the cat was given steroids. The cat was transformed. She was jumping over walls, hanging off the curtains. Ann joked with the vet, "Can you get me some of that?" The vet replied, "Where do you think these athletes got the idea from." Pixi passed away at the ripe age of 19.

"I was at the World Track and Field Championships in Gateshead. There was an American woman there; the Irish lads called her the tractor thrower because of her build. She was checked out – was she a man or a woman? She was a woman! But was done for drugs. One of her compatriots said to me, it was because she was a Texan cattle farmer and fed her cattle with angel dust. I told her it was banned in Ireland."

Somewhat predictably, people get in a tizzy about Ann's age and unusually active lifestyle. But to her, age is irrelevant. Nonetheless it draws regular comment. Remarkable people often draw remarks upon them!

"They call me the Galloping Granny! And they say, 'Look at her … she's my age!' and 'I'm glad you've let your hair go grey. You finally look your age.'"

She recalls bringing her daughter, who smoked at the time, to run the mini-marathon. Ann encouraged her throughout the race. "Not long to go now, come on!" The daughter was really feeling it. She struggled on towards the finish line. Ann bounced along beside her. They crossed the finish line together. A photographer snapped the pair as they crossed the line. The photograph appeared in the paper the following day. The caption read something like, "Daughter Helps Mum Across Finish Line", much to Ann's amusement.

"I wouldn't say I am naturally energetic, I just do it because I want to do it. I have the get up and go.

"I really love the Phoenix Park. It does something for me. It is under appreciated by people and under used. Talk to the deer, kick up the leaves! Be free.

"My friends and I don't sit around having coffee. We meet in the park and go for a run and tell all our tales. It really is therapy. I don't think I'm old. It's just a number. I say my age and I might as well be saying I'm 40.

"I remember when the park rangers used to have bikes and cycle around the park. They have Jeeps now. Myself and a few friends used to run together in a group, they used to call us the Miss Marples. You'd sometimes see kids on the mitch from school. There was one day when a kid ran out of the bushes. A man emerged from the bushes too, pulling his trousers up. The kid had money. The man was roaring after him and roaring at us. It was very frightening. We surrounded the boy and we ran with him in the centre. We scolded him. 'Don't ever do that again!' We rang the schools to let them know what we had witnessed. We never heard anything about it after that.

"Another time we were running along and there was a naked man panned out on the grass. A friend of ours was running a bit behind and we thought, 'Oh God, she's going to see that. We'd better slow down here in case she gets a fright.' Along came our friend around the corner, completely oblivious. When we told her about the naked man, she said, 'Do you think I might get lucky if I go around again?'

"In the 1970s all the talk was about liberating women. Nell McCafferty and friends went up North and brought back condoms etc. *The Irish Times* and Irish Ferries decided to do something practical and had a competition, 'Why I should Be Liberated from the Kitchen Sink'. I wrote an article and was one of 14 women highly commended. I didn't win but I did get to meet Maeve Binchy – a wonderful woman."

After a lifetime's desire to attend college, Ann finally got her wish. In recent years, she attended Trinity College and studied Greek.

Where can your legs carry you to? For Ann, they've transported her around the world and carried her along on her great adventure. Here are just some of Ann's achievements.

Major Achievements

World Road Championships, Birmingham (1992). Won Silver medal in 10,000m.
World Masters in Durban, (July 1997). Placed 4th. "The experience of a lifetime!"
Russian Indoor Championships, Indoors in Moscow (1998). Won Gold and Silver medals. "My first experience running indoors."
European Indoor Championships in Malmo, Sweden (1999). Two Bronze medals, 1500m and 800m.
European Track and Field in Arhus, Denmark (2004,). Came 4th in 800m race.
World Indoors in Linz, Austria (2006). Came 4th in 3000m and 1500m race.
World Track and Field in Lahti, Finland (2009). Won Bronze.
Two silver medal world championships Poland indoors 2015
European 1,500 M indoor European Champion 2016 Ancona, Italy

About the Author

MICHAEL GYGAX

Date of Birth: 19/11/1961

Life Energised by Sport and Story Telling

In times of great stress or adversity, it's always best to keep busy, to plough your anger and your energy into something positive. – Lee Iacocca

One of my fondest childhood memories is that of listening to stories of "the good old days" from my maternal grandfather, Michael McCabe. Born only one year into the twentieth century, he described an Ireland, of fair grounds, farmers, farm labourers, of sports days, tug war and a rather rigid social order. He was of an era where the parish priest, bank manager, shopkeeper, lawyer and accountant where part of the upper echelons of the social hierarchy. Granddad himself was one of the first recruits into a Garda Siochána and climbed the ranks to garda superintendent. His saddest day was day he retired at sixty six such was his love and devotion to his job. Granda McCabe as I called him, brought me to run in my first race, a cross country in the Phoenix Park, such was my enthusiasm to impress, that I started like a cannonball fired from a big gun, only to flop after a half a lap, the entire field passed me, I finished a distant last. Granddad instilled in me a love of learning and it is only now that I appreciate the rich repertoire of stories that he recounted on a regular basis. Awareness that so much history can be lost with death and the passing of time, this ritual which he partook in is certainly is part of the inspiration of the writing of *A Golden Era.* The span of this book crosses many generations, living memories of a rich tapestry of social, cultural and sporting history, whose stories bring me back to memories of listening to Michael, my grandfather all through my boyhood into adulthood.

My paternal great granny, "Granny Ward", was the local midwife in Greystones, a role that seemed to emerge organically as a result of the early death of her husband, when she went to Holles Street Hospital to train in nursing and midwifery and my paternal grandmother Rose Ward [Gygax] gave up school at twelve to look after her younger siblings, the youngest who was not born at the time of his father's death. Rose's own husband, Ernst Gygax, a Swiss national, also died when my father's youngest siblings were still a tender age leaving Rose a widow. I often wonder is part of my great granny's legacy the interest and love of healing which drew me to Chinese medicine and physical therapy, and three out of four of my siblings to nursing and medical science. My sister Ciara works in Holles Street Hospital today as a neo-natal nurse.

My parents, Fred and Josephine, are well and pushing on into the autumn of their lives. Dad still plays golf twice weekly and they both regale stories of their youth and adulthood, not the good old days, for now the present moment, is often the best of times and they have always through thick and thin, time and energy for their children and family, sharing laughter and concern as life dishes out rations of fortune and adversity in equal measure.

There is some history in my father's family in running. Dad (Fred) did some running around Glasnevin but it was his brother Derek who had the distinction of being on the same relay team as Ronnie Delany running for O Connell School. Derek went to USA where he enlisted with the US military, where he was posted to Germany in the 1950s. In his own words, "the greatest time of my life, I was paid to run and race." Derek was a fine athlete and sportsman all his life and my interest and participation in athletics meant that I always kept a close eye on his personal best times, in order to see if I could emulate him. Derek is married with three children, multiple grandchildren and still resides in Maryland and is now eighty, the same age as Ronnie Delany.

I started running when I first joined De la Salle school but there was always a seed in me that wanted to be a runner which was latent, not yet germinated until secondary school. I joined the now dissolved Grange Athletic Club and my first introduction to Tom O'Connor coach, now deceased, and it was Neil Farrell, my then business teacher and now by serendipity, one of the authors in this book. Tom O'Connor was a very knowledgeable coach, a person I owe a lifelong gratitude for the depth of understanding of coaching, a lifetime in athletics and learning leaves me humbled by his methodology that is still relevant today. I had modest success in school winning the school's north Leinster 800m, the height of my athletic success but not the pinnacle of my ambition.

Michael Gygax

My teens were a battlefield with my parents, as the family retail business called me and all my siblings to work weekends and weekdays in the shop. Our shop was open from 8.00 am to 10.00 pm seven days per week, my parents work ethic meant that they and all my siblings rarely had what is now known as "time off". This meant my requirement to work, study and train became a source of conflict and my parent's requirement for me to work always trumped my preference to train and compete. When I left school after leaving cert and started to work, initially for VHI, I started to train twice daily, in order to see how good I could become. My second job in the early eighties as a rookie social welfare inspector brought me all over the country for the first two years, an odyssey which taught me many life skills, brought me novel experiences and made me a lot of friends and acquaintances.

Success in athletics did not come early or easily to me, I always finished mid pack or worse in cross country, track or the road. My father regularly reminds me that as a youngster I wore callipers and was not able to walk properly until I was two years old. Even today I find my proprioception (sense of inner balance poor) and I often feel uncoordinated in my movements. It is not surprising that an ambition to go to America on scholarship or join the army cadets to pursue athletics further, was met with a certain "get real". My primary education was enjoyable but I remember going home on a regular based and been asked a certain question, "what did you learn today" and the truth to the question was very little. I spent most of my days daydreaming, about being great at something, but the specifics I do not know. Staying back a year and some remedial one to one tuition, brought me up to speed. I believe now that I did not always take things in the first time, but when I do learn something, I never forget what I learn. In my own mind I was below average student with poor sporting potential.

The second Dublin Marathon in 1981 swept me off my feet when I was nineteen years old; my ambition was to break three hours. I just picked this time out of the air. I was delighted with my time of 2.43 and placing of 172. A few months later I went to London to watch my friend Dominick Gallagher compete in the London Marathon. Unfortunately, he was ill, so I took his number and ran 2.40 as a training run. Dublin City in 1982 saw me finish 32 places in 2.31. Two years later I ran 2.30 for a 26th place finish. I did not run another marathon for another 8 years.

In 1985 I decided that I wanted to see the world and experience something of eastern culture, particularly in relation to yoga, meditation and the healing arts. I took a year out from work and engaged in voluntary work, working as an outreach person engaging with people with drug-related issues. The place I stayed in was an ashram run by a palatine father Joseph Bockenhoff or "Anand" as we called him. The time spent there was a retreat, doing yoga, meditation, running twice a day, swimming in the sea and largely living a Spartan and monastic lifestyle. I immersed myself in discussions, reading books on philosophy and eastern and western mysticism. I learnt about drugs, addiction and was probably overloaded with social and cultural dynamics that were completely new to me in my new environment. I ate simple vegetarian food, prayed, chanted and meditated. After half a year, in April 1985 I decided to go to the Himalayas where I spent five weeks climbing, succeeding in reaching Kali Patar, 20,000 ft. on my journey to Everest Base camp. I went alone to Nepal and tagged along with some experienced climbers. I was really fit, but had little experience climbing, so it was ironic that on one fateful day, our group got stranded on a ledge at minus 40 degrees. I found I had an uncanny knack of getting out of trouble and rolling on my stomach found a way down the mountain. I was able to travel huge distances in the mountains, so I reckoned I could keep up with any man. I met up with a certain Austrian climber Peter Habeler and walked with him for a day, covering more than three times the distance recommended for a top mountaineer. Peter commented that he was taking it easy. My legs were sorer than after any of my marathons, so I let him off on his own the next day. One of the climbers in the hostel came over to me and confided that he was the first man to climb Everest without supplemental oxygen. This event happened in 8 May 1978, together with Messner, which had previously been thought as impossible.

The rest of my Indian continent odyssey was engaged in doing short-term development projects in Sri Lanka which included working in an orphanage, building roads, visiting local communities and Buddhist temples. I raced about ten times while in India and stretched my run to over 3 consecutive years running every day without missing a day, a streak that was broken on my return home when I ended up in hospital with dysentery for over two weeks. I remember coming home and was unable to get up the stairs I was so weak, much to the consternation of my parents.

I was intensely lonely when I was away; I missed my family, friends and running mates. After such a colourful and diverse cultural christening I also felt a little displaced on my return. The fact was that the transition was made really easy by my continued engagement with Raheny Shamrocks and the general athletic scene, particularly training at lunchtime in the grounds of Trinity College with many great athletes, complementing my run to and from work.

In hindsight, I always seem to be a little bit ahead of my time or at the beginning of great social and cultural developments. My father developed part of his retail business into a health food shop which brought many, new age and yoga types into his shop. This aroused an interest in food, nutrition, massage, meditation, yoga and various forms of healing. At fourteen I did my first course in massage, shiatsu and an Eastern form of bodywork called Do In. By eighteen I had done my first course in Swedish massage with the Irish Health Cultural Society which was running their first course. Tony Quinn was one of the principals behind this company. I immediately started working with athletes and developed a lot of skill through practice on a wide range of subjects. Over time I developed "sports massage therapy" from experimenting with different techniques and learning from different teachers and therapists. This was well before "sports massage" and "physical therapy" became a genre in the realm of sports medicine. India was a revelation for me, as I visited many yoga Cure and nature centres when I was there and learnt many things from traditional practitioners. On my return home from India I enrolled in one of the first detailed course in acupuncture in Europe and was very fortunate to study under the world famous Giovanni Macciocci whose books are now used as the mainstay of acupuncture texts in the western world. After three years' study, I spent two months in Chinese Hospitals in Nanjing doing clinical work with some wonderful knowledgeable doctors. I have been practicing now for over thirty years, combining Chinese medicine, physical therapy and manipulation. Working with people like Dr Tony Crosbie for four years, Dr Bill Scogens Chiropractor and MD and other practitioners in my clinic have greatly enhanced my understanding of the treatment of injury, illness and the maintenance of good health. I have always endeavoured to get some "maintenance treatments" which has helped to keep me in good health and relatively injury free. I have been positively educated in certain aspects of psychology by various hypnotherapists working in my clinic, techniques that I use with my patients and with charges that I have coached at various times.

John Shields took over coaching me on my return from Asia and over a decade transformed my performances on the track and road beyond recognition. His stable of athletes all home grown were running excellent times at national level. John contributed to Raheny Shamrocks being one of the foremost clubs in the country in the late eighties, early nineties. I remember running 3.54 for 1500m in 1989 and only being 7th fastest time in the club that year. The pinnacle of my racing career was wining the Dublin 5000m in1988 and the Dublin 10,000 in 1989. I had become a good athlete but was never a great athlete. Any notions I had in that respect were kept in check by a frequent inability to make the Raheny A team. I do pride myself however of having the distinction of winning national (team medals) from 800m to marathon, on road, track and cross country. My first couple of years as a master over 40 were particularly productive winning Dublin titles over 800, 1500, 5,000 and 10,000 in the same season. I also won the Leinster 1500 and second in national 1500 to Gerry Robinson who was then the reigning European champion. I won multiple titles with Raheny on the road track and cross country in my early master years.

Every day there are new lessons to learn, a valuable addition to any day. Diverse voices have shone a light on my granddad's time through the lifestyle, experiences of the older folk. I found it surprising how young so many of subject born in the thirties, forties and fifties left school and made their way in the world with little formal education we have today. Those people who went to do their leaving certificate, usually attended university. The USA college system is less of a draw today for our elite athletes than it was before and the army and FCA influence athletic development has practically died out. Thankfully the guns of division and discord have been put away in Northern Ireland and there is unity and cooperation between sporting bodies replacing animosities, discord that historically compromised sporting development and excellence. Many of the older masters in this book attended boarding schools, institutions which contributed to their sporting success and participation. Running clubs are now the vanguard of athletic development. Women in my grandfather's time generally did not participate in sport and rarely did they do so in their twilight years. These women are true pioneers of sport and life. The larger world view too has changed; the eastern blocs are no longer a united force politically and sportingly, now competes locally and internationally as newly formed nation states.

The world of my grandfather has changed immeasurably. People are now giving up cigarettes and taking up jogging. The times of European runners are slower now than former years at the elite level, but the volume of people out there doing their own thing is greater than ever before. The popularity of the radio has been usurped firstly by the black and white TV, then coloured one, and later by the computer, laptop, tablet and phone. The world has become a global village. By intelligent budgeting and planning most working people can travel and experience a multiplicity of geography and culture The variety, quality and availability of food and drink has improved the quality of our existence when consumed in the correct quantities. If we make the right lifestyle choices we can be fitter, stronger and healthier than former generations. I have taken advantage of these changes and have travelled widely and usually cheaply often to participate in mountain or track championship races. Other trips have been a pleasure, time out to learn history, geography, walk, track and time to share valuable time with friends and family.

Ireland is a small place but it has had an extraordinarily dominant in producing great athletes over the years. I have been very fortunate to have treated many of Ireland's greatest athletes – Eamonn Coghlan, T.J. Kearns, Frank Murphy, Jerry Kiernan, Noel Carroll, David Mathews, Jimmy McDonald, Dick Hooper, Neil Bruton, Noel Berkley, Fionnuala Brittan and many others too numerous to mention. I like to think that I contributed to part of their success by keeping them injury-free and getting them back on the road when they were injured. I have had the privilege of training with Caitriona McKiernan when she was at her best and rubbed shoulders with three generations of Irish athletes which has greatly enhanced my enjoyment and appreciation of sport. Meeting and staying with Br. Colm O'Connell in Kenya was a game changer, an experience that brought me to have a better understanding of the development of athletics on the highest level.

In 1992 I decided that I would run another marathon. I had improved greatly as an athlete and had been breaking seventy minutes on a regular basis for a half marathon, my best been 67.47. Again it was Dublin City Marathon that I chose and for most of the race I was flying. At half way in the race, I went through in 70 minutes and a second, on a very cold blustery wet day, forging ahead; I went through twenty miles in 1.49.20. Ten minutes later I was in seventh place but the wheels came off, and I hobbled in in 2.35 in 35th place. When crossed the line I cried uncontrollably, it was like a deep trauma had overtaken me. Raheny, with me as third scorer, won the team prize that day, but I was never the same athlete again. For the next two years I suffered from what I would call a mild form of ME. I ran three more marathons, the New York Marathon in 1994, 2.42 [fastest Irishman], The 100th Boston 2.49 [training run] and finally the National Marathon in Waterford in 1999, finished twelfth again in 2.42, Dick Hooper second, Mick Traynor third and Raheny Shamrocks won the team again.

I have been fortunate to experience the company of many people who have attained a great excellence in many fields of endeavour in their lives. This reoccurring theme of excellence shines through the many stories and characters in this book, many who are acquaintances, others are people who I feel privileged to call my lifelong friends.

My son Fiachra was born in 1995 the week my grandfather passed away, my daughter Fionnuala was nearly three years old. Both are now in their twenties, Fionnuala studying drama and acting, Fiachra is doing business in DCU.

It is my hope that fitness will always be a theme in their lives and that they follow the paths that will bring them contentment and resilience.

For most of my life I feel I have been blessed with good fortune, oceans of energy and good health. I used to take three months off every summer, term time from Social Welfare to write my first book, *Beyond a Singular Truth*, a cross cultural perspective on massage, traditional medical systems and bodywork, run and compete, spend time with children and catch up on things that were being left behind. Running down Dollymount Strand early on a summer's morning followed by swimming in the sea, I often reflected what a lucky man I am. Everything I touched at various stages turned to gold, I seemed to have the Midas touch. The tide turns for most people in life, and like most I experienced grief, for me it came in the form of separation and breaking up of family. There were many dark days and nights that seemed interminable, where the Midas touch seemed to be replaced by a curse with everything I touched turned to slush. There were times of deep loneliness fraught with moments of real despair. I have learnt that it is through darkness we learn who we really are; we learn skills that help us be resilient beyond what we thought possible. Most of all it teaches us empathy, humility and a deeper appreciation of the good times, the good people and loved ones around us. In a strange sort of way this process can be transforming, the old coat moulted and the new vision is brighter, warmer and wiser. Out of my chaos came greater insight into the human condition, a greater resilience and a creativity that has catalysed a creative spark to write great poetry, as well as *Changing Tensions*, a book which explores a bridge between bodywork and psychotherapy which is not quiet complete. I scribed a play, *Cutting Links*, and set about writing and project managing volumes one and two of *A Golden Era: Profiles of Irish Master Athletes*.

Major Achievements
Three senior Dublin championships 5km/10km/1,500 [b] championship
Leinster master 1,500
National Silver 1,500
Dublin Master Championship
800, 1,500, 5,000, 10,000 same year
Clonliffe 2 miles 8.47 3rd place
National senior team medals 800m to Marathon
Multiple Master medals with Raheny Shamrocks
Marathon: 2.30.26
Half Marathon: 67.47

About the Contributors

P.J. Browne

P.J. Browne, from Bruff, County Limerick, has worked as a sports journalist nationally and internationally for four decades. A regular contributor to *Irish Runner* magazine, his depth of understanding of athletics and deep insight into the human condition always gives his audience a great read. P.J.'s contributions to *A Golden Era* have significantly added to the quality of this book, and his continuous presence and support was a key factor in getting the final product over the line.

Joe Conway

Joe Conway was born and raised in Portlaoise, County Laois. He competed for his local club, Ballyfinn Athletic Club, and later for Clonliffe Harriers. He now resides in the USA and competes for Ireland at masters level. He has promoted Irish masters sport through his blog.

Eamonn Delahunt

Eamonn graduated with a 1st Class Honors Degree from the UCD School of Physiotherapy in 2003 placing first in his class. He currently works as a Senior Lecturer in the UCD School of Public Health, Physiotherapy and Population Science, and acts as the programme coordinator for the BSc Health and Performance Science Degree programme. Eamonn also has extensive clinical experience having previously worked as a Chartered Physiotherapist in ExWell Medical.

David Dwyer

David is a native of County Limerick who is now living in East Cork. In athletic terms by his own account his achievements are modest to say the least, however in the context of this book his bronze medal in the National Masters 5000m M35 category in 2009 is a noteworthy achievement. David is a long-term member of the East Cork AC and has scored on a number of Masters Cross Country and Road Championships winning teams.

Neil Farrell

Neil Farrell is a retired secondary school teacher in De La Salle Raheny where he taught Michael Gygax economics. He actively helped students engage with Grange Athletics Club during his early years at the school. He has a keen interest in writing and is part of a writing club. Living in Clontarf he is an active member of Slender Health gym and goes sailing during the summer. An astute observer of human behaviour, his work on Hugh Gallagher and Willie Dunne with Michael Gygax greatly enhanced the vision of *A Golden Era* where he regularly gave Michael his ear.

Peter Gleeson

Peter Gleeson is a reporter for the *Nenagh Guardian* and has been a journalist for over 30 years, having worked for regional and national newspapers, including the *Irish Examiner*, where he worked in the Cork office for six years. A runner all his life, he is a member of Nenagh Olympic Athletics Club and is a former Tipperary and Munster senior 400m senior champion.

Colin Griffin

Colin represented Ireland at the 2008 and 2012 Olympic Games in the 50km walk. Other career highlights include top 12 performances at the 2010 European Championships, 2012 World Race Walking Cup as well as top 10 performances at World Youth Championships and European Junior Championships. Colin is an active coach, having coached a fellow Leitrim race walker to 19th at the 2012 London Olympic Games and 6th at the 2013 World University Games.

Kevin Humphreys

Kevin Humphreys, a native of Dublin, attended Colaiste Mhuire Parnell Square and began his running career there. In 1969 he won the Irish schools senior miles in a record 4 min. 16 sec. Later that year he set a junior record of 3 min. 51.8 for 1500m. That year he joined the Irish Air Corps and qualified as a pilot in 1971. He reset the Irish record junior record at 3.45.7 in 1970. Between 1968 and 1978 he represented Ireland at 800m and 1500m at schools junior and senior level. He retired from the Air Corps in 1987 and joined the Department of Transport.

Kieran Kelly

Kieran Kelly is a Chartered Civil Engineer currently working in the telecommunications industry across Ireland and is an active member of Brow Rangers AC. His mother Rose and father Murty had a huge influence, sporting-wise, on him and his two older brothers.

Jim Kelly

Jim is the current president of Dublin Business Houses Athletics Association and a member of Raheny Shamrock AC. He played Gaelic football and soccer before becoming a soccer referee. While training he got to know runners from several athletic clubs. He became a road race runner and acknowledges that he was more enthusiastic than good. For many years now he has been the race promoter for Dublin City Council's BHAA annual races and is also involved in other race events.

Cillian Lonergan

Cillian is a Clonliffe Harriers athlete and the club statistician. He was National medal winner at Juvenile, Junior and Senior level and an Irish international at Schools, Junior and senior level. He has personal best times of 13.47 and 28.37 for 5000m and 10000m and is currently living in Switzerland.

Caoimhe Lynch

Caoimhe Lynch is a 23-year-old journalism graduate just about to finish a masters in marketing in Dublin. She is passionate about fitness and spends a lot of her time in the gym. She recently ran her first 5k and plans to run many more.

Frances Macken

Frances Macken is a writer originally from Claremorris in County Mayo, now residing in Skerries, County Dublin. At the time of publication, she is studying at the University of Oxford for a Masters in Creative Writing. She has a Degree in Film and Video Production from the Dun Laoghaire Institute of Art, Design and Technology.

Malcolm McCausland

Malcolm McCausland has been athletics correspondent of the *Irish News* since 2001, having previously worked for the *Belfast Telegraph*. He is a regular contributor to BBC local radio and *Athletics Weekly*. As an athlete he was twice Northern Ireland senior 800m champion and won numerous Irish titles as a veteran/master. He was also a member of a British Milers' Club team that set a world record for 4 x 1500m. He continues to compete and can be seen at races all over the country and beyond.

Peter McDermot

Peter is a retired school teacher. He ran for UCD and won 5 college titles over 5000m and cross-country. He joined Clonliffe in 1972 and was captain in 1979-80 and 1991 to 2001. He won 4 National Senior medals as a scoring member of the Clonliffe cross-country, road relays and marathon teams. He was National Endurance Coach from 1997 to 2002 and was coach to the Irish International Cross-Country teams from 1997 to 2002.

Sean McGoldrick

Sean McGoldrick joined North Leitrim AC while still at school. Later when he moved to Dublin he joined Raheny Shamrock AC and competed at distances as diverse as the 800m and the Comrades Marathon. He served as the club's PRO for several years. A journalist for the last 37 years, he writes on sport for the *Sunday World*.

Patsy McGonagle

Patsy has been involved in athletics in Donegal and has been part of the management team in BLE and AAI for a number of decades. He has been instrumental in the development of athletics in Donegal and nationally. He has been manager to a number of Irish teams at the Olympic Games.

Owen McLoughlin

Owen McLoughlin has been Chairperson and Development Manager of Rathfarnham WSAF AC for a number of years. He is responsible for Track & Field athletics in Dublin (Senior) since 2010 as an officer of the Dublin Athletics Board. He has been a keen masters' competitor since turning 40 in 2004 on road, track and country.

A personal highlight was a club masters' team victory nationally in the Dublin City Marathon in 2011. By day he is a primary school principal in Rathfarnham.

Willie McNelis

Born in Glenties, County Donegal in 1945, the eldest of six children, Willie was educated in the local boy's National School and later at the Hugh McDevitt Institute. He played minor football with County Donegal. In 1964 he came to Dublin to train as a draughtsman in the ESB where he met his wife Evelyn.

Zoë Melling

Zoë Melling has been a member of Rathfarnham Athletics Club since 2002 when she moved to Ireland from New Zealand. A great lover of the outdoors, she started running at age 31 after looking for a new challenge and hearing about a long distance mountain race in one of her favourite wilderness locations. She still loves mountain running although she also participates in cross country, road and track events, and is happy to run on any type of terrain. Aside from running, she enjoys hill walking, travel, reading and writing, and is a librarian by profession.

Lindie Naughton

Lindie Naughton is a well-known national sports journalist. She is an active member of DSD (and previously Crusaders) as a coach and mentor. She has had a very robust influence in the development and promotion of the Dublin Ladies Mini-Marathon through her advice and reporting in the national newspapers. She keeps active daily and competes in orienteering events. Her books include *Let's Run: A Handbook for Irish Runners*; *Faster, Higher, Stronger: A History of Irish Olympians* with Johnny Watterson; and *Lady Icarus: The Life of Mary Heath Irish Aviator*, which formed the bases for an award winning documentary film in 2014.

Ciaran O Coigligh

Born and reared in Finglas, Ciaran was educated by de la Salle Brothers. He has worked in the Irish Departments of NUI Galway and NUI Dublin and the Department of Irish Folklore, NUI Dublin. He is the author of 10 collections of poetry, three novels and one collection of short stories. He took up running at age 28 and his best time for the mile is 5.49; 2 miles, 12.19; 3 miles, 19.25; marathon, 3.30. He was the third fastest over 10k in Ireland for over fifty-fives in 2008 and was the winner of Raheny Road Race League, Division 3, in 2008.

Fergus O Donovan

Fergus O Donovan's introduction to athletics was winning the mile (5.12) in South Munster Sports in 1956, his last year in school. As a spectator he went to four Olympics in Tokyo (1964), Mexico (1968), Munich (1972) and Montreal (1976); and four European championships in Budapest (1966), Athens (1969), Helsinki (1971) and Rome (1974). In coaching he initiated training/coaching weekends in Gormanston College, which became The Bears Club and continued twice yearly for more than 20 years. He served on the BLE National Coaching Committee for several years and on Cork City Sports committee for 10 years. After a 20-year "sabbatical", he has been coaching one day a week for the last 12 years and is trying to support revival of the track and field league in Cork.

Ian O'Riordan

Ian O'Riordan is a second generation national sports journalist currently writing with *The Irish Times*. Ian's father Tom was an Olympian and multiple national champion who hailed from Kerry. Ian went to Brown University where he studied journalism and partook in an athletic scholarship. Ian trains daily to keep fit.

Hugh Parnell

Hugh Parnell is the elder son of two boys and some would say the least athletic, despite sporting activity being the pulse in his household. He did history and English in college, and he was glad that through the writing of his mother's and father's achievements that many Irish sporting heroes will no longer be "a hidden history". Only time will tell if his own sporting excellence will shine in later years.

Brian Timmons

Brian Ó Tiomáin lives in Rathfarnham, Dublin with the three women in his life – his wife and two daughters. He is a writer/director in Irish and English and has won several Oireachtas awards for Irish language plays, radio plays, screenplays and prose. He is currently finishing a novella in Irish based on the Aran Islands, and is also working on a screenplay of the same story.

John Walshe

John started running in 1971 with Middleton AC, now with the East Cork club. He has run 31 Dublin Marathons (1980-2010) with a best time of 2:37:59 (1985), and also ran 2:39:59 after turning 40 in 1991. He still enjoy the shorter races, although he is happy nowadays to get under 80 minutes for 10 miles. He was involved with the first Ballycotton race (five miles) in August 1977, Ballycotton '10' started the following March and the rest is history. He is a long-time contributor to *Irish Runner*, and also covers local athletics for the Cork *Evening Echo* along with the *Irish Examiner* and various other publications.